BISMARCK

BISMARCK
THE MAN AND THE STATESMAN

A.J.P. TAYLOR

SUTTON PUBLISHING

This book was first published by Hamish Hamilton in 1955

This edition first published in 2003 by
Sutton Publishing Limited · Phoenix Mill
Thrupp · Stroud · Gloucestershire · GL5 2BU

British Library Cataloguing in Publication Data
A catalogue record for this book is available from the British
Library

ISBN 0 7509 3274 0

Printed and bound in Great Britain by
J.H. Haynes & Co. Ltd, Sparkford.

Bismarck in 1855

Bismarck in 1865

Bismarck in 1890

Bismarck in 1895

THE BOY AND THE MAN

OTTO VON BISMARCK was born at Schönhausen in the Old Mark of Brandenburg on 1 April 1815. Both place and date hinted at the pattern of his life. Schönhausen lay just east of the Elbe, in appearance a typical Junker estate —some sheep and cattle, wheat and beetroot fields, with woods in the background. Life seemed to follow a traditional rhythm, far removed from the modern world. Yet if Bismarck had been born two years earlier, the kingdom of Westphalia, ruled by Jerome Bonaparte, would have been just across the river. French troops had occupied Schönhausen during the wars; French revolutionary ideas lapped to the edge of its fields. The true Junkers lived far away to the east, in Pomerania and Silesia. These Junkers were a Prussian speciality—gentry proud of their birth, but working their estates themselves and often needing public employment to supplement their incomes. They looked with jealousy at the high aristocracy with its cosmopolitan culture and its monopoly of the greatest offices in the state. We may find a parallel in the English country-gentry with their Tory prejudices and their endless feud against the Whig magnates; but the Junkers were nearer to the soil, often milking their own cows and selling their wool themselves at the nearest market, sometimes distinguished from the more prosperous peasant-farmers only by their historic names.

Schönhausen was an estate of this kind, but the winds of the modern world blew round it. Though Bismarck was born a couple of miles on the Junker side of the Elbe, he was always the Junker who looked across it—sometimes with apprehension, sometimes with sympathy. The date of his birth was also significant. A fortnight earlier Napoleon had arrived in Paris for his last adventure of the Hundred Days. The old order had a narrow escape. Bismarck, despite his appearance of titanic calm, was always aware of the revolutionary tide that had threatened to engulf the antiquated life of Schönhausen. The kingdom of Prussia, of which he was a subject, had risen again into the ranks of the Great Powers, but it had been almost snuffed out by Napoleon. Her statesmen feared that the same fate might come again. It became their dogma: 'Unless we grow greater we shall become less'. This was no basis for a confident conservatism.

The very geography of Schönhausen also shaped Bismarck's character and political outlook. It was unmistakably in north Germany, in a district entirely inhabited by Protestants. Bismarck never came to regard the south Germans as true Germans, particularly if they were Roman Catholics. Yet Schönhausen also lay far from the sea. Its inhabitants looked to Berlin as their metropolis; and the connexion which Bismarck later established with Hamburg was always rather artificial. If Germany was to expand at all, he preferred that it should be overseas rather than down the Danube; yet both were alien to him. The eastern expansion of Prussia, which had shaped her history, was equally remote for him. Unlike the Junkers of Silesia or West Prussia, he never had a Pole among his peasants. The Poles whom he denounced from personal experience were educated revolutionaries, not workers on the land; it was because of them that Bismarck disliked intellectuals in politics.

There was a similar contradiction in his family heritage. His father Ferdinand was a typical Junker, sprung from a family as old as the Hohenzollerns—'a Suabian family no better than mine' Bismarck once remarked. Schönhausen itself symbolized their humiliation; for they had received it as compensation for their original family estate, which a Hohenzollern elector had coveted and seized. The Bismarcks had done nothing to gain distinction during their long feudal obscurity. Ferdinand did not even exert him-

self to fight for his king. He left the Prussian army at 23;
and missed both the disastrous Jena campaign in 1806 and
the war of liberation against Napoleon in 1813. The efficient
management of his rambling estates was beyond him, and
he drifted helplessly into economic difficulties. It needed a
vivid imagination for the son to turn this easy-going, slow-
witted man, with his enormous frame, into a hero, representing all that was best in Prussian tradition.

Wilhelmine, the mother, was a different character. Her
family, the Menkens, were bureaucrats without a title, not
aristocrat landowners. Some of them had been university
professors. Her father was a servant of the Prussian state,
prized by Frederick the Great and later in virtual control of
all home affairs. His reforms and quick critical spirit
brought down on him the accusation of 'Jacobinism'.
Wilhelmine was a town-child, at home only in the drawing
rooms of Berlin. She had a sharp, restless intellect, which
roamed without system from Swedenborg to Mesmer. At
one moment she would be discussing the latest works of
political liberalism; at the next dabbling in spiritualist experiments. Married to Ferdinand von Bismarck at sixteen,
she developed interest neither for her heavy husband nor in
country life. All her hopes were centred on her children.
They were to achieve the intellectual life that had been
denied to her. Her only ambition, she said, was to have 'a
grown-up son who would penetrate far further into the
world of ideas than I, as a woman, have been able to do.'

She gave her children encouragement without love. She
drove them on; she never showed them affection. Otto, the
younger son, inherited her brains. He was not grateful for
the legacy. He wanted love from her, not ideas; and he was
resentful that she did not share his admiration for his father.
It is a psychological commonplace for a son to feel affection
for his mother and to wish his father out of the way. The
results are more interesting and more profound when a son,
who takes after his mother, dislikes her character and standards of value. He will seek to turn himself into the father
with whom he has little in common, and he may well end up

neurotic or a genius. Bismarck was both. He was the clever, sophisticated son of a clever, sophisticated mother, masquerading all his life as his heavy, earthy father.

Even his appearance showed it. He was a big man, made bigger by his persistence in eating and drinking too much. He walked stiffly, with the upright carriage of a hereditary officer. Yet he had a small, fine head; the delicate hands of an artist; and when he spoke, his voice, which one would have expected to be deep and powerful, was thin and reedy —almost a falsetto—the voice of an academic, not of a man of action. Nor did he always present the same face to the world. He lives in history clean-shaven, except for a heavy moustache. Actually he wore a full beard for long periods of his life; and this at a time when beards were symbols on the continent of Europe of the Romantic movement, if not of radicalism. In the use of a razor, as in other things, Bismarck sometimes followed Metternich, sometimes Marx. Despite his Junker mien, he had the sensitivity of a woman, incredibly quick in responding to the moods of another, or even in anticipating them. His conversational charm could bewitch tsars, queens and revolutionary leaders. Yet his great strokes of policy came after long solitary brooding, not after discussion with others. Indeed he never exchanged ideas in the usual sense of the term. He gave orders or, more rarely, carried them out; he did not co-operate. In a life of conflict, he fought himself most of all. He said once: 'Faust complains of having two souls in his breast. I have a whole squabbling crowd. It goes on as in a republic.' When someone asked him if he were really the Iron Chancellor, he replied: 'Far from it. I am all nerves, so much so that self-control has always been the greatest task of my life and still is.' He willed himself into a line of policy or action. His friend Keyserling noted of his conversion to religion: 'Doubt was not fought and conquered; it was silenced by heroic will.'

He felt himself always out of place, solitary and a stranger to his surroundings. 'I have the unfortunate nature that everywhere I could be seems desirable to me, and dreary and boring as soon as I am there.' He loathed the intellectual circles of Berlin to which his mother introduced him, and in 1848 said to a liberal politician: 'I am a Junker and mean to have the advantages of that position.' But the years he spent as a Junker, managing his estates, were the most miserable of his life; and when, as Chancellor, he retired to his beloved countryside, he was happy only so long as the state papers continued to pour in on him. He spent the twenty-eight years of supreme power announcing his wish to relinquish it; yet no man has left office with such ill grace or fought so unscrupulously to recover it. He despised writers and literary men; yet only Luther and Goethe rank with him as masters of German prose. He found happiness only in his family; loved his wife, and gave to his children the affection that he had been denied by his mother. He said in old age that his greatest good fortune was 'that God did not take any of my children from me.' Yet he ruined the happiness of his adored elder son for the sake of a private feud, and thought nothing of spending a long holiday away from his wife in the company of a pretty girl; indeed he was so self-centred that he boasted to his wife of the girl's charm and good looks. He claimed to serve sometimes the king of Prussia, sometimes Germany, sometimes God. All three were cloaks for his own will; and he turned against them ruthlessly when they did not serve his purpose. He could have said with Oliver Cromwell, whom he much resembled; 'He goeth furthest who knows not whither he is going.' The young Junker had no vision that he would unify Germany on the basis of universal suffrage; and the maker of three wars did not expect to end as the great buttress of European peace.

Bismarck was not brought up as a Junker, despite his constant assertions of this character in later life. The family moved soon after he was born to the smaller estate of Kniephof in Pomerania. Here there was a smaller house with no architectural pretensions and hard practical farming. The Junkers, unlike the English gentry, did not live on rents. They worked the land themselves, and their peasants

were, in reality, agricultural labourers, many of whom did
not cultivate any land of their own. Bismarck experienced
this idyllic existence only till he was seven. Then his
mother set up house in Berlin, no doubt much to her own
satisfaction, but ostensibly to send her sons to school in the
capital. This exile from the country gave Bismarck a lasting
grievance against his mother. The education which she
chose for him was another. A Junker's son usually went into
a cadet corps and, later, joined a cavalry regiment, even if
he was not destined for a permanent military career.
Wilhelmine, however, insisted that her children should have
an intellectual education suited to the grandsons of the
great Menken; and Bismarck went to the best Berlin
grammar school of the day where he mixed with the sons
of middle-class families. His mother revived her connexions
with the court; and Bismarck led a privileged existence,
mixing on intimate terms with the younger Hohenzollerns.
This counted in his later career. Despite his sturdy affecta·
tion of independence, he was always inside the royal circle
and was treated as one of the family.

The spirit of the Enlightenment still dominated Prussian
education; and Bismarck left school 'as a Pantheist and if
not as a republican, with the belief that a republic was the
most reasonable form of state.' His mother once more imposed her intellectual standards by sending him out of
Prussia to the university of Göttingen in Hanover, the
greatest liberal centre of the day. Bismarck at first took a
radical line. He defied university discipline both in behaviour and ideas. What was more, he joined the *Burschen-
schaften*—students' unions which tried to keep alive the
revolutionary spirit of the war of liberation. He soon
turned the other way. It was one thing to pose as a young
radical in the court circles of Berlin; quite another to accept
these ill-bred students from the middle class as his equals.
Personal relations changed Bismarck's political outlook, as
was often to happen in his later life. He suddenly discovered
pride of blood and joined an aristocratic students-corps. He
still led a disorderly existence. He drank a great deal; had

some passionate *affaires*; and, like the young Disraeli, wore
fantastic and colourful clothes. He was always ready for a
duel, though the only time he was injured he characteristically alleged that it was a foul blow—an allegation which he
maintained unforgivingly even thirty years later. After
three terms, debts drove him back to Berlin, where he could
live at home; and here he put in a second academic year.
In May, 1835, when he was just twenty, he scraped through
the examination which qualified him for entry into the
Prussian civil service.

Though Bismarck was never a great scholar, his years at
the university left their mark. He read widely, despite his
boasts of idleness, though he read more history than the law
that he was supposed to be studying. He liked Schiller,
admired Goethe, and ranked Shakespeare and Byron above
either of them—tastes characteristic of the Romantic
movement. Scott was his greatest favourite of all, romance
and history blended in the right proportions. Bismarck's
classical learning was scanty; his scientific knowledge almost non-existent. All the historical references in his
speeches are to the three hundred years since the Reforma-
tion; his occasional echoes of Darwinianism only what he
could pick up from a newspaper. Philosophy never interested him; and he was one of the few Germans to escape
the influence of Hegel. People were always more important
to Bismarck than books; and he made at the university the
only two lasting friendships of his life, both with men who
were—like him—in a strange environment, fish out of
water. Alexander Keyserling was a German baron from the
Baltic and later a distinguished naturalist. John Motley
was a budding American diplomat, who became the historian of the Dutch republic. Bismarck trusted himself only
to these strangers. The ties of affection between these three
never weakened, despite years of separation. Bismarck was
writing to 'dear old John' with undiminished enthusiasm
forty years later; and even when he became Imperial
Chancellor would throw aside the cares and dignity of office
to make Motley welcome. Keyserling was less demonstra-

tive; but he, too, was faithful. After Bismarck's fall from power, Keyserling, though nearly eighty, left his Baltic retreat to console his old friend; and his visit gave Bismarck a last experience of quiet happiness.

Bismarck grew up into the Germany of reaction. The great storm of the Napoleonic empire had been followed by 'the quiet years'. Germany was divided into thirty-nine states, the survivors after much Napoleonic reconstruction. Most of them were tiny; half a dozen were of medium rank; and, overshadowing them, the two great states, Austria and Prussia. The congress of Vienna had tied them all together into a loose confederation, which was supposed to settle internal disputes and even to provide a federal defence force in case of foreign war. In practice its only function turned out to be the suppression of German liberalism; and it did even that ineffectively. Austria was the presiding Power in the confederation. She had the greater historic prestige—an emperor as ruler, and Metternich, the most famous statesman of the day, as chancellor. She had the army of a Great Power, supposedly capable of challenging that of France, as it had often done—unsuccessfully— during the Napoleonic wars. But the Austrian empire was in decay—its finances shaky, its administration rigid and out-of-date, its very existence menaced by the rise of Italian and German nationalism.

Prussia had been the more severely mauled by Napoleon; and remembrance of this kept her policy safely on the conservative line with Austria. She hardly counted among the Great Powers. In 1815, there were only ten million Prussians, as against thirty million Frenchmen and almost thirty million subjects of the Austrian emperor. Her army was not of much esteem. The other Powers relied on conscripts chosen by lot, who served for fifteen or twenty years. Prussia made up for her weakness in manpower by giving all, or most, of her subjects a three-year training and recalling them for service in time of war. Though this was to be the pattern of all subsequent military development, it was despised by contemporary experts as providing little more than a civilian militia. Frederick William III, who reigned until 1840, was timid and unimaginative, clinging anxiously to Metternich's coat-tails for protection. During the excitement of the war of liberation he promised his people a constitution. But he soon repented of his promise and did not carry it out. All that remained of it was a promise that the Prussian state would not incur any new loan without the consent of some sort of popular assembly. The eight provinces of Prussia had diets elected on a class basis and with few real functions. For all practical purposes Prussia continued to be run by a narrow bureaucracy, its standards of efficiency and honesty higher than any other in Europe, but remote from popular feeling.

Germany was still overwhelmingly rural, even Berlin only an overgrown garrison-town. The French had begun to develop the coalmines of the Ruhr when they controlled the Kingdom of Westphalia. But the few great capitalists of Germany drew their wealth from commerce and banking on the artery of the Rhine. The customs-union (*Zollverein*) which Prussia had organized by 1834 got rid of most internal tariffs, but trade was on a modest scale—mainly the import of British manufactured goods in exchange for German wool and wheat. There was some intellectual stir in Germany, despite this economic stagnation. The German universities were at this time the best in Europe. The Prince Consort rightly took them as his model when he attempted, somewhat ineffectually, to reform Oxford and Cambridge. Most of the students affected a hazy radicalism. Even Bismarck did not escape this influence. He jeered at the bureaucracy and said to Keyserling: 'A constitution is inevitable. This is the way to honour in the world.' Like most of his generation, he thought that Prussia would come to dominate Germany by her liberalism, not by her strength.

His short career in the civil service was not a success. In 1836, after a few weeks of training at Potsdam, he was sent to Aachen in the Prussian Rhineland. This territory had been acquired by Prussia only in 1815, as compensation for the Polish lands which Russia insisted on retaining. The inhabitants had no attachment to Prussia. They were Roman Catholics, much influenced by French liberalism and impatient with reaction. They had been included in France for twenty years and indeed retained the Napoleonic code until 1900. The Prussian administrators were despised and disliked. But Bismarck did not trouble himself much with the inhabitants. Cosmopolitan travellers passed through Aachen on their way to more fashionable spas; and Bismarck neglected his official duties to mix with this wealthy crowd. He imagined himself in love with one rich English girl after another, allegedly flying as high as a niece of the Duke of Cleveland. Soon he claimed to be engaged to a young lady from Leicestershire. Taking a fortnight's leave, he followed his betrothed across Germany. He ran heavily into debt and overstayed his leave by three months. The affair came to nothing, and he was left only with a knowledge of colloquial English. He was too proud to return to Aachen with a request for forgiveness. It is easy to guess what he would have said, as Chancellor, of a subordinate who slipped off in this way. Bismarck merely replied to complaints: 'He by no means intended to give the government an account of his personal relations.'

He found a simple means of evading Aachen. Prussians with a secondary education had to serve for a year in the army as officers; and Bismarck still had this hanging over him. He tried to escape by pleading a muscular weakness: 'I have told them I feel pain when I raise my right arm.' The plea did not work, and Bismarck joined the garrison at Potsdam. He found it tedious and, never having been to boarding-school, railed fiercely against the hardships of life in barracks. Yet he led a privileged existence, constantly invited to the royal palace, where he strengthened his acquaintance with the crown prince—soon to be Frederick William IV—and perfected the arts of a courtier. His only achievement in the field was to rescue a corporal who had fallen into a ditch; he received a medal for life-saving—the only military decoration that he ever earned. His later admiration for the military virtues was certainly not based on personal experience or taste; and when his sons did their military service, he lamented their fate with civilian bitterness.

In 1839, when his year of service was completed, he resigned from the Prussian bureaucracy. He found high grounds for his action. The Prussian official, he said, was only a member of an orchestra. 'But I will play music the way I like, or none at all.' His ambition was to have 'the career of a statesman in a free constitution, such as Peel, O'Connell, Mirabeau, etc.' A strange trio! Peel, seeking a compromise between the old England and the new, one can understand; even Mirabeau, struggling to create a strong constitutional monarchy in the storm of the French Revolution. But how did Bismarck hit on O'Connell, the radical tribune of Irish nationalism? Evidently principles did not matter to him. The important thing was to take part in 'energetic political movements'.

Bismarck was now 24, at a loss for a future. His mother died the same year, with her hopes for her son disappointed. The family fortunes had fallen into disorder through his father's incompetence and neglect. Bismarck and his elder brother established the old man at Schönhausen and took over the Pomeranian estates themselves.[1] Here was the Junker life which had always been Bismarck's ideal; and he anticipated an idyllic existence. 'I shall be happy in the country surroundings of my family; *car tel est mon plaisir.*' It soon turned to dust and ashes. He confessed later to his wife: 'I learnt only from experience that the Arcadian life of a dyed-in-the-wool landowner with double book-keeping and chemical experiments was an illusion.' The eight years that he spent as a working landowner were the most wretched and barren of his life. Unlike Cavour in similar circumstances, he never tried to take the lead in agrarian improvements. As he showed later, country life was for him

---

[1] In 1845, when Ferdinand von Bismarck died, Otto moved to Schönhausen and left the Pomeranian estates in the hands of his brother. He later sold his share, insisting on the full market price.

a matter of display, not of genuine economic activity; and he would overspend on his estate at the slightest excuse. In these years he and his brother restored the family finances by plodding economy, not by any striking initiative. This vegetating life was not enough to satisfy Bismarck's energy. He was driven crazy with boredom and with the futility of his existence. He found the society of his Junker neighbours intolerable; and they in turn distrusted him. His only public achievement was to become keeper of dykes on the Elbe—symbolic, perhaps, but trivial. He read enormously—history for the most part and classical English novels. *Tristram Shandy* especially took his fancy; and he saw himself as the same sort of eccentric. He rode hallooing through the woods at night and seduced the peasants' daughters. He released a fox in a lady's drawing-room. These wild escapades won him the title of 'the mad Junker'. When money ran to it, he travelled—once to England, where he saw the new industries of Lancashire. He thought of joining the British forces in India; then asked himself, 'what harm have the Indians done to me?', and refrained.

In 1844 he returned to the Prussian civil service, only to leave it again after a fortnight. His simple explanation was: 'I have never been able to put up with superiors.' By now he was 30, bitter, cynical and neurotic, his gifts running to nothing. New life came unexpectedly with religion, a wife, and a revolution. Bismarck learnt religion from the only neighbours for whom he cared—devout Lutherans who developed a quietist religion in a Quaker spirit. He was impressed by their content and peaceful confidence. Hoping to discover their secret, he spent much time in their company; and he found there a wife, Johanna von Puttkamer. His open avowal of religious belief was, no doubt, made partly to win her hand. After baring his soul to his prospective father-in-law, he wrote lightheartedly to his sceptical brother: 'I think I am entitled to count myself among the adherents of the Christian religion. Though in many doctrines, perhaps in those which they regard as essential, I am far removed from their standpoint, yet a sort of treaty of Passau has been silently established between us.[1] Besides, I like piety in women and have a horror of feminine cleverness.' This letter, too, was a piece of diplomacy, with its repudiation of their mother in the last sentence. Yet there can be no doubt that, whatever reserves he might have for his brother, Bismarck's faith became strong and sincere.

His religion was far removed from Christianity, or rather from the humanitarian Christianity of the twentieth century. There was in it little love, except for his own family. He believed in the God of the Old Testament and of the English puritans, the God of battles. Luther or Oliver Cromwell would have understood Bismarck's religion, though it is less easily grasped by those for whom religion is simply a high-flown form of liberalism. Bismarck certainly used war as an instrument of policy and exercised secular power to the full. Anglo-Saxon sentimentalists are therefore inclined to suggest that his religion was sham. Yet the overwhelming majority of Christians have agreed with Bismarck in both theory and practice for nearly two thousand years. Lutheranism especially never claimed to lay down moral principles for public policy. It taught that service to the state and to the appointed ruler was a high religious duty. Bismarck felt this himself: 'I believe that I am obeying God when I serve the King.' His religion gave to his unstable personality a settled purpose and a sense of power. He said just after Sedan: 'You would not have had such a Chancellor if I had not the wonderful basis of religion.' He believed that he was doing God's work in making Prussia strong and in unifying Germany. The belief itself brought power. God was on his side; therefore he could ignore the opposition of men. Like others who have had this belief, he easily persuaded himself that whatever suited him at the moment was God's purpose and, indeed,

[1] The treaty of Passau, made in 1552, first allowed Lutheranism and Roman Catholicism to exist side-by-side in Germany. It symbolized a grudging and resentful religious toleration.

that he understood this purpose a great deal better than did God Himself.

Marriage brought to Bismarck lasting and secure happiness. Unlike most men, Bismarck did not marry his mother, but her opposite—a simple, devoted woman, endlessly patient and ready to put up with anything. Under his rough exterior, he was deeply emotional, a man of the romantic movement. He had grown up just when the Byronic legend dominated the continent. He was the contemporary of Heine and Wagner. Like Gladstone, he was much given to tears at any public or private crisis; no doubt he too would have wept over *East Lynne*. He broke down sobbing after his first public speech and again after the battle of Sadova. He wept when he became Prime Minister and even more when he left office. William I and he often sobbed together, though Bismarck always got his way. Music affected him deeply, the more because he could neither play nor read it. And by music he meant a soft glow of feeling when the sonatas of Beethoven were played with more expression than accuracy. He agreed with his wife's verdict on Anton Rubinstein, the greatest pianist of the age: 'The playing was masterly both in control and attack and in everything you like, and yet "the heart, the heart remains homeless".' Johanna gave him a home for his heart, and it was very homely indeed. Though he played high drama on the public stage, his private setting resembled a Victorian boarding-house. Even in that tasteless age contemporaries commented on the banality of Bismarck's surroundings.

When Bismarck proposed marriage to Johanna von Puttkamer, he supposed that he was offering her a life in the country. But political activity called him even before the wedding, and the Bismarcks never knew uninterrupted country life until his retirement at the age of 75—and then much to his regret. Frederick William IV, who succeeded his father as King of Prussia in 1840, was far removed from the usual Hohenzollern stamp. He had an intellect above the average and a fine gift of phrase. Though he asserted his divine right, he strove also for popularity and dreamt of restoring the glories of an imaginary middle age, as described in the novels of Sir Walter Scott, when the King was surrounded by his loyal vassals. He thought to ward off a parliament by reviving the Estates of the Realm—estates which had never existed in Prussia and had long perished elsewhere. This would get round his father's promise of a constitution and, as a more practical point, allow him to raise a loan for a railway to the eastern provinces of Prussia. In 1847 he summoned the provincial estates to meet as a 'united diet' in Berlin. Bismarck had little prestige among his fellow Junkers, and they had not made him a member of his local diet, only a substitute in case any regular member fell ill. He did not receive the call to Berlin. But in May a regular member retired, and Bismarck took his place. Only the illness of Herr von Brauchitsch launched him into history. Bismarck said so himself in 1881: 'No one would ever have heard of me in my rural retreat, if I had not become a member of the united diet by chance.'

Bismarck had often expressed his dislike of the absolutist bureaucrat state; and he might have been expected to join with those who were demanding a modern constitution for Prussia. But those who demanded control over the public accounts and regular meetings of the diet were themselves bureaucrats. Indeed in a community without political experience, it would have been impossible to provide a quorum for the diet if state servants had been excluded from it. Thus, when Bismarck attacked the liberals he was attacking his old enemies. He was a true rebel, though for himself, not for others—always better at destructive criticism than at creation, and never willing to co-operate. Now he found himself, somewhat to his surprise, the champion of 'historic' Prussia, asserting what were in fact the very recent rights of the Crown and the nobility. He liked nothing better than to face a hostile assembly; and he got his wish in full measure.

Bismarck resisted every liberal proposal. He denounced the emancipation of the Jews and defended the game laws.

When a speaker argued that the Prussian people had merited freedom by their services during the war of liberation in 1813, Bismarck answered: 'He had thought that the oppression against which they fought then came from abroad. Now he was taught that it was at home, and he was not grateful for the lesson.' It did not need Bismarck to bring the united diet to deadlock. The majority would not authorize a railway loan without the guarantee of regular meetings; and Frederick William IV would not make this concession to liberalism. At the end of June the diet was prorogued. Bismarck had made a name for himself in a narrow reactionary circle. He had high Tory principles, yet a gift of sharp expression that would have become a Jacobin. Perhaps his gift was a little too striking; slow-witted squires distrust cleverness even when it is displayed on their side. With the diet out of the way, he was free to marry and to go on honeymoon. He met Frederick William IV at Venice and received the King's approval for his attitude at the diet. His future as a reactionary seemed secure.

But the old world of monarchy was coming to an end. The continent of Europe had recovered from the exhaustion of the Napoleonic wars. Everywhere men wanted to take up the work of the French Revolution and to assert the ideals of individual and national freedom. The year of revolution was approaching. In January 1848, revolution stirred in Italy. On 24 February, the French monarchy was overthrown and a republic established in Paris. The revolution soon spread to Germany. A group of learned men called for a German national parliament. On 13 March Metternich, symbol of the old order, was overthrown in Vienna. Prussia was more stable than Austria, its army strong enough to put down any disorder. But Frederick William was not the man for a stern conflict with the revolution. Street-fighting in Berlin soon made him lose his nerve. On 18 March he ordered the army to withdraw; announced that 'Prussia merges into Germany'; and agreed to call a Prussian parliament. Bismarck's liberal enemies of 1847 had won. He himself was in the country when the revolution broke out. His first thought was to rescue the king with the aid of his 'faithful peasants'. It was sentimental Jacobitism to suppose that untrained peasants could succeed where the army had failed.

Bismarck hurried off to Potsdam and even entered Berlin, wearing a national cockade. He tried to persuade the commanding generals to stage a counter-revolution; but, as on many later occasions, the Prussian generals would not meddle in politics without an order from above. Each would act only if the other generals acted first. They were moved, but not to action, when Bismarck picked out the notes of a cavalry-charge on the piano. Finally, he managed to see the king for a few minutes. The queen lamented that the king had been unable to sleep for three nights from worry. Bismarck answered: 'A King *must* be able to sleep.'[1] In desperation he planned a reactionary stroke. Frederick William was childless; his brother William, Prince of Prussia, had gone into exile in England. Bismarck sought out Augusta, William's wife, and proposed that Frederick William should be pushed aside; William should renounce his rights; and their young son should be put on the throne as the figurehead of reaction. A similar manœuvre made Francis Joseph Emperor of Austria in December. In March it was too early; and Augusta in any case too loyal both to her husband and to her brother-in-law. She rejected the idea indignantly and harboured a lasting resentment against Bismarck which was to hamper him throughout his career.[2]

There seemed nothing to be done. Liberalism was in the ascendant. A German national assembly and a Prussian parliament were elected, both by universal suffrage; and the electors did not choose Bismarck for either. As a gesture

[1] But did he really say it? In the first draft of his recollections, the remark appears as: 'A King *must* not sleep.' Perhaps the whole dialogue only occurred to him some forty years later.

[2] Here again Bismarck improved on reality when he came to write his recollections. According to him, Augusta proposed putting her son on the throne with herself as Regent; and he loyally defeated the proposal. But the contemporary record is against him.

of defiance against the revolution, he began to sign himself *von* Bismarck for the first time. This was his only concrete achievement during the revolutionary year. Throughout the summer he drifted round Berlin, attempting to organize the Prussian conservatives and engaging in futile court intrigue. In the autumn Frederick William plucked up courage. He ordered the army to reoccupy Berlin and dissolved the radical parliament. But he did not intend to restore absolutism. He issued a constitution which provided for a parliament with more restricted powers; the electorate was also limited, and the elections were made indirect—the primary electors did not choose their representative, but only an electoral committee. This gave Bismarck his chance. He was elected to the new parliament by 152 votes of the committee against 144. He was still hostile to Frederick William's attempts at compromise. Later on, he claimed to have acted as a secret adviser in forming the conservative ministry. The king's real opinion of him was expressed in the comment; 'red reactionary, smells of blood, only to be used when the bayonet rules.'

Frederick William kept up an appearance of liberalism in the hope of leading the movement for German unity. He was always a German nationalist, though he learnt his nationalism from the romantic movement and not from the French Revolution. Here, too, Bismarck was hostile. He was, he said, 'a decided opponent of the German swindle in every form' and believed only in 'the specifically Prussian'. He denounced the attempt 'to force on Prussia the role which Sardinia had played in Italy'. Instead he wanted a conflict between 'authority by the grace of God' and 'revolution and popular sovereignty'. Frederick William hoped to reconcile the two. While the revolution was at its height, the national assembly at Frankfurt had tried to create a united German state which would include also the German provinces of Austria. At the end of 1848 reaction triumphed in Vienna; and Felix Schwarzenberg, the Austrian prime minister, would have nothing to do with German nationalism. The Frankfurt assembly had to accept a 'lesser Germany' without Austria, whether they would or not; and in April 1849 they offered the Imperial throne to Frederick William IV. The Prussians jumped at this chance of aggrandisement, even with its liberal coating. On 2 April the members of the Prussian parliament appealed to Frederick William IV to accept the Imperial crown; even Bismarck put his name to the letter. But Frederick William stuck to his monarchist principles. He would accept the crown, he replied, only if it were offered to him by the German princes. Bismarck hastily trimmed his sails. He, too, denounced the Frankfurt assembly. Though he admitted that everyone who spoke German, including himself, wanted the unification of Germany, 'yet with this constitution I do *not* want it.'

He did not need to worry. Frederick William's refusal of the Imperial crown ended the Frankfurt national assembly. The moderate liberals, who were in the majority, went home in despair. The radical rump tried to put the imperial constitution into effect without either an army or an emperor. The Austrian forces were still fully engaged against the revolutions in Hungary and Italy. All the German princes clustered under Prussia for protection. The radicals had once planned to capture the Prussian army. Now this army turned them out of Frankfurt and suppressed the risings in Saxony and Baden. There was, in a sense, a Prussian conquest of Germany, but it was a conquest achieved against those who believed in German unification. Frederick William and his intimate adviser, Radowitz, tried to turn the situation to some account. The German princes were dependent on Prussian protection; therefore they could be induced to 'consent' to Prussia's leadership of Germany, yet—with the defeat of the radicals —this could be presented as a respectable, even a conservative, programme. The princes had no choice so long as Austria was without weight in Germany; and Radowitz badgered them into setting up the Erfurt Union, a 'lesser Germany' with a parliament, elected on a limited suffrage, and its armed forces under Prussian control. This was al-

most exactly the Germany which Bismarck created twenty
years later. But at the time he could not denounce it
enough. 'We are Prussians and want to remain Prussian.'
Instead of challenging Austria, they should return to the
system of Metternich—'the agreement of Austria and
Prussia to control the whole of Germany.' Another saying
of his in the Prussian parliament was to read oddly later.
Opposing civil marriage, he declared: 'I hope to see the ship
of fools of the age wrecked on the rock of the Christian
church.' He was always ready to challenge the liberal
politicians with some provocative phrase. Yet in 1849 he
took a step on the road to professional politics and away
from a quiet Junker life. He farmed out the lands at Schönhausen which had come to him on the death of his father
in 1845 and rented a house in Berlin.

The parliament of the Erfurt Union actually met in
April 1850. The liberals from the Frankfurt assembly were
in the majority and Bismarck protested against everything
as usual. But the struggle for mastery in Germany had still
to be fought. The Austrian empire had recovered its
strength. Italy and Hungary were subdued, and despotic
Austria enjoyed the favour of the tsar. Schwarzenberg was
determined to reassert Austria's pre-eminence in Germany.
He revived the diet of the old confederation which had
fallen into oblivion at the beginning of the revolution, and
looked round for a conflict. He soon found one. The Elector
of Hesse, once a member of the Erfurt Union, was at odds
with his subjects. He appealed to the confederation to
restore order, and the diet authorized Austrian and
Bavarian troops to intervene. This was a vital challenge to
Prussia. For, apart from the question of the Union, the
Prussian military road which joined the Rhineland to
Brandenburg ran through Hesse. Frederick William was at
first all for resistance. Radowitz was made foreign minister,
and preparations were made to mobilize the Prussian army.
Shots were exchanged between Austrian and Prussian
soldiers for the first time since 1778. The king's conserva-
tive advisers soon revolted. They shrank from a war in

which they would have to call on revolutionary France and even on Sardinia against the two legitimist Powers, Austria and Russia. The minister of war discovered that the army was not prepared for war; and Bismarck, 'as a lieutenant of the reserve', felt it his duty not 'to raise his voice against a general'. Radowitz resigned; and his successor, Manteuffel, met Schwarzenberg at Olomouc (Olmütz). He agreed to disband the Erfurt Union and to join in restoring the old confederation.

The course of Prussian aggrandisement was temporarily arrested. Even the most conservative felt the 'shame' of Olomouc. When Manteuffel came to defend it in parliament, he said ruefully: 'The efforts of Prussia have not been crowned with success. . . . There is always something sad in the failure of a policy.' Bismarck had no such regrets. He alone defended the settlement of Olomouc without reserve. He repudiated the notion that Prussia 'should play the Don Quixote for offended parliamentary celebrities'. The Erfurt Union would not have united Germany. It 'would have made us shoot and kill our German fellow-countrymen in the South', and he praised Austria as 'a German power which had the good fortune to rule over foreign races'. Bismarck regarded Olomouc as a decisive defeat for the revolution of 1848. Liberal dreams of German unity had been shattered, and the conservative system of Metternich had been restored. Historic right had triumphed over national freedom. Yet at heart Bismarck had no sympathy with this outlook. When one of his conservative friends said that Austria had right on her side, he answered: 'I don't recognize any right in foreign policy.' And he said in his parliamentary speech: 'The only healthy foundation for a great state is egoism, not romanticism, and it is unworthy of a great state to dispute over something which does not concern its own interest.'

There was no doubt a case to be made against Radowitz and the policy of the Erfurt Union. Prussia lacked allies; the tsar would perhaps have supported Austria; the German liberals were strong only in words; the Prussian army was inadequate.[1] Yet, reviewing Bismarck's arguments, it is difficult to resist the impression that the policy of uniting the lesser Germany without Austria had one overriding fault in his eyes: it was being conducted by Radowitz, instead of by Bismarck. He declared in words worthy of John Bright:[2]

> 'Woe to the statesman, who at this time does not seek a cause for war which will still be valid after the war. . . . Will you have the courage then to go to the peasant in the ashes of his cottage, to the cripple, to the childless father, and to say: "You have suffered much, but rejoice with us, the constitution of the Union is saved!" '

Powerful rhetoric! But could not a critic have said the same of the wars which Bismarck conducted in 1866 and 1870? Yet Bismarck was not insincere. Like many great men before they find their vocation, he specialized in denunciation and harsh invective. The elder Pitt confessed late in life the injustice of the attacks on Walpole by which he made his name; Mussolini, who opposed the Italian conquest of Libya in 1911, himself conquered Abyssinia in 1935; Lloyd George, the pro-Boer of one war, was 'the man who won the war' of the next; and Stalin rejoiced in 1945 at having revenged the tsar's defeat in what he had once called the 'criminal' Russo-Japanese war. Men see things very differently when they are themselves in power.

[1] This opinion was not held by all good judges. The Prussian minister of war opposed the war on principle and therefore found technical arguments against it, as soldiers can always do. But Prince William, who was somewhat of an authority, believed that the army could defeat Austria; and the Russian general Paskievich, who had seen the Austrian army in action in Hungary, thought that Prussia could take on both Austria and such Russian forces as could be spared for a war in Germany.

[2] The parallel is closer than either man would have liked. During the Crimean war, Bright denounced the quixotic idea of Lord John Russell that Great Britain should defend the liberties of Germany: 'What a notion a man must have of the duties . . . of the people living in these islands if he thinks . . . that the sacred treasure of the bravery, resolution, and unfaltering courage of the people of England is to be squandered in a contest . . . for the preservation of the independence of Germany, and of the integrity, civilization, and something else, of all Europe.'

It did not yet occur to Bismarck that he would ever attain power. After Olomouc he remained the provocative and irresponsible critic. His last words in parliament as a private member were thoroughly in character: 'Be sure, gentlemen, that we shall know how to make the name of Junkerdom honoured and respected.' When parliament adjourned, he puzzled for some means of adding to his income, in order to support his growing family—a son and a daughter, with another son born in 1852. He even thought of returning to the state-service which he had given up so emphatically twelve years before. Opportunity came unexpectedly. With the restoration of the German confederation, Prussia needed a delegate to the federal diet at Frankfurt. It would be a thankless task to acknowledge in daily practice the Austrian supremacy which had been recognized at Olomouc. Who so suitable as Bismarck, the one Prussian who apparently had a genuine belief in co-operation with Austria? He had had only six months' experience of administration and none of diplomacy. In all the history of the Prussian monarchy he was the only man ever appointed to a high diplomatic post without previous service. However, his training might be enough to handle the economic questions, which were the only important German issues for the men in Berlin. If he failed, no one would be the worse for it. Bismarck was not alarmed. 'I shall do my duty. It is God's affair to give me understanding.' For once he could say with truth: 'I have not sought it, the Lord wished it', though the Lord's name was invoked primarily for its effect on his wife. She would have liked him to give up all public affairs and settle down in the country. He, without knowing it, had turned his back on a quiet life for good and all. He was to serve Prussia, Germany, and God without interruption for more than thirty-nine years. In other words, his feet were at last on the ladder of power. He was 36.

THE DIPLOMAT

WITH the meeting of the federal diet at Frankfurt, the old order in Germany seemed to have been restored unchanged. This was far from being the case. Though the great revolution had blown over, the men who ruled in Vienna and Berlin had been shaped by their experiences in it. Frederick William IV went on dreaming of some impossible stroke by which he could make Prussia dominant in Germany with Austrian consent. Though he would never go against Austria, he would also never accept subordination to her. Manteuffel, the foreign minister, knew nothing of foreign affairs. He was an old-style civil servant, who had been pushed into the office on the sudden death of Brandenburg in November 1850, and he had no plan of foreign policy. All he wanted was to keep out of difficulties; but he, too, had a sturdy Prussian pride and would not accept Austrian orders.

There was a greater change on the Austrian side. Her rulers had acquired new confidence from their victories in Hungary and Italy. They despised Metternich's gentle methods and thought that rudeness was the best diplomatic method. Schwarzenberg, who directed Austrian policy until his sudden death in 1852, planned to include the entire Habsburg monarchy in the German confederation; and a conference to achieve this was held at Dresden early in 1851. But the smaller states, who had welcomed Austrian support against Prussian encroachment, were equally opposed to Austrian control and voted solidly against her plans. The confederation had to be carried on unchanged. The federal diet had seventeen members—the larger states one each, the smaller lumped together with five delegates.[1]

---

[1] The *plenum* of all thirty-nine states met only to approve changes of the federal constitution—and none was ever made.

Previously Metternich had run the diet in partnership with Prussia and arranged the business, such as it was, with her delegate beforehand. Now the Austrians asserted their presidential position and planned to control Prussia with the votes of the smaller states. In any international organization it is easy to forget in peacetime the realities of power; and, since Prussia had only one vote, the Austrians assumed that she was on the same level as Bavaria or even Schaumburg-Lippe.

Bismarck, perhaps, went to Frankfurt with the sincere intention of co-operating with Austria. For him, at any rate, the perils and humiliations of the revolutionary year were not forgotten. More probably, he had not thought about his future policy. He always lived in the moment and responded to its challenge. In the Prussian parliament the liberals had been his enemy; and he answered them by preaching co-operation with Austria. Now, at Frankfurt, his opponent was the Austrian delegate; and he reacted at once without thought for consistency. He did not weigh Prussia's strength or her position in Europe. He saw only his immediate opponent and wanted Prussian policy to be subordinated to his own needs. He was always quick to take offence personally; and Austria's airs as 'the presiding power' were enough to offend a less sensitive man. The Austrian delegate arranged the business and often settled matters without consulting his colleagues. Bismarck insisted, like the Russians at the United Nations, on knowing every detail.

A trivial gesture announced the coming struggle for mastery in Germany. Only the Austrian delegate smoked at meetings. Bismarck pulled out a cigar and asked the Austrian for a match. His act showed that he was a man of a new sort. Previous Prussian delegates had been high aristocrats and, like all the men of the old order, non-smokers. Only Austrian aristocrats smoked—a habit they acquired when they inherited the tobacco-monopoly from Napoleon in Lombardy. Bismarck had learnt to smoke from the radical students whom he otherwise despised; and his cigar was a reminder that he really belonged to the world of the *Burschenschaft* despite his affectation of sympathy with the principles of Metternich. The conflict was repeated in every conversation. Thun, the Austrian, sneered at 'the legacy of Frederick the Great' and compared Prussia to a man who, having once won a prize in a lottery, based his annual budget on it. Bismarck replied: 'If that is what they think in Vienna, Prussia will have to speculate in the said lottery again.'

The Austrians did not take Bismarck's complaints seriously, nor admit that their policy had changed. They perhaps behaved with more arrogance than in the days of Metternich; but they had always behaved with much. Even Metternich did not really regard Prussia as Austria's equal. He flattered her because flattery was his way; but he thought of Austria as the only Great Power in Germany. Bismarck unconsciously confessed that the change originated in himself, not in the Austrians. He wrote in February 1852: 'Since the month of September of last year, Austria has abandoned the ground on which we used to meet.' But nothing had happened in September 1851 so far as Austria was concerned. The only significance of the date was that Bismarck then received official confirmation of his appointment as Prussian representative. Once more he changed his policy simply because of his personal feelings. He had advocated co-operation with Austria when he was attacking Radowitz. He swung over to Radowitz's programme of a lesser Germany when he felt that the Austrian representative was not treating him as a social equal; and this personal resentment was at once translated into high-flown political terms. 'I conceived the idea of withdrawing Germany from Austrian control, at least that part of Germany united by its spirit, its religion, its character and its interests to the destinies of Prussia—northern Germany.' He made no pretence as yet that this was what the Germans wanted. He admitted frankly that 'the best thing for the confederation would undoubtedly be to put ourselves and all German governments under Austria militarily, politi-

cally and economically'; but 'advantage for the confederation cannot be the guiding-line of Prussian policy'. His
aim, in fact, was to divide Germany with Austria, not to
unite it.

The conflict on which he set out could not be settled by
votes at the Frankfurt diet. The smaller states, with no
real strength of their own, went with Prussia against any
Austrian attempt to unify Germany; they swung round just
as much to the Austrian side if Prussia made any positive
proposals. Bismarck wrote to Berlin: 'Only outside Germany can we find the means to strengthen our position in
the interest of Germany itself.' He had no faith in public
opinion or in liberal support. Foreign alliances, not an
appeal to German feeling, would solve the German question.
Hence Bismarck concentrated on European diplomacy, not
on the intricacies of federal politics. His guiding principle
was the aggrandisement of Prussia 'according to the principles of Frederick the Great'; and he acknowledged loyalty
neither to legitimacy nor to German nationalism. He never
acted as a traditional ambassador, carrying out the instructions of his government. Soon after going to Frankfurt
he wrote with becoming modesty: 'the river of history flows
as it will, and if I put my hand in it, this is because I regard
it as my duty, not because I think I can change its course.'
In reality he soon set out to devise the policy which his
government ought to follow. After all, he had no experience
of the diplomatic service until he stepped into the highest
rank; and he never troubled to learn the trade. His notes of
conversations with others were unsatisfactory all his life on
a technical standard—invaluable for revealing the current
of Bismarck's own thought, unreliable as a record of the
other man's point of view.

His reports from Frankfurt carried this to extremes. He
never troubled to report what was going on there or what
the other representatives said. His sole concern was advocacy. He preached to Frederick William IV and to
Manteuffel the policy which seemed to him right and
criticized them when they rejected it. A Prussian diplomat

who behaved like this when Bismarck was in power would soon have run into trouble. Soon after becoming prime minister of Prussia, he wrote to Goltz in Paris: 'Policy can only be made once, and it must be that on which the ministry and the king are agreed.' This was not at all his line when at Frankfurt; and it earned him no rebuke. Frederick William liked contradictory advice. Manteuffel preached timid inaction; Gerlach, his unofficial adviser, upheld legitimism and a struggle against the revolution; Bismarck wanted conflict with Austria; and Bunsen, the King's closest friend, advocated from London a 'liberal' alliance with Great Britain. Frederick William dodged among them all, appreciating their ideas without following them. He commented on one of Bismarck's reports: 'a masterpiece of its kind', though he did not accept its proposals. Bismarck, while ostensibly loyal, was driven to exasperation by his elusive master; and, when written argument failed, would hurry to Berlin in the hope that personal persuasion might succeed. In his own words, he went from Frankfurt to Berlin like the pendulum of a clock—an early instance of the changes brought to diplomacy by the railway train. But, unfortunately for Bismarck, not all his efforts could make the clock strike.

Bismarck scored an early success against Austria—negative, but decisive. The great Prussian advance of 'the quiet years' had been the building of a German customs-union, the *Zollverein*. This included nearly all the German states except Austria; and it inevitably turned German trade from the Danube valley to the ports of the North Sea. Metternich had foreseen the political weakening of Austria that must follow; but he could do nothing so long as the Austrian empire was itself divided by a separate tariff-barrier with Hungary. This barrier was swept away in 1850 after the revolution; and the Austrian government now asked to be included in the *Zollverein*. The demand was justified if the policy of Olomouc had any real meaning. Bismarck took the lead against it. He went on a special mission to Vienna, gave the Austrians many soft words, but

held out on the essential point. It was fortunate for him that
Schwarzenberg died suddenly just when the negotiations
began. Buol, the new Austrian foreign minister, had less
grasp of affairs; 'sharp, but neither broad nor deep', was
Metternich's description of him. Austria was bought off
with a post-dated cheque. The *Zollverein* was maintained
unchanged, but the inclusion of Austria was to be considered again when it next came up for renewal in 1863. By
then Bismarck had the decision in his own hands. He did
not appreciate the full importance of the decision at the
time, nor perhaps even later. He considered the German
question in political and, to some extent, in military terms.
Yet the economic division was the greatest of all. Germany
of the *Zollverein*, which was later Bismarck's Reich, became an economic power of the first order as the coalmines
of the Ruhr expanded; Austria remained relatively backward. Two Germanies would have come into existence,
even if Bismarck had never been born—though their
political character might have been different.

Bismarck at Frankfurt was absorbed in 'grand policy',
not in economic questions. He recognized that he was on
the way to becoming a professional diplomat and in 1852
did not seek re-election to the Lower Chamber. Though he
was given a seat in the Upper House, he never spoke there.
Indeed, he never spoke again in the Prussian parliament
except from the bench of ministers. It was a grave handicap
to him later that he had experience of parliament only as a
factious critic and none of working with a political group.
At Frankfurt, too, he fought very much for his own hand.
There was not much sense in his endless petty quarrels with
the Austrian delegate so long as Prussia and Austria were
forced together by the international situation. European
politics seemed to have reverted to a fixed system after the
upheavals of 1848. On the one side was revolutionary
France, now under Napoleon III; on the other the conservative alliance of Russia, Austria, and Prussia, 'the
three Northern courts'. This conservative union had forced
Prussia to accept the agreement of Olomouc, and she had no

freedom of movement so long as Russia and Austria held together.

In 1853 this rigidity was dissolved. A conflict started in the Near East, first between Russia and France, soon between Russia and the two western Powers, France and England. The tsar assumed that Austria and Prussia would support him unquestioningly for the sake of 'the Holy Alliance'. Both failed him. Austria wished to maintain the integrity of the Ottoman empire and to keep the mouth of the Danube out of Russian hands; indeed, she wanted Russia to be defeated, though without bearing the risks or the blame herself. Prussia, alone of the Powers, had no stake in the Near East. She was concerned neither to defend Russian claims in the Near East nor to thwart them. The Holy Alliance had been all very well so long as it implied Russian aid to Prussia against a possible French threat on the Rhine. It became a danger if it made Prussia face a war against the western Powers for the sake of Russian interests in the Near East. When the Crimean war broke out early in 1854, Russia found herself alone. The Holy Alliance was dissolved.

Frederick William was at the centre of a turmoil which he much enjoyed. Gerlach urged him to fight on the side of Russia; Bunsen on that of the western Powers; Manteuffel sought security by making an alliance with Austria. Bismarck rejected all three lines. He wanted Prussia to remain in isolation and to profit from it. 'Let us frighten Austria by threatening an alliance with Russia, and frighten Russia by letting her think that we may join the western Powers.' With his mind concentrated on the disputes at Frankfurt, he was fiercely opposed to alliance with Austria. He wrote in February 1854: 'I should be alarmed if we sought protection from the approaching storm by tying our neat seaworthy frigate to Austria's worm-eaten old battleship.' He urged Frederick William to mobilize 200,000 men in Silesia, ostensibly as a threat against Russia; then he should demand from Austria the headship of Germany, and neither she nor the other Powers, fully engaged in the Near East, could withstand him. Frederick William replied: 'A man like Napoleon could pull off this sort of stroke, but not me.' On 20 April 1854—three weeks after the outbreak of war— Prussia concluded a defensive alliance with Austria for three years.

Bismarck was in high agitation. He believed that the subtle politicians of Vienna had taken Frederick William prisoner. But the outcome was not very different from what Bismarck had wanted. Frederick William would not join either side in the war, and he calculated rightly that Austria, too, would be more reluctant to enter the war if she had the Prussian alliance behind her. The Crimean war would have led to a gigantic European upheaval if the two Germanic Powers had fought on either side. As it was, their neutrality prevented any real decision. The Crimean war was localized and had to be fought in a detached peninsula of the Russian empire. The Austrians regretted this limited outcome. Time and again they tried to pull Prussia into war; time and again Prussia pulled them back into neutrality. In December 1854 Austria made an alliance with the western Powers, by which she promised to impose peace terms on Russia. She followed this up by trying to involve all the states of the German confederation in her troubles. The diet was asked to mobilize the federal forces in defence of Austria. The lesser states disliked this threatened burden; and Bismarck had an easy time persuading them to remain neutral. This was certainly a score for Prussia, but one without novelty. It had been shown often enough that the smaller states would always vote with whichever of the great Powers wanted to do nothing.

At the end of 1855 Austria was driven into action by pressure from the western Powers. She sent an ultimatum to Russia, threatening to enter the war if Russia did not agree to the allied peace-terms. Russia was exhausted and gave way. A Congress met at Paris, and Prussia who had remained neutral was at first excluded. She entered the Congress only when the rule of the Straits was discussed, and the treaty of London of 1841, to which she was a

signatory, had to be revised. This seemed a humiliating
outcome. Prussia had been treated almost as though she
were not a great Power. This appearance was deceptive.
Russia was grateful for Prussia's neutrality, which had
given her security in Poland; the western Powers soon
forgot their resentment. On the other hand, Russia would
not forgive the threats from Austria; while the western
Powers blamed her for not fighting on their side. Frederick
William and Manteuffel had, in fact, followed the policy
of neutrality which Bismarck himself had advocated. He
could have taken no different line if he had been in office.
Only his later successes enabled him to establish the
myth of Manteuffel's timidity and Frederick William's
blunders.

In April 1856, when the war was over, Bismarck reviewed
the European situation, seeking—though in vain—to
dictate policy to the men in Berlin. The German confederation, he insisted, had broken down. Austria and Prussia
were rivals. 'Germany is too small for us both.' Prussia
must therefore look outside Germany for allies; and it
would not be difficult to find them. Tsar Alexander II was
anxious to overthrow the peace settlement that had just
been made at Paris; Napoleon III was even more resolved
to destroy the settlement of 1815. Though they had
recently been enemies, the two emperors would soon come
together in a revisionist alliance; and Prussia should make
a third in the partnership. Alliance with Russia did not
shock Frederick William IV's legitimist principles. Alliance
with Napoleon seemed to him mortal sin. Bismarck attacked the idea of basing foreign policy on principle in
letter after letter. 'My ideal for foreign policy is freedom
from prejudice, the independence of our decisions from
impressions of dislike or affection for foreign states and their
governments.' He jeered at the doctrine of resisting the
revolution. All states had a revolutionary origin. The Habsburg monarchy itself was built on conquest. Even the German princes 'cannot find any completely legitimate origin
for the ground which they have won partly from the

Emperor and the Empire, partly from their fellow-princes, partly from the Estates.' Again, with characteristic ruthlessness: 'We cannot make an alliance with France without a certain degree of meanness, but in the Middle Ages very admirable people—even German princes—used a drain to make their escape, rather than be beaten or strangled.'

It would be rash to conclude from these arguments that Bismarck had no principles or that he had abandoned the cause of conservatism. He always concentrated on the task in hand, and when he was following a trail would reject every scent that led away from it. Conflict with Austria was the only thing that mattered to him during his years at Frankfurt; and he judged all international affairs from this angle. Besides, his argument was founded on fact. The 'legitimism' which Austria preached was fraudulent. The Austrians had no objection to an alliance with France so long as this worked against Russia in the Near East, not against themselves in Italy; and they insisted on conservative principles only to ensure that Prussia should trail in their wake. The Russians did much the same. In August 1857 the Tsar Alexander II met Napoleon at Stuttgart with every mark of intimacy. The whole world talked of 'the Franco-Russian entente'. Why should Prussia alone be fooled by principles which others did not practise?

Moreover, Bismarck had grown up when Prussia was the least of the great Powers; the memories of the Napoleonic wars always at the back of his mind. He underrated Prussian strength and overrated that of others. He knew nothing of the industrial revolution in the Ruhr which would in time make Germany economically dominant on the continent. It never occurred to him that the aggrandisement of Prussia or the unification of Germany might come naturally by force of economic circumstances. Rather he expected a new partition of Prussia—such as Napoleon I carried through in 1807—to be the most likely outcome if things were left to drift. He did not suppose in these years that Prussia could defeat Austria unaided. What he counted on was a war of Russia and France against Austria in which Prussia would make easy gains. Prussia had nothing to lose by such a war. It would not matter to her if Russia controlled the Straits and the mouth of the Danube. In 1857 Bismarck visited Paris and discovered Napoleon's aims. Napoleon had little interest in expansion on the Rhine. He wanted to expel Austria from Italy and to make the Mediterranean a French lake 'or very nearly'. These ambitions, too, did not conflict with Prussia's interests, however much they might injure Austria or Great Britain. On the contrary, Napoleon was prepared to offer Hanover and Sleswig-Holstein to Prussia in return for her neutrality. It was a reasonable speculation that Prussia could achieve the mastery of northern Germany as reward for assisting a Franco-Russian revision of the map of Europe, or perhaps even for tolerating it.

The two emperors, Alexander and Napoleon, seemed to dominate Europe already, despite the Crimean war. Bismarck thought that he was going with the tide. But in 1858 the tide turned against him so far as Prussia was concerned. Frederick William had always listened fascinated to Bismarck's ideas and, with his incurably speculative mind, might ultimately have been won for them. In 1858 he fell hopelessly insane, and his brother William became regent. William was a simpler and less intelligent man than his brother, with some understanding only in military matters. Frederick William once said: 'If we had been born as sons of a petty official, I should have become an architect, William an N.C.O.'[1] Though reputed a reactionary in 1848, William had none of his brother's high-flown conservatism. In 1854 he had wished to go to war with Russia on the side of the western Powers. Now he thought it his duty, as a good German, to co-operate with Austria, especially in the defence of her lands in Italy. At home, he intended to give Prussia a more liberal government and so to make her more popular in Germany; he planned a policy of 'moral con-

[1] Of the other two brothers: 'Charles would have gone to prison, Albrecht become a drunkard.'

quests'. He dismissed Manteuffel and opened 'the new era' by appointing a liberal ministry.

Bismarck's career seemed to be ended. He could not work with Austria at Frankfurt. He was equally unwilling to return to Berlin as a liberal minister. William regarded him as a wild reactionary. Augusta, the regent's wife, had a deep-seated hostility to him and, at this time, held her husband firmly against him. Schleinitz, the new foreign minister, had been nominated by Augusta and shared her outlook. Still, Bismarck could not be turned loose. He was consoled early in 1859 by being made Prussian minister to St. Petersburg. His final gesture of contempt was to leave the Diet without the customary formalities of farewell. On his way through Berlin, he said to a liberal politician: 'The only reliable ally for Prussia is—the German people.'

St. Petersburg was poor consolation for Frankfurt. At Frankfurt Bismarck had been fighting a diplomatic campaign against Austria, not unsuccessfully; and he had always had the illusory hope that one day his arguments would impress Frederick William. Moreover, he had enjoyed the life. Frankfurt was the nearest thing to an international capital that Germany possessed; and Bismarck liked clever company whatever his Junker affectations. He had always been exuberantly well, despite his energetic way of living. He smoked Havana cigars from morning to night; drank much 'Black Velvet'—the mixture of stout and champagne which he invented; rode in the woods and swam in the Rhine; wrote endless reports. Yet never a day's sickness. At St. Petersburg he was, in his own words, 'put on ice'. There was, as yet, no through railway, and the journey to Berlin took five days. He could no longer argue with the regent and the ministers in person, and he was removed from events while they pursued a 'German' policy of supporting Austria. He tried to console himself by reflecting on the triviality of all human affairs. 'Peoples and men, folly and wisdom, war and peace, come and go like waves and the sea remains. Our states and their power and honour are nothing to God but ant-heaps and beehives, which are trampled by an ox's hoof or snatched by fate in the shape of a honey-gatherer.' These reflections did not restore his peace of mind. He fell desperately ill of a nervous complaint, sure sign of strain and frustration that was often to be repeated. Characteristically, he attributed his illness to poison from an incompetent doctor, whom he imagined to be in Austrian pay; and he refused to convalesce at Carlsbad for fear of further Austrian tricks. He disliked the damp gloom of St. Petersburg, particularly as the Prussian minister was more poorly paid than other diplomatic representatives and could not hold his own with the Russian aristocracy. Bismarck always worried about his private finances, and never more than at St. Petersburg.

Yet curiously enough the years there did not turn him into an enemy of Russia. This was a unique exception. The Frankfurt diet had made him hate Austria and despise the smaller states. A fortnight in Paris was enough to produce revulsion against 'the modern Babylon'; and he never developed any affection for Napoleon III, despite their intimacy. He said himself that England was the only foreign country for which he cared, but this was romantic humbug, an imaginary longing for the 'old England' of roast beef and Burke's classical constitution. Bismarck regarded the contemporary British statesmen with special hostility. Yet Russian arrogance did not offend him. He was flattered by attentions from the imperial family, and at this time even got on well with Gorchakov, the foreign minister. He learnt Russian and grew so fond of it that he used it to record his most private thoughts. He even claimed to like the Russian people. Perhaps there was some deep psychological link. The Russians, despite their emotional instability, present to the outer world a stolid resolution, which may be peculiarly satisfying to neurotic Germans. Or perhaps it was simply a political calculation. Bismarck regarded the Polish lands as essential to Prussian power and knew that they were secure only so long as Prussia and Russia were on good terms. At any rate, the fact is inescapable. St. Petersburg was the only capital which Bismarck left without hating it and without resolving to be revenged for his humiliations. He made a good impression on his side. Alexander II even offered him a high post in the Russian diplomatic service. Accepting this offer would have had curious historical results.

Circumstances made it easy for Bismarck to like Russia, and to be liked. He never had to dispute with the Russian government; he was too busy disputing with his own. Relations between Prussia and Austria reached a crisis just when Bismarck went to St. Petersburg. In January 1859 France and Sardinia made a secret alliance to liberate northern Italy from Austrian rule. In April Austria was provoked into launching war against them. German feeling was deeply disturbed. All the traditions of German nationalism were bound up with the war of liberation against Napoleon; and many Germans drew an analogy between the present war and the Italian campaigns of Bonaparte which had paved the way for his conquest of Germany. The regent William had himself fought as a boy in 1813 and thought that those great days had come again. Even Moltke, chief of the Prussian general staff, wrote: 'The next French step will be against Prussia, just as the campaign of 1806 followed that of 1805.' Prussia, it seemed, must go to the aid of Austria if she were to remain popular in Germany; and those Prussians who were indifferent to German opinion advocated the same course for reasons of self-preservation.

Only Bismarck opposed this course. He wanted to seize supremacy in northern Germany, while Austria was busy in Italy. He wrote on 5 May: 'The great chance has come for us again, if we let Austria get embedded in war with France and then march south, setting up the Prussian frontier-posts either on Lake Constance or where Protestantism ceases to predominate.' And a week later: 'I regard our connexion with the German confederation as an illness of Prussia, which will have to be cured sooner or later *ferro et igni*, unless we take treatment for it at a favourable opportunity.' No one in Berlin took any notice of him. He was

the only important Prussian diplomat who was not recalled to Berlin for advice on the critical situation. The
army was mobilized and the Prussian government proposed
to 'mediate' between the two sides, as a preliminary to supporting Austria. Instead, Bismarck's policy triumphed,
though not from his exertions. The regent William demanded a reward from Austria for his support: Prussia
must be given supreme command over all the German
forces north of the Main. There was not much sense in this
condition from a military point of view. The forces of the
little German states were not worth quarrelling over. But
it had profound political significance. It implied equality
between Prussia and Austria and therewith the partition
of Germany between them—a return to the policy of the
Erfurt Union, which had been discarded at Olomouc.
Francis Joseph, the emperor of Austria, would not pay this
price, even to keep his lands in Italy. In July he made a
hasty peace with Napoleon III and surrendered Lombardy.

Prussia had made the worst of both policies: she had
neither exploited Austria's difficulties nor made 'moral
conquests' by supporting her. The prince regent would not
admit this. He went on striving for partnership with Austria
against France, but always attached the military supremacy over northern Germany as a condition. In July 1860
things got so far that a defensive alliance between Prussia
and Austria was actually drafted. But negotiations broke
down in April 1861 when it came to a military convention.
Yet still neither side realized that conflict was the inevitable
alternative to alliance. Neither understood that the other
was serious in its attitude; and this lack of understanding
went on until the very outbreak of war in 1866. The Prussians, including even Bismarck, could not believe that
Austria would let things come to a war and would risk her
vital interests in Italy and the Near East rather than
concede to Prussia command over the trivial forces of north
Germany—a command which she did not aspire to exercise
herself and which was of no benefit to anyone. Similarly,
the Austrians could not believe that Prussia would refuse

to see the danger from France and would go to war for the
sake of this military triviality. The issue was certainly unreal. Austria would have agreed to it at any time if it had
not carried with it the implication of her equality with
Prussia. But, of course, the Prussians would not have
made the demand unless it had carried this implication,
however unspoken.

The prince regent was certainly still unconscious of this
challenge. Bismarck paraded himself as an enemy of
Austria. This ruled him out as a minister in the regent's
eyes. But William was driven towards Bismarck for reasons
of domestic policy. With his military training and experience, he was anxious to reform the Prussian army, which
Frederick William IV had neglected. The population of
Prussia had almost doubled since 1815; the annual intake
of 40,000 recruits had remained unchanged. By 1859
23,000 young men were escaping military service each year.
William and Roon, his minister of war, proposed to increase
the number of regiments and the barracks provided for
them, so that every Prussian should receive his three years
of military training. There was no conflict with the Prussian
parliament about this. The Prussian liberals admired the
tradition of Scharnhorst and Gneisenau, and regarded
universal military service as an enlightened measure. The
dispute between William and the parliament was quite
other. It had been an essential part of the Scharnhorst
system that every Prussian citizen should pass, after three
years' active service and two in the reserve, into the
Landwehr—a sort of territorial army with its own units and
its own officers, most of them not drawn from the nobility.
The *Landwehr* was a symbol of democratic nationalism.
Roon despised it. It was, he said, 'all wrong as a military
institution, because it lacked the genuine soldierly spirit
and had no firm discipline.' Moreover, now that Prussia was
a constitutional country, the members of the *Landwehr*—
especially the officers—were also voters. But, as Roon said,
'the armed forces do not deliberate; they obey.' Roon
therefore proposed to increase the years spent in the regular

reserve and to whittle the *Landwehr* to almost nothing. The liberals, on the other hand, wished to reduce the period of active service to two years and to make the *Landwehr* the core of the Prussian army.

The constitutional conflict which now began was not a conflict over the size of the army. It was a conflict over its character and particularly over the class-origin of the officers. The regular army had exclusively Junker officers; the *Landwehr* officers from the middle-class. Roon introduced his proposals in 1860. The Chamber was mollified by an assurance from the minister of finance that no fundamental changes would be made if it granted the extra money for a single year. The money was granted. Roon went ahead with his plans despite his colleague's promise. In 1861 the Chamber protested. Once more it granted the extra money for the next year, but with a clear warning that it would refuse further supplies if its conditions were again disregarded. 1862 would be the year of crisis. William had to look round for a man who would defy the Chamber and break its opposition. Bismarck was clearly the man. With his reactionary reputation and his unrivalled courage he would not shrink from infringing the constitution. But he cared nothing for this military dispute. Himself without military experience or devotion, he knew that Roon was fighting a class battle, not a technical one, and expected the *Landwehr* to give a good account of itself in wartime—as proved to be the case. He would become minister and give William and Roon the army they wanted only if he could have his own way in foreign policy: challenge to Austria and alliance with France and Russia. William would not stomach this condition, despite his failure to make the Austrian alliance.

The bargaining dragged on for more than two years. It was relentless, though never consciously formulated. Bismarck waited ruthlessly until William was forced to the wall. Time and again Bismarck was summoned to Berlin in order to take office; time and again he demanded a free hand in foreign policy and was sent back to St. Petersburg.

The first call came in May 1860 when Roon put forward his proposals. Bismarck horrified William with the remark: 'If the kingdom of Italy did not exist, we should have to invent it.' He was at once ordered back to St. Petersburg. In July 1861 he appeared again. This time he advocated a German parliament, elected by universal suffrage, to sweep away all the little princes. He spoke of their 'sovereignty-swindle' as 'completely unhistorical, without divine or human right', and said: 'I am loyal to my own prince even to the Vendée, but as for the others I don't feel in one drop of my blood the slightest obligation to lift a finger for them.' William had become king in January 1861 and was now planning his coronation with legitimist pomp; he was outraged by these subversive remarks, and once more Bismarck returned to St. Petersburg. Early in 1862 the Chamber refused to pass the budget. It was dissolved, and Bismarck was summoned again. He was offered the post of prime minister, but without control of foreign affairs. He refused. He said in 1868: 'I was not absolutely sure that the king would go with me through thick and thin.'

Still, William wanted Bismarck near at hand in case of a crisis. St. Petersburg was too remote. In May 1862 Bismarck was appointed Prussian minister to Paris. At once he began to make out that he had been sent to promote an alliance between Russia and France, with Prussia as the third party. William was again alarmed. He said: 'Tell Bismarck that I will never reconcile myself to alliance with France.' Bismarck decided that he would be better out of the way; he would lie low until despair drove the king to accept his terms. In June he visited London and told Disraeli: 'I shall declare war on Austria, dissolve the German confederation, subjugate the middle and smaller states, and give Germany national unity under the control of Prussia.'[1] In July he went to Biarritz. He met there Katherine Orlov, wife of the Russian ambassador at Brussels, and fell passionately in love with her. No doubt

[1] This story, which comes from Disraeli, was perhaps manufactured later, like many of Bismarck's own.

it was innocent in the law-court sense. The men of the
nineteenth century had the art, now lost, of displaying
violent emotion without carrying it to its logical conclusion.
Kathi was with her elderly husband. She was 22, gay,
pretty, irresponsible. Bismarck was nearly fifty, his nerves
on edge with anxiety, and uncertain of his future. She called
him 'Uncle' and sent him sentimental messages. Johanna,
in the remote German country, knew the truth. She wrote
to a friend: 'If I had any inclination to jealousy and envy,
I could be tyrannized to the depths now by these passions.
But my soul has no room for them, and I rejoice greatly
that my beloved husband has found this charming woman.
Without her he would never have known peace for so long
on one spot or become so well as he boasts of being in every
letter.' Probably Bismarck was as genuinely in love as he
was sincere in politics or religion. That is to say, he was
sincere and pretended at the same time.

For whatever reason—love or political tactics—Bismarck
remained in the south of France and failed to answer
letters. In Berlin affairs reached their crisis. The new
Chamber had a larger liberal majority than before. It again
refused to authorize the additional military expenditure.
The ministers declared that they could not carry on without
a constitutional budget. All of them, including Roon, were
ready to give way on the three-year service if the Chamber
would then grant the full estimate. William would not be
moved. He had preached universal three-year service from
the time when he was a young officer; and he threatened to
abdicate rather than yield. Yet abdication would settle
nothing. The crown prince, though more liberal in talk,
was as firm on the three-year service as his father. The
ministers were in despair. They might soon find themselves
at odds with the Chamber and repudiated by the king, yet
with no alternative government in sight. It is not surprising
that some of them hankered after Bismarck, with his
boasted strength of will. He might defeat the Chamber,
or overcome the king's reluctance; he would break the
deadlock one way or the other. On 16 September Bernstorff,

who had succeeded Schleinitz as foreign minister in 1861,
telegraphed to Bismarck: 'The king wants you to come
here, and I advise you to come at once.' There was no reply,
no sign of life. On 17 September Roon offered a compromise
to the Chamber; on 18 September he withdrew it, on the
king's orders. He was at the end of his tether. He wired to
Bismarck: 'Periculum in mora. Dépêchez-vous.' This time
Bismarck took notice: perhaps in response to the appeal
from his friend, perhaps because he had parted from Kathi
Orlov at Avignon. She gave him an onyx medallion which
he wore on his watch-chain to his dying day. On 20
September he arrived in Berlin.

William knew nothing of this. He was still far from accepting Bismarck's terms. He had promised his wife not to
make Bismarck a minister. When he repeated this to his
son, the crown prince replied that Bismarck was pro-
French as well as anti-liberal. William answered: 'That is
another reason for not appointing him.' On 20 September
Roon came to the king to explain that the deadlock could
not continue. He wanted William to give way. William
wanted to force Roon on the path of unconstitutional
action and said provocatively that Bismarck would do it.
'But, of course,' he added consolingly to himself, 'he is not
here.' Roon called the bluff: 'He is here and is ready to
serve Your Majesty.' William had to see Bismarck. But he
still intended to tie him down. He prepared a detailed programme of domestic and, more important, of foreign policy
to which Bismarck was to pledge himself; and Bernstorff
was to remain as foreign minister. William also drafted a
deed of abdication. This, too, was bluff. He meant to produce it when Bismarck made difficulties and counted on
Bismarck's being swept away by monarchist devotion.

On 22 September Bismarck met William at Babelsberg,
a summer palace just outside Berlin. It was their first
struggle, a rehearsal for their future relations. Bismarck
gave the king no time to read his prepared papers. 'Royal
government or the supremacy of parliament' was, he said,
the only issue; and he would bring the first to victory.

William was carried away. He tore up both his act of abdication and his political conditions. He consoled himself
with Bismarck's promise that 'he would always submit to
the king's orders in the last resort even if he disagreed
with them.' William supposed that he was still free to forbid
Bismarck's wild ideas in foreign policy; but Bismarck had
retained the right to put them forward. Both men remained
uncommitted. The future would show which 'in the last
resort' was master.

Bismarck returned to Berlin as prime minister. A fortnight later he became foreign minister also. He was to
remain in supreme power for twenty-seven years.

III

PRIME MINISTER OF PRUSSIA

BISMARCK was 47 when he became prime minister. No man has taken supreme office with a more slender background of experience. He had never been a minister and had spent only a few months of rebellious youth in the bureaucracy nearly twenty years before. During his short time in parliament he had merely voiced extreme reactionary views; he had not tried to win votes or to work with others. At Frankfurt he had fought Austria, not practised diplomacy in the usual sense. He had no friends or social circle, except for a few sycophants who wrote at his dictation. Where an English prime minister spent the recess going from one great country house to another, Bismarck withdrew to his own estate and saw no one. In later years he was absent from Berlin for months, once for ten months, at a time. He is often called a Junker and certainly he liked to present himself as a landowner. But he had a poor opinion of his fellow Junkers and jettisoned their interests without hesitation whenever it suited his policy. His aim was to succeed in whatever he turned his hand to or, as he called it, 'to accomplish God's purpose'; and he certainly did not think that every Junker prejudice was a divine ordinance. The only check on him was the king's will, but he meant to see to it that the king should will what he wanted.

He was too old to learn political habits. He stood outside party or class, a solitary figure following a line of his own devising. He had no colleagues, only subordinates. The Prussian council of ministers rarely debated policy. It was called together only when it was necessary to pass a unanimous resolution or to force the king on some distasteful course. Bismarck conducted foreign policy in autocratic isolation, easily roused to anger if some ambassador tried to influence him. He knew nothing of internal affairs or of economics when he became prime minister; and he left these matters entirely to other ministers until some event suddenly drove him to intervene with devastating effect. Even then his policy was the outcome of private reflection, uninfluenced by others. Discussion always brought on a nervous crisis, which ended in tears or the breaking of china; and he preferred to do all his work on paper.

Opposition infuriated him. Bismarck never respected an opponent or listened to his argument. If a minister raised objections, then the critic's position was undermined with the king and he was soon dismissed. To parliamentary critics Bismarck always attributed unworthy motives, jeering at their ambition for office, their financial difficulties, or their personal appearance. One fearless critic, Lasker, was pursued with hatred even after his death. Bismarck developed a petty malignity during his years of office, until at the end of his life he seemed concerned only to carry on his personal feuds. Yet he did not show gratitude for the most unwavering support. Lothar Bucher, an extreme radical of 1848 now convinced that Bismarck alone could unite Germany, gave him thirty years of devoted service. He once received a word of praise. All others, including the most responsible ministers, were used so long as it suited Bismarck's purpose; and were then flung casually aside.

Nor did Bismarck take part in parliamentary debates as this is understood in England or France. The Prussian ministers were not members of the Chamber. They sat aloof on the ministerial bench; and Bismarck delivered his Olympian speeches without any contact with the members. He stated his policy. He did not try to argue or to convince. The effect was increased by his thin, high voice, like a professor lecturing his class. Though he admitted the right of members to question him, he refused to listen to their criticism and withdrew ostentatiously to his own room when the debate turned against him.

Yet, on the other hand, he had great personal charm

when he cared to use it. He bewitched Alexander II, Napoleon III and Queen Victoria—all of whom had started out with strong prejudice against him. He had been trained as a courtier in his youth; and those who met him in old age were astonished to find under his rough exterior all the formal grace of a Talleyrand or a Metternich. Foreign statesmen and German radicals alike succumbed to his magic. He would catch a politician in the corridor of the parliament-house or casually in a railway carriage and talk to him as though they were the most intimate friends in the world. Of all the great public figures of the past he is the one whom it would be most rewarding to recall from the dead for an hour's conversation. With all his brusqueness, no man was more skilful at evading a storm. When a member was preparing to move the adjournment of the Chamber owing to Bismarck's absence, Bismarck put his head round the door and said: 'I can hear everything you are saying.' He once caused an uproar by saying that a critic 'was associated with the refusal of taxes in 1848'. The president of the Chamber interrupted him. Bismarck repeated the phrase. The president declared that he would suspend the sitting if the phrase were repeated again. There seemed no alternative between humiliation and defiance. With a disarming smile, Bismarck said: 'It is not necessary for me to repeat my words again. Everyone heard them'; and he went on with his speech. Gladstone could not have managed things better.

Bismarck had no settled views on domestic policy when he became prime minister. It was a matter of indifference to him whether men served for two or three years in the army. His only concern was to have a free hand in foreign policy. For this he had to keep his hold over the king. Therefore the constitutional conflict must continue. If it were once settled, William could get rid of Bismarck or, at the very least, refuse to follow his advice in foreign affairs. Bismarck disliked his dependence on the king; he always feared that Augusta might reassert her influence over her husband. Bismarck had no real devotion to the monarchy, despite his legitimist phrases. As he himself often said, he was 'by nature a republican'; and he accepted the monarchy only as he disciplined himself to accept reality in so many ways. He was quite prepared to use the Chamber against the king if it on its side would back him over foreign policy in return. If the bait of uniting Germany under Prussia would make the Chamber swallow the military programme, then William would be helpless. He, too, would have to follow Bismarck's foreign policy. A parliamentary assembly was easier to manage than the king in the long run, as Bismarck found in later life. With his usual impetuosity, he tried out this idea as soon as he took office. He fell into talk with a leading liberal and compared the king to a horse who 'takes fright at an unaccustomed object, will grow obstinate if driven, but will gradually get used to it.' The unaccustomed object was, of course, a rivalry with Austria.

On his first appearance in the Chamber, Bismarck pulled out of his pocket a leaf of olive and offered it as a gesture of conciliation. It was also, although no one knew it, a gesture of sentiment: Kathi Orlov had plucked the leaf for him at Avignon. So, in Bismarck's life, one hand washed the other. Were his thoughts now on political tactics or on the pretty girl at Biarritz? On 29 September he appeared in the budget commission and tried to brush aside the constitutional dispute. 'Germany does not look to Prussia's liberalism, but to her strength.' And then, in his most famous sentence: 'The great questions of the day will not be decided by speeches and the resolutions of majorities— that was the great mistake from 1848 to 1849—but by iron and blood.'[1] This was a statement of fact, not of principle. The liberals dreamt of uniting Germany by 'moral conquests'. Yet whoever has examined the Austrian records must recognize that the Habsburg statesmen would never have admitted the equality of Prussia except by blood and iron, though it might well have been the iron force of economic power rather than the bloody victory of war

[1] For some reason unknown to me, the accepted version soon became 'blood and iron'.

which forced the decision. All the great questions of our own day, from the defeat of Hitler to the checking of Soviet expansion, have been determined by blood and iron. It is the task of the idealist to put moral clothing on the victor.

Bismarck never acquired this art. He was always inclined to call things by their real names, and when he was excited he found frankness irresistible. Later in life he could afford to enrage the Reichstag; but at this time he had meant to persuade the deputies. He was amazed when even Roon found the phrase too provocative. Bismarck replied: 'I only meant that the king needs soldiers. It was not an appeal to use force against the other German states.' Roon's disapproval was not the worst. William I, who was at Baden-Baden, read of 'blood and iron' in the newspapers; it convinced him that Augusta's view of Bismarck was right, and he took train for Berlin to dismiss his new Prime Minister. Bismarck sensed that he was lost if William I were once firmly back among the Prussian politicians. He went to meet the king, travelling in an ordinary carriage and waiting at a deserted junction with the buildings still unfinished for William I to change trains. It would have been useless to make out to William I that the phrase had meant nothing: the king would reply that he could not afford a prime minister who committed such indiscretions unintentionally. Bismarck, therefore, played things the other way. The phrase, he claimed, had been an assertion of royal authority. William I said mournfully: 'I see how it will end—on the gallows. You will suffer the fate of Strafford and I of Charles I.' Bismarck countered skilfully: 'Better that than surrender.' And the trick was turned. The soldier-king could not run away from a fight. He drew himself up, according to Bismarck's account, like an officer responding to the command of a superior.

William I would have been bewildered if he had known that Bismarck was still trying to settle the dispute by compromise without a fight. Despite 'blood and iron' Bismarck offered the liberals something like a fresh start. He would withdraw the budget of 1863; the army reforms, hitherto carried out by executive action, would be submitted as a parliamentary bill; and the budget for 1863 would be brought forward again before the New Year. This was typical of all Bismarck's compromises. While his opponents would escape humiliation, he would keep open his path to the future. The constitutional crisis would be evaded. The Chamber could, if it liked, amend the army law. But it would have surrendered its fiscal weapon, and Bismarck no doubt hoped to win it over by some stroke of foreign policy. The liberals refused to be caught. On 7 October the Chamber demanded the immediate submission of the budget, pruned of the army estimates. Bismarck answered by carrying the budget in the Upper House. There was now, he said, 'a hole' in the constitution. Money could be spent only with the agreement of the king and the two Houses. They had failed to agree. Therefore the king must spend the money until they reached agreement. This was a tawdry piece of constitutional theory, and Bismarck himself did not take it seriously. The liberals had defied him. Now he defied them. On 13 October parliament was adjourned. Bismarck was securely in power, defending the cause of hereditary monarchy. But he was more dependent on William I than he liked. The hold which the constitutional conflict gave him over the king might be shaken if he moved too fast in foreign policy; and, in fact, it took him nearly four years to break William's reluctance.

It is often said that the Prussian liberals failed at this decisive crisis, but there was nothing they could do. The constitution of 1850, within which they had to work, did not establish parliamentary sovereignty; it was not even undefined, like the English constitution of the seventeenth century. The taxes were not granted annually by parliament; they were laid down permanently in the constitution. Any refusal of taxes would have been illegal. The expenditure of money which had not been authorized by the Chambers was certainly unconstitutional; but not even the most fervent liberal wanted to disband the Prussian state and the Prussian army—just as the Whigs of the British parliament shrank in 1784 from refusing supplies to the younger Pitt. The Prussian liberals desperately wanted a compromise. When the Chamber met in the following year, they offered to agree to the increased army and even to the three-year service if the *Landwehr* kept some of its importance. Roon accepted the compromise. Bismarck was in dismay. He could not allow the constitutional conflict to be ended until either the king or the Chamber accepted his line of foreign policy. He went down to the Chamber and behaved so provocatively that the compromise was withdrawn. It was never in sight again. The Chamber continued to meet regularly, though with occasional dissolutions, which did not shake the liberal majority. It continued to reject the budget. And Bismarck continued to spend the money. Far from the conflict embarrassing him, it was the essential condition of his political existence.

Bismarck did not attempt a *coup d'état*; the liberals did not attempt a revolution. The constitutional struggle was fought within the constitutional framework. The liberals were not solid country squires like the English parliamentarians of the seventeenth century. They were intellectuals from the professional classes—lawyers, journalists, university professors, many of them actually drawing a salary from the Prussian state.[1] In earlier times a revolutionary struggle could perhaps be confined to the established classes. The events of 1789 and 1848 had shown that now the masses broke in when revolution raised its head; and the liberals were further removed from the masses than any other section of the community. Indeed, the only man who thought of calling in the masses was Bismarck himself. He had no more respect for the constitution than for hereditary monarchy and said maliciously to the crown prince, who was himself a liberal: 'I have sworn to observe the constitution conscientiously, but what if my conscience tells me not to observe it?'

[1] Bismarck most outraged the liberals by proposing that civil servants should not receive their salaries while they worked in the parliamentary opposition; and even Bismarck did not carry out the suggestion.

Bismarck had thought of playing off the conservative
peasants against the town radicals even during the revolution of 1848. Since then he had watched Napoleon III's
success in using universal suffrage to destroy a liberal
republic. He agreed with Proudhon: 'universal suffrage is
counter-revolution.' He spent long hours during 1863 in
discussion with Lassalle, the revolutionary socialist. Lassalle urged that only the educated middle-classes cared for
constitutional niceties; the masses wanted material re-
wards. 'Give me universal suffrage and I will give you a
million votes.' These votes would certainly swamp the
propertied voters; but Bismarck counted on the peasants
in turn swamping the urban proletariat. Both Bismarck
and Lassalle wanted to ruin the liberal *bourgeoisie*; then the
strange allies would round on each other. In 1863 the idea
was too new. A working-class movement hardly existed.
As Bismarck said later of Lassalle, 'what could the poor
devil offer me?' Besides, universal suffrage was even more
abhorrent to William I than conflict with Austria. Bismarck might have been driven to it if foreign affairs had
stagnated. As it was they served his turn.

If universal suffrage were ruled out on the one side and
revolution on the other, only foreign affairs could break the
constitutional deadlock. On this at least Bismarck and his
opponents agreed. The liberals calculated that Prussia
would have to take a liberal line at home in order to win
Germany. Bismarck planned to succeed in Germany so as
to drown the liberal opposition at home. In foreign politics
at any rate his rule marked the real 'new era'. His first act
as foreign minister was to instruct Prussian representatives
abroad that they must henceforth write their reports in
German—previously they had been in French. This was a
formal sign that Prussia now claimed a German national
character. Bismarck could not, of course, make a new
foreign policy. Though he alleged in 1870 that he had
planned the war against Austria from the first day he took
office, his contemporary opinion rang truer: 'Events are
stronger than the plans of men.' Conflict with Austria had

certainly the attraction that it might win liberal support, both in Prussia and beyond. Moreover, there was the strong negative argument that co-operation with Austria offered no concrete reward. In Bismarck's words: 'Even if we are victorious against a Franco-Russian alliance, what should we have fought for?' He certainly did not aspire to more Polish lands and it did not occur to him at this time to take seriously the Romantic national claim to Alsace.

But these arguments and still more the abstract debate between a conservative or a revolutionary course in foreign policy with which his admirers later credited him were remote from the day-to-day facts. What mattered in 1862 was that Austria seemed hostile to Prussia and that the Franco-Russian partnership favoured her. Events were stronger than the plans of men. Francis Joseph of Austria had been trying to work a liberal constitution in his empire since February 1861. He needed the support of the German liberals in Austria for this; and the conflict in Prussia increased the temptation for him to woo German liberalism. Austrian plans for strengthening the German confederation proliferated at the diet; and the Austrian statesmen, who had a clear grasp of economic realities, pressed hard for the fulfilment of the promise made ten years before that Austria should be included in the *Zollverein*. Bismarck defied them by pushing through a commercial treaty between Prussia and France. The low tariffs which followed from this made economic co-operation with Austria almost impossible. But Bismarck did not invent the conflict with Austria. It had been in existence ever since 1849. Every Prussian statesman had insisted that equality was the necessary condition for Austro-Prussian friendship. Manteuffel refused to back Austria during the Crimean war; Schleinitz demanded military supremacy north of the Main in 1859; Bernstorff repeated this demand in 1861. All three shrank from admitting that they could achieve this aim only by war; and Bismarck, too, did not yet face this hard fact. In December 1862 he told the Austrian ambassador that it would come to war between them 'unless Austria

shifted her centre of gravity to Hungary'. This was not a
demand that Austria be excluded from Germany. After all,
Bavaria was nearer to Budapest than it was to Berlin. It
was the old demand for dividing Germany at the line of the
Main.

In 1862 Bismarck hoped and believed that this demand
could be achieved without war. The Austrian empire was
having a fairly easy time of it at the moment, after losing
Lombardy in the Italian war of 1859. This easy time was
not likely to last. The new kingdom of Italy still claimed
Venetia; and her claim would be backed by France when
Napoleon III had another burst of nationalist enthusiasm.
At the other extremity of the Austrian empire, Russia
resented the loss of Bessarabian territory at the Congress of
Paris and might even revive the claim to dominate the
territory at the mouth of the Danube which she had ad-
vanced before the Crimean war. This claim threatened
Austria's vital economic outlet to foreign markets. Bismarck assumed that one challenge or other would soon blow
up—perhaps both. Then he could take advantage of
Austria's difficulties, either by aiding or attacking her.
Even in the conversation of December 1862, when he
threatened Austria with war, he also offered to guarantee
her interests in Italy and the Near East if she would divide
Germany at the Main. But he talked just as often of making
a third in the Franco-Russian alliance.

The reality of this alliance was indeed Bismarck's basic
assumption when he took office in September 1862. He
had matured as a diplomat during the years of the Franco-
Russian *entente*. He prophesied its coming during the
Crimean war; he saw his prophecy fulfilled immediately
afterwards. There was nothing unique in this. Every statesman in Europe regarded France and Russia as the two
dynamic, restless powers, who would turn the continent
upside down—Napoleon III driven on by the explosive
spirit of the French revolution, Alexander II dominated by
resentment against the peace of 1856. The difference between Bismarck and his predecessors lay only in the

deduction to be drawn. Manteuffel and Schleinitz had held, as William still did, that the Franco-Russian alliance crippled Prussia; she must stand by Austria and forget the German question so long as this alliance existed. Bismarck took the opposite line. He had always preached, though hitherto in vain, that Prussia should join in revolutionizing the map of Europe. After all, Venetia and the Danubian principalities were not her affair. Control of Germany north of the Main would be cheap at the price. No doubt Bismarck was vague about the ultimate outcome. Sometimes he talked of going to the rescue of the Austrian empire when it had been sufficiently weakened. At other times he suggested that the dismemberment of the Austrian empire would be no great catastrophe. He had no regard for any traditional state except Prussia—perhaps not even much for her.

Bismarck was to establish himself in history as a great conservative statesman, but he was conservative in an unusual way. Though he admired traditional beliefs and institutions, he had no faith in their strength. The revolutions of 1848 gave him a shock from which he never recovered; and he always supposed, like any radical, that fresh, more violent revolutions were only a matter of time. In so far as he had any vision of the future, he held that Europe would not be at peace until her peoples had been sorted out into nationalities or, as he preferred to put it, into 'tribes'. The difference of words is not a triviality. The advocates of nationalism claimed to be preaching a high moral principle—Mazzini equating nationalism and Christianity merely carried this to its extreme. Bismarck did not regard nationalism as high or moral; he merely accepted it as inevitable and wished to be on the winning side. His calculations have proved correct. The 'tribes' have won all over Europe; the sorting-out has even been completed artificially by the compulsory moving of populations; yet politics are no more moral than they were before.

Bismarck's error was in his timing. Dynamic himself, he always overrated the dynamism of others. He could understand the conservatism of high principle; he could not understand the conservatism of inertia. He supposed that men would burn down churches as soon as they lost faith in God, and would cut off the king's head as soon as they substituted the rights of man for the divine right of kings. In practice men are too lazy to act on their convictions, or lack of them, unless driven to it by extreme necessity. Bismarck had intended to be a Cavour on a greater scale. Within a few years he found himself cast for the role of Metternich. The transformation began as soon as he entered office. He came into power with the urgent conviction that the great national upheaval was at hand. He had spent ten years craving to conduct a diplomatic campaign against Austria; and now he planned an immediate challenge at the diet. Against her feeble plans for a stronger confederation, he proposed to launch a German parliament based on universal suffrage—the revolutionary constitution of 1849. Almost his first act was to inquire in Paris what the French would do 'if things grew hot in Germany'. Here was the revolutionary alliance with France which King William had determined to resist. But events did not at all follow Bismarck's programme. Napoleon III was losing his revolutionary zest. The clericals at the French court, led by the Empress Eugenie, had just got rid of Thouvenel, the foreign minister with nationalist sympathies. Drouyn de Lhuys, his successor, wanted a conservative alliance with Austria. Bismarck's inquiry was met with cold indifference; his revolutionary policy had misfired.

Even the Austrians disappointed him. They failed to live up to their aggressive pretensions. In January 1863 the smaller German states voted down the Austrian plans for federal reform; and Austria took her rebuff quietly. Bismarck's career as a statesman begins from this moment, not from September 1862. During his first few months of office, he had been trying to carry out a preconceived plan— a plan formally advocated by him for more than a decade. Now he discovered that events would not conform to his plans; and he began to live with reality instead of trying to force his will upon it. He did not face reality all at once. He continued to exaggerate the aggressiveness of Austria and the revolutionary spirit of Napoleon III; indeed, he exaggerated dangers of every sort to his dying day. But in January 1863 he came to realize that European politics could not be forced into a pattern even by a man of ruthless will, impatient with long years at the federal diet.

There was a more urgent practical reason for Bismarck's retreat from his preconceived plans in January 1863. Revolt broke out in Russian Poland; and this disrupted the Franco-Russian *entente*. Napoleon III had to protest for the sake of French opinion; and he tried to drag the other Powers along with him. The dynamic alliance which Bismarck had hoped to join disappeared; the 'Crimean coalition'—most baleful of combinations for Prussia—threatened to take its place. But Prussia had been indifferent to the eastern crisis itself; this time a vital interest of her own was at stake. The revolt might spread to Prussian Poland; and Bismarck held that, while Russia could still be a Great Power without her Polish lands, Prussia could not. Indeed, with his endless ingenuity in discovering dangers that were largely imaginary, he even suspected that Gorchakov, the Russian chancellor, was planning to liberate both Russian and Prussian Poland in order to recover the friendship of France. Prussia would be dismembered; France and Russia would join hands across the continent. Bismarck had welcomed the Franco-Russian alliance so long as it was directed against Austria; he had to destroy it when it threatened to turn against Prussia. As a final provocation to him, the Prussian liberals—like the radicals of 1848—inclined sentimentally towards Poland. Bismarck goaded them on, so as to discredit them further with the king; and he recognized more clearly than they did that the defeat of Poland would be a crushing blow also against Prussian liberalism.

Bismarck acted with his usual impatience. General Alvensleben was sent to St. Petersburg, and on 7 February concluded with Russia a convention for joint action against

3

the Polish revolution. Bismarck later claimed that by this pact he had defeated Gorchakov as well as Napoleon III; he had played off the 'anti-Polish monarchist against the polonizing Panslav forces' at the Russian court. This was a characteristic exaggeration. Gorchakov had no real plans in favour of Poland; and the anti-Polish party at the Russian court would have carried the day without Bismarck's assistance.[1] As it was, Alexander II felt little gratitude for Prussia's patronage. It reminded him humiliatingly of Russia's protection of Austria against the Hungarian revolution in 1849. Moreover, the convention threatened to turn European resentment against Prussia. France could not act against Russia, even if she would; she could easily move against Prussia on the Rhine. Bismarck had to ask Gorchakov to cancel the convention; and within a month he was assuring the other Powers that it was 'a dead letter'. After March 1863 he kept out of the Polish affair—left Russia to suppress the revolt herself and drew his profit from her ensuing isolation.

The Alvensleben convention showed Bismarck in all his strength and weakness: a lightning grasp of any possible danger, but also excessive haste in meeting it. In later life, though he never lost his speed of vision, he learnt to control his immediate impulse and to let events do the work for him. Even in this case, he recovered from his initial blunder. He kept clear of both sides from March 1863 until the end of the affair. England and France continued to make impotent protests against the Russian treatment of Poland. Austria joined them, even more ineffectually. She was a partner in the partition of Poland, but she could not

---

[1] Ever resourceful, Bismarck had an alternative policy which he thought of applying if Russia acted weakly towards Poland. In that case, he would proclaim the liberation of Poland and would unite Russian and Prussian Poland under Hohenzollern sovereignty. This was no doubt little more than a sketchy improvisation; but it is a curious thought that, if things had run differently, Prussia, not Austria, would have been 'the Dual Monarchy'. It was not so preposterous as may appear in retrospect. Bucher, Bismarck's closest assistant, had advocated it in 1848; and Bismarck was often ready to steal from the radical programme.

resist the prospect of reviving 'the Crimean coalition'. As in the Crimean war, she ended by estranging everybody. England and France were angry that Austria had not translated her protests into acts; Russia was angry that she had protested at all. The Polish revolt ruined the Franco-Russian alliance. Even more important from Bismarck's point of view, it ended what fragments of monarchical solidarity remained between Russia and Austria. It was certain after 1863 that Russia would tolerate a war between Prussia and Austria if Prussia chose to fight one. Bismarck's gain should not be exaggerated. Prussia performed an inestimable service to Russia merely by remaining neutral; and Russia would henceforth repay in kind. She would not do more. She would not protect Prussia against Austria or France. In fact, like Italy in 1848, Prussia was only free 'to do it herself'. Still, a Power with three strong neighbours has a great advantage when one frontier is firmly neutral; and Prussia enjoyed this advantage between 1863 and 1871.

It did not look much like an advantage in the summer of 1863. Austria, not Prussia, took the lead in Germany. Prussia seemed to need protection, not a free hand. The Polish affair had forced Austria towards a choice between France and Russia; she tried to escape as she had done during the Crimean war, by uniting all Germany behind her. Francis Joseph invited the German princes to meet at Frankfurt, there to consider a reform of the federal constitution. There was to be an executive directory of five (Austria, Prussia and three others) and an assembly drawn from the parliaments of the individual states. It was the last and greatest attempt to unite Germany by consent—the consent of princes who owed their sovereign existence solely to the fact that Germany was not united. Francis Joseph and his advisers might make out that Austria was putting herself on a level with the others. In fact, Austria would be the presiding power; the princes would lose their existing right of veto; German power would be at Austria's beck and call. In particular, the Prussian claim for military supremacy north of the Main would be circumvented. All German forces would be merged in a new federal army; and these troops would be fighting for Austria, one day in Italy, the next on the Danube. The Austrians guessed that Prussia might raise objections. Therefore they concealed their plans and delayed the invitation to King William till the last moment.

William was at Baden-Baden near Frankfurt when the King of Saxony arrived to deliver the invitation in person. William was swept away by his monarchical emotions: 'Thirty reigning princes and a king as messenger? How can I refuse?' Bismarck fought with the king his first and most severe battle. He won the day by arguing that, if William went to Frankfurt, surrender to the Prussian parliament must follow—there would be no point in quarrelling over an army that had no longer an independent existence. When William gave way, Bismarck broke off the door handle as he left the room and then, smashing a jug against the wall, burst into hysterical sobbing. It was worth the effort. Bismarck had ruined the Austrian plan. Without Prussia the Frankfurt meeting achieved nothing. The German princes agreed to surrender their sovereignty only if Prussia did the same—an easy and unshakable excuse. When Francis Joseph left Frankfurt on 22 August 1863, Austria had lost the initiative in Germany for ever.

Bismarck had not yet won it. His first year in office was a watershed in European affairs—the moment when moderate liberalism faltered and began to run backwards. The Prussian chamber had been checked; the Franco-Russian alliance had crumbled; Austria's plans for a liberal Germany had miscarried. European anarchy and confusion was at its height. In November 1863 Napoleon III invited the Great Powers to a Congress which should consider every European problem. No one troubled to turn up. France had certainly lost the leadership of Europe. But Bismarck had not yet discovered how he could take the lead himself. He tried the idea of a German parliament elected by direct universal suffrage. The initiative fell as flat as those of others. The middle-class liberals, who were alone vocal in Germany, would not trust Bismarck so long as he was in conflict with the Prussian parliament. He beat about wildly, consulting Lassalle, the extreme reactionaries, even the liberals, for something that would raise a storm and get things moving. Events came to his rescue. In November 1863 Frederick VII of Denmark died. The question of Sleswig and Holstein was opened; and Bismarck stumbled, without knowing it, through the door that led to victory.

IV

THE DEFEAT OF AUSTRIA

THE affair of the Danish duchies, which opened in January 1864, led by logical steps to the defeat of Austria in July 1866. This is far from saying that Bismarck knew at the outset where he was going, whatever he might claim later on. The future is a land of which there are no maps; and historians err when they describe even the most purposeful statesman as though he were marching down a broad highroad with his objective already in sight. More flexible historians admit that a statesman often has alternative courses before him; yet even they depict him as one choosing his route at a crossroads. Certainly the development of history has its own logical laws. But these laws resemble rather those by which flood-water flows into hitherto unseen channels and forces itself finally to an unpredictable sea. The death of Frederick VII opened the flood-gates; and Bismarck proved himself master of the storm, a daring pilot in extremities. In his own words: 'Man cannot create the current of events. He can only float with it and steer.'

Sleswig and Holstein, the two 'Elbe duchies', had long been a pivot of German national feeling. They had been in personal union with Denmark for many centuries. Holstein, inhabited entirely by Germans, was a member of the German confederation; Sleswig was not, though Germans predominated in its southern half. In 1848 they had risen against the King of Denmark; and all Germany had rallied to their side. Even Prussia fought for them. The non-German Great Powers were then united on the side of treaty-rights. They had threatened to support Denmark. Prussia had given way, much to her discredit in Germany; the revolution had been humiliated; and the duchies were restored to union with Denmark by the treaty of London in 1852. Now times had changed and new legal issues had arisen. Frederick VII was the last King of Denmark in the male line; it was argued that the Salic law applied to the duchies, though not to Denmark itself. Moreover, Christian IX, the new king, opened his reign by confirming a constitution which incorporated Sleswig in a unitary 'Greater Denmark'. This was a breach of the treaty of London. The German liberals thought that their chance had come. They had found a cause which would arouse the enthusiasm of the masses. The German Powers would have to support the Duke of Augustenburg, the rival claimant, and so liberate the duchies from Danish rule. The unification of Germany on liberal lines would surely follow.

Bismarck had no sympathy with this policy: 'It is no concern of ours whether the Germans of Holstein are happy.' He certainly did not wish to help in manufacturing a new small state which would vote against Prussia at the diet. He said from the outset that only annexation of the duchies would justify Prussia's going to war. This was not crude land-hunger on his part; it was an appeal to William I —the only argument that might keep him from succumbing to nationalist feeling. For not only the liberal crown prince, but even William himself, was affected by the prevailing enthusiasm. When Bismarck spoke only of Prussian interests, William asked reproachfully: 'Are you not a German as well?' William looked back with humiliation to the failure of 1848–50 and wished to avenge it. When Bismarck was negotiating his alliance with Austria, he said that the king would not allow a new reference to 'the hated treaty of 1852'. This has usually been regarded as a clever trick by which Bismarck shook himself free of treaty obligations; but the objection was genuine enough. Again and again Bismarck had to hold William back from openly supporting the claim of Augustenburg; and if this had happened, reconciliation between William and the Prussian liberals would have followed at once. Though this might have given Germany a better future, it would also have led to Bismarck's fall—a consideration for him of some importance.

Bismarck therefore had to do something in the duchies—something which would satisfy the king without satisfying the liberals. Yet, with his mind always dominated by recollections of 1848, he feared the other disaster of that year. If Prussia took the lead against Denmark, the Great Powers would unite against her, as they had done in 1848. Bismarck found a way of escape. He would co-operate with Austria to enforce the treaty of London. There should be war against Denmark, but only to destroy the unitary Danish constitution. The other Powers could not object to a war for a treaty which they themselves had made. Moreover, the unity of the Powers would be broken: 'It is better to be two against three than one against four.' Most important of all, Austria would be tied down, taken prisoner for the conservative cause. Bismarck's anxiety may seem surprising. Austria lives in history as the conservative, Prussia as the revolutionary, power. But it did not look like that in 1864. Bismarck was condemned to conservatism by his quarrel with the Prussian chamber; Austria had a liberal constitution, ostensibly in full operation, and Francis Joseph was being strongly urged to bid for the leadership of liberal Germany. Bismarck himself wrote to the king: 'Austria is trying to outbid us in the Danish question.'

His apprehensions were, as usual, exaggerated. Francis Joseph was weary of German liberalism after the failure at Frankfurt in August 1863. Rechberg, his foreign minister, feared that the nationalist arguments used against the Danes could be turned against Austria in Venetia. He wished to restore the conservative partnership of Metternich's time, as Bismarck had perhaps wished to do in 1850. Alliance between Austria and Prussia, previously so difficult, suddenly became easy. Both countries dropped the conditions on which they had hitherto insisted. Austria did not get a Prussian guarantee of Venetia; Prussia did not demand military supremacy north of the Main. These conditions seemed to have become irrelevant. Venetia was not endangered by a war against Denmark; and there was no point in arguing over the federal forces just when they were being brushed aside. The alliance, signed on 16 January 1864, provided only for joint action against the Danish constitution and that the two allies should settle the fate of the duchies together.

This alliance has always been regarded as Bismarck's master stroke. Certainly it prevented either Austria or William I from going over to German liberalism. But in international affairs it increased Bismarck's difficulties rather than lessening them. Even he could not yet appreciate how completely the concert of Europe had been disrupted by the Crimean war. He still went on fearing a united European front against Prussia, when in fact her alliance with Austria was the only thing that offended the three non-German Powers. All three were friendly to Prussia, though for different reasons; all three were hostile to Austria and wanted to see her isolated. Russia favoured Prussian aggrandisement, which she thought would make her more secure; Napoleon favoured the national principle; Great Britain wanted a liberal Germany under Prussia. Prussia's stock went down when she made the alliance with Austria; it mounted again only as it became clear that the alliance would not last. If Prussia had acted alone, she could have acquired the duchies and defeated Austria without the diplomatic alarms of the following years. Bismarck was certainly a political genius. But he often displayed the genius of a pavement-artist who first ties himself up in knots and then brilliantly escapes from them.

Nor was the alliance designed as a trap for Austria. There was no reason to suppose that joint control of the duchies would necessarily lead to a quarrel. Powers usually learn from working together how to work together. The partition of Poland was there to prove it. Poland was the strongest bond between Russia and Prussia; it even enabled Russia and Austria to tide over innumerable crises in the Near East

without war. It had been the only cement in the Holy
Alliance. Why then should Sleswig and Holstein not be the
cement of a new conservative partnership? The alliance
was a test for Austria rather than a trap. Bismarck
answered the criticism of Goltz, his ambassador in Paris:
'You do not trust Austria. Nor do I; but I think it right to
have Austria with us now; we shall see later whether the
moment of parting comes and from whom.' This might only
mean that Bismarck wished to prove to the king that co-
operation with Austria was impossible; it is more likely that
he needed also to prove it to himself. After all he—along
with others—had been posing the choice for the last ten
years: either a revolutionary alliance with France and
Russia, or a conservative partnership with Austria. The
revolutionary alliance was no longer on offer. Therefore
only the conservative alliance remained. No one, not even
Bismarck, foresaw a third course—that Prussia should
defeat Austria without the help of either France or Russia.
But Austria had to show that she was more friendly to
Prussia than in the days of Schwarzenberg and Buol.
When the Italian ambassador complained: 'You don't need
us. You have chosen another,' Bismarck replied: 'Oh, we
have hired him.' 'Gratis?' '*Il travaille pour le roi de Prusse.*'
Here surely was the truth. If Austria would help Prussia
to conquer the duchies and would surrender northern
Germany to her, then Bismarck would maintain Austria as
a Great Power elsewhere—in Italy and the Near East.
Though this has often been dismissed as a preposterous
dream, it was in fact the ultimate outcome in 1879.

The war against Denmark opened on 1 February. Though
the Danes could not withstand two Great Powers, they
counted on the others to help them. Not altogether in vain.
The signatories of the treaty of London allowed Austria
and Prussia to overrun the duchies; but they protested
when the invading armies reached the frontier of Denmark
itself. An armistice was signed; and an international conference met in London on 25 April. Then the Danes over-
played their hand. Still confident that the Great Powers

would support them, they refused to restore the autonomy of the duchies; and this Danish repudiation of the treaty of London enabled Austria and Prussia to repudiate it also. Bismarck has sometimes been given the credit for provoking the Danes into obstinacy; but they needed little provocation. The conference broke up, and war was resumed. None of the Powers came to Denmark's assistance. Napoleon III would not go against the national principle; Russia would not go against Prussia, her only friend; and British isolationist opinion silenced the feeble attempts of Palmerston and Russell to repeat their firm stand of 1848. The Danes, left to themselves, were again defeated. They made peace at the beginning of August, surrendering the duchies to Austria and Prussia jointly.

So far the conservative partnership had been successful. The two German Powers had been able to ignore European opinion and to have things in the duchies their own way—a great improvement on the events between 1848 and 1850. But now Austria and Prussia had to work together in peace. On 23 August, Bismarck and Rechberg, with their two royal masters, met at Schönbrunn, the Habsburg palace just outside Vienna. Bismarck claimed the duchies for Prussia. Rechberg answered by demanding a Prussian guarantee of Venetia and, as well, that Prussia should help to reconquer Lombardy for Austria in case of a new war against Italy. Bismarck agreed. Perhaps, as most historians think, he was not sincere. But it is difficult to resist the conclusion that, with his usual impetuosity, he was now running full tilt after the conservative alliance, as he had run full tilt after the revolutionary alliance in earlier years. At any rate, the scheme was wrecked by the two monarchs. William said shamefacedly, 'he had no right over the duchies,' and, with all the stubbornness of his limited intelligence, revived the claim for Prussian military supremacy in northern Germany. Francis Joseph would not swallow the German aggrandisement of Prussia which her annexation of the duchies would involve, for any price short of the surrender of some Prussian territory. He would not, in short, compromise in Germany for the sake of his lands in Italy; and as a result lost both.

Rechberg and Bismarck had to drop their proposed treaty. No agreement was reached except that the two Powers should hold the duchies jointly until something turned up. At Schönbrunn the conservative policy reached high-water—and passed it. Bismarck realized this. While still in Vienna, he said to the French ambassador: 'We Berliners do not now look on Vienna as a German city.' The conversation, made sharper by the fact that it took place in Rechberg's own drawing-room, was Bismarck's first approach to France for nearly two years. The tide soon began to run fast the other way. The treaties on which the *Zollverein* were based expired at the end of 1865. Rechberg pressed hard for the fulfilment of the promise to include Austria that had been made ten years ago. Bismarck was ready to meet him or, at any rate, to renew the promise; it was 'an inexpensive act of friendship'. The Prussian ministers in charge of economic affairs objected. They were eager to shake off the conditional promise to Austria and to press further on the Free Trade course. Bismarck did not usually allow his colleagues to dictate policy to him. This time a strange thing happened. He went off to Biarritz, where he once more enjoyed the company of Kathi Orlov; and, though he urged the Prussian ministers to agree to Austria's request, he acquiesced when they turned it down. Was he exhausted? Did he feel economic questions beyond his ken? Or, recognizing that this was a vital decision, did he prefer to place the responsibility on others? We can never know. But certainly the breach over the *Zollverein* made a greater cleavage than any of the political actions in these years. The tariff frontier between Austria and the *Zollverein* became the frontier between two worlds. Austrian trade went down the Danube and into the Balkans. Germany turned to the world market across the North Sea. Political division was bound to follow even if Bismarck's diplomacy had failed.

The check over the *Zollverein* ruined the Austro Prussian

alliance. Rechberg resigned. Mensdorff, his successor, was in the hands of his professional advisers; and they were determined to resist Prussian claims. Biegeleben, the most outstanding of them, wrote contemptuously: 'Austria would have to give up the presidential dignity, as she gave up the Imperial dignity half a century ago, and conclude an alliance with the Prussian German Reich.' To this indeed Austria was to come, but only after defeat in war. The breach was not welcomed by Bismarck. He would have preferred to let things drift in the duchies until compromise was forced on Austria by new difficulties in Venetia or the Near East. As he wrote to Goltz in February 1865: 'I think it wiser to continue the existing marriage with Austria for the time being despite little domestic quarrels.' But Russia and France did not oblige him. Both remained inactive. Russia was busy subduing Poland. Napoleon III, ill and dispirited, was playing at imperialism in Mexico. Neither was in the mood to revolutionize Europe. Austria seemed free to take the offensive against Prussia.

Mensdorff and his advisers had no clear picture of their plans for Germany. Conservative in outlook, they disliked German nationalism; yet equally disliked the upstart Prussia, and resented the way in which they had been involved in the affairs of the duchies. They took to patronizing the claim of Augustenburg, more to provoke Prussia than for any constructive purpose. Bismarck tried to strike this weapon from their hands. In February 1865 he offered to recognize Augustenburg as duke of Sleswig-Holstein, but on condition that Prussia had military control of the duchies. Augustenburg was confident of German liberal support; he was encouraged even by the Crown Prince of Prussia and dreamt of becoming a truly independent ruler. Bismarck has described their interview. He greeted Augustenburg as 'Your Royal Highness'; lowered his tone to 'Your Highness' when Augustenburg proved obstinate; and saw him off at the door as 'Your Excellency'. The Austrians approved Augustenburg's obstinacy. Biegeleben said that he would sooner plant potatoes than be duke on

such terms. Soon afterwards, the Austrian delegate at
Frankfurt voted for a federal resolution supporting
Augustenburg; this was a breach of the Austro-Prussian
alliance in all but name.

Bismarck had to contemplate war against Austria, or at
any rate to threaten it. He asked the general staff for an
appraisal of Austrian strength, and received an encouraging
reply. On 29 May the Prussian Crown Council discussed
future policy. Bismarck described Austria's mounting
hostility and urged William to claim the duchies. He
urged his old line of the revolutionary alliance: 'If war
against Austria in alliance with France is ruled out of the
diplomatic vocabulary, no Prussian policy is possible.'
William saw the trap. If he claimed the duchies, he would
have to pay Bismarck's price and agree to alliance with
France, a course that was abhorrent to him. He therefore
declared that he had no moral claim to the duchies, though
he would accept them if Austria offered them to him. This
was an unlikely contingency. Bismarck had to play a
game of bluff against Austria—not authorized to claim the
duchies, forbidden to negotiate with France, yet giving the
impression that he intended to go to war with Austria for
some reason or other. He talked threateningly and even
proposed alliance to Italy through the Austrian post
office.

The Italians were not taken in. They suspected that Bismarck was not ready 'to play the great game'. The Austrian
ministers, however, drew back. They had no clear-cut plans
for war against Prussia and, besides, wanted to settle their
internal difficulties in Hungary. The lesser states were even
more alarmed; and a Bavarian came forward as mediator.
His mediation was successful; and Austria and Prussia
struck a bargain when Bismarck was on holiday on
Austrian soil. The treaty of Gastein, signed on 14 August
1865, divided the administration of the duchies—Holstein
to Austria, Sleswig to Prussia; Lauenburg, the third fragment of territory, was ceded to Prussia outright. William
was delighted. He exchanged pledges of 'loyal and honest

understanding' with Francis Joseph, and made Bismarck a count for having saved the peace of Germany. No doubt Bismarck was rather less pleased; and yet rather better pleased than is sometimes made out. Though he spoke slightingly of the treaty of Gastein as 'papering over the cracks', he did not seek to widen the cracks himself. After all, Gastein gave some territory to Prussia; it ignored Augustenburg; and the administrative division prepared the way for a more lasting partition if Austria ran into difficulties. Bismarck had a deep sense of moral responsibility—certainly deeper than any other continental statesman of the time; and he would not disrupt the existing order in Europe unless events drove him to it. In his own words to Friedjung many years later: 'I had to try every way one after the other—the most dangerous last.' The treaty of Gastein was a further opportunity—almost the last—for Austria to accept Prussia as an equal. The Austrians did not mean to do so; it was they, not Bismarck, who refused to treat Gastein as a step on the road towards agreement.

It may seem paradoxical to describe Bismarck as having a deep sense of moral responsibility; and certainly it was of an unusual sort. Most statesmen seek to show that they have acted from high-minded motives, but have failed to live up to them. They do not plan wars; they drift into war and think it an adequate excuse to plead that this was unintentional. Bismarck aspired to control events. He would go to war only 'when all other means were exhausted' and then for 'a prize worthy of the sacrifices which every war demands'. This may shock those who judge by motives instead of by results. But Bismarck's planned wars killed thousands; the just wars of the twentieth century have killed millions. Moreover, Bismarck disliked war, though not primarily for the suffering that it involved. War was for him a clumsy way of settling international disputes. It deprived him of control and left the decision to generals whose ability he distrusted. A civilian to the core, he always wanted to back a certain winner; and Moltke, the greatest

Prussian general, told him repeatedly that nothing was certain in war.

Gastein gave Bismarck some hope that he might succeed without war; but only if he could increase Austria's difficulties elsewhere. It was clear to him that Russia would not be stirred to move in the Near East; therefore Napoleon must be roused over Venetia. In September 1865 Bismarck again went to Biarritz—for the last time. Kathi Orlov failed to meet him, much to his annoyance.[1] He even blamed her for his political talks with Napoleon III and for the upheaval that followed. If she had been there, he would have had something better to do—a preposterous example of the way he liked to put the blame on others. Bismarck wished to push Napoleon into action over Venetia so that Prussia could get the duchies peacefully. Napoleon had the opposite aim. He regarded the quarrel between Austria and Prussia as providential—'a stroke of luck which it seems should never arise;' and he wanted to push the two German Powers into war so as to get Venetia peacefully for Italy.

Both men talked vaguely of their future plans; neither succeeded in tying the other down. It is often said that Bismarck cheated Napoleon at Biarritz by hinting at territorial concessions on the Rhine. This is not so. Napoleon was not interested in the Rhine; he was obsessed with liberating Venetia and so, he supposed, distracting Italy from Rome. But he wished to accomplish this miracle without war—at least without war in which France was involved. This was for Bismarck the real importance of the meeting at Biarritz. He realized for the first time that Napoleon wanted to avoid war, not to promote it. Hitherto Bismarck had preached alliance with France in and out of season; now he saw that this alliance was not on offer in any positive form. Instead of the revolutionary alliance, Prussia 'must do it herself'. Napoleon would offer neutrality, no more. Previously Bismarck had believed that this was not enough; now, he had to make do with it, and in any

---

[1] There was an alarm of typhoid at Biarritz, and Kathi took her children to Sidmouth instead.

case Moltke's assurances had perhaps convinced him. At Biarritz, not earlier, Bismarck came round to the view that Prussia could defeat Austria without French assistance. Of course, he still preferred to get his way peacefully and would have rejoiced at a Franco-Italian attack on Venetia. Neither Napoleon nor Bismarck committed himself to war at Biarritz. They struck a negative bargain, which left each free to act if he wished to do so; and of course, each wished the other to act first. Bismarck promised not to give Austria a guarantee of Venetia; Napoleon promised not to make an alliance with her. This was the agreement of Biarritz. Bismarck kept his word; Napoleon later repented.

When Bismarck returned from Biarritz, he said to the Austrian ambassador: 'Either a genuine alliance or war to the knife.' The Austrians refused the first; they shrank from the second. They stirred up agitation in favour of Augustenburg, though without any clear appreciation that war must follow. This certainly pleased German opinion, but it also helped to convince William I of Austria's hostility. Bismarck answered by stirring up Italy in Austria's rear. His motive was not primarily military, though Moltke pointed to the obvious advantage of dividing the Austrian army by having Italy on their side. The advantage was not great; for the Austrians must have kept on their guard against Italy even if she remained neutral. Bismarck's main concern was to give a further pledge to Napoleon. He still feared that Austria might recover French favour by surrendering Venetia without a war. The Italians had the reverse fear that Austria might consolidate her position in Venetia by agreeing to Prussia's demands north of the Main. Both Prussia and Italy, in fact, wanted to tie the other down without being tied themselves. Each wanted to bluff Austria into surrender. Napoleon gave the final push which brought them together. He told the Italians that alliance with Prussia would make the balance more even in Germany and so open the road to Venetia. On 8 April 1866 the Italians gave way. Italy promised to attack Austria if Prussia went to war within three months; Prussia only promised to continue the war (if it occurred) until Italy gained Venetia.

Italy was caught: she had to go to war if Prussia chose to do so. But others had also lost their freedom of manœuvre. Austria could no longer buy Italian neutrality by surrendering Venetia; she could only buy Prussian neutrality by giving way in Germany. And no doubt Bismarck had still a faint hope that she might do this. But he could no longer rely on time to do his work for him. He must either settle with Austria or fight her within three months before the alliance with Italy ran out. He had always held that the duchies alone would not justify a great war; for that, he must open the German question. On 9 April— the day after concluding the Italian alliance—he proposed a German parliament elected by universal suffrage. The stroke miscarried once more. Few Germans would take Bismarck seriously as a radical. Public opinion was against him not only in Germany, but even in Prussia itself; and William I, not German nationalists, made the war of 1866 possible. The king had no desire to unify Germany, but he resented Austria's threatening attitude. The Austrians were manœuvred into this by the clumsiness of their military machine. Their army needed six weeks to mobilize; Prussia's needed only three. Therefore the Austrians had to start the race to a war which they feared and did not want. They tried to escape the trap by proposing mutual disarmament. William accepted joyfully. Bismarck saw precious time slipping away. He was saved by the Italians. They began to mobilize, and the Austrians therefore refused to disarm. William was now finally convinced of Austrian hostility.

In May Bismarck offered Austria a peaceful settlement for the last time. It was on the old terms: Prussia to command all German forces north, and Austria those south, of the Main. The Austrians answered with the old condition: Prussia must guarantee Venetia. Earlier Bismarck would have agreed to this. Now his hands were tied by his promise to Napoleon at Biarritz. Napoleon had won the diplomatic competition, or so it seemed: Venetia would be liberated without any French exertion. Bismarck's last negotiations with Austria were abandoned, wrecked on the question of Venetia. The same question barred every way against a peaceful settlement. The Austrians offered Venetia to Italy in exchange for her neutrality; but she was bound by the Prussian alliance. When Napoleon had a pacific qualm and tried to prevent the war by proposing a European Congress, the Austrians insisted that no territorial changes, and therefore no surrender of Venetia, be discussed. The congress failed to meet, much to Bismarck's relief. Finally, the Austrians reached the despairing conclusion that only war with Prussia would end their difficulties—as indeed it did, though not to their advantage. On 12 June they promised to cede Venetia to Napoleon if he would allow them to have their war against Prussia first. Thus both sides paid the same price for a neutrality which Napoleon did not, in any case, mean to abandon.

By the time the Austrians made their treaty with Napoleon, war in Germany had virtually started. On 1 June the Austrians placed the question of the duchies before the federal diet and asked for a federal decision on their future. This was a formal repudiation of the Austro-Prussian alliance, which had provided that the two allies should settle the fate of the duchies between themselves. Bismarck had won the waiting game after all. Austria had made the first open gesture of hostility. Prussia could claim to be acting defensively. William I was at last convinced of Austria's ill-will. Even Bismarck spoke of 'freeing Germany from Austrian domination', and attributed the war to God's inscrutable will, not to his own doing. In one particular Bismarck waited too long. He had intended the war to start in the duchies, so as finally to win the king to his policy; and he answered the Austrian action at the diet by ordering the invasion of Holstein. The Prussian general there moved slowly, and the Austrian troops got away, much to Bismarck's annoyance, before a shot could be fired. However, the Austrians were determined to provide Bismarck with his war. On 14 June they called for federal mobilization against Prussia. The smaller states temporized to the last. Though they agreed to mobilize, they cited the armaments of both Prussia and Austria, and proposed to defend their own neutrality. Bismarck did not respect their nice point. He declared the confederation dissolved and sent an ultimatum to the states that had voted for mobilization. There was no formal declaration of war against Austria. The Prussian armies advanced through Saxony and, when they reached the Austrian frontier their commander sent a message to the nearest Austrian officer that a state of war existed. All wars are a struggle for power, but a practical occasion for their outbreak is usually found. In 1866 there was no disguise; Austria fought for her primacy, Prussia for equality.

The campaign lasted barely a fortnight. On 3 July the Austrian armies suffered catastrophic defeat at Sadova or, as it is called in German, Königgrätz. Prussian policy had to be decided literally on the battlefield. William I accompanied the armies, theoretically commander-in-chief, with Moltke as chief-of-staff; and Bismarck went along with him. Though only a lieutenant in the reserve, he was hastily made a temporary major-general and tried to behave as a soldier during the campaign. His real concern was to keep his hands on the king, and this proved difficult. The smell of powder made William almost uncontrollable. A small incident showed it. William refused to withdraw when under fire; and he was unmoved by the accusation that he was endangering the life of his civilian prime minister. Finally Bismarck gave William's horse a sharp, unperceived kick in its flank; and William obeyed this protest. It was a perfect parable of relations between king and minister—outward obedience, secret kicks. Bismarck was anxious to end the war as quickly as possible. He still could not believe that Russia and France would allow the remaking of central Europe without their participation. Therefore he kept to the modest aims that he had before

the war. He took some steps which might have heralded
the breakup of the Habsburg monarchy; he organized a
Hungarian legion and even talked of a Czech national state
in Bohemia. But these were simply precautions in case
Francis Joseph proved obstinate. Essentially Bismarck's
terms remained the same: Prussian hegemony in Germany
north of the Main. The only advance was that, whereas
previously he would have left Austria supreme south of the
Main, he now insisted that she withdraw from Germany
and leave the south to enjoy 'an independent international
existence'.

The Austrians made little difficulty over accepting these
terms. Francis Joseph was angry with the German states,
which—apart from Saxony—had given him no effective
help. It troubled him little to renounce the last scraps of
Habsburg supremacy in Germany; and he was quite ready
for Prussia to annex all north Germany, so long as his one
loyal ally, Saxony, was spared. Nor did Russian complaints
prove serious. Bismarck invoked William's family ties with
the tsar, and threatened to raise Poland if Russia tried to
intervene. The Russians acquiesced in sulky silence. France
seemed a graver danger. Napoleon III had got what he
wanted—the liberation of Venetia, the aggrandisement of
Prussia, and the triumph of 'the national principle' in
which he believed. He would have been content to let well
alone. But his advisers insisted that France would be
humiliated and his prestige ruined, unless he imposed himself on the combatants and claimed territorial compensation
for France. Unwillingly he followed their advice. On 4 July
he announced that Austria had appealed to his mediation
and that he had agreed. This was a breach of the neutrality
which he had promised at Biarritz. Bismarck exclaimed:
'I will be revenged on the Gauls when opportunity offers.'
He discussed the possibility of a war on two fronts with
Moltke and prepared to rouse German feeling by resurrect-
ing the revolutionary constitution made at Frankfurt in
1849. The alarm did not last. Napoleon might have been
pushed into action, despite the inadequacy of the French

army, if Prussia had stood alone. But Italy was also in the
war. The Italian army had been defeated by the Austrians
at Custoza, and occupied Venetia only when the Austrian
troops were recalled to defend Vienna after Sadova. Now
the Italians wanted a victory of their own and dreamt of
conquering south Tyrol. Napoleon could never go against
Italy, his own creation. Therefore he swung round to his old
line and welcomed the triumph of nationalism. He even
pushed Bismarck to make higher claims. Where Bismarck
would have been content with military hegemony in north
Germany, Napoleon urged full annexation; and thanks to
him, four million Germans became 'compulsory Prussians'.
Napoleon made two conditions: south Germany should be
independent, and there should be a plebiscite in northern
Sleswig. Bismarck agreed to both. He had no ambitions
south of the Main; and he himself believed in the national
principle particularly where the territory concerned had no
strategic importance.[1]

A fortnight after Sadova, Austria had accepted Bismarck's terms; France approved of them; Russia did not
object. Yet Bismarck's greatest struggle was still to come.
The obstacle which almost broke his will was William I.
The king had never understood Bismarck's far-reaching
plans and had been dragged reluctantly into war. He had
given way only when convinced that Austria and her
German allies were planning to attack him. Now he regarded them as wicked and insisted that they be punished.
For him, as for many lesser mortals, war was a matter of
moral judgement, not an instrument of power. It seemed to
him immoral that Austria should be allowed to end the war
without losing some territory, and even without a march
of the victorious Prussian army through her capital. On
the other hand, the dethronement of the north German
princes seemed to him excessive; it would be a more bitter
and more appropriate punishment for them to survive
diminished. Bismarck had no scrap of this outlook. Resent-

---

[1] The plebiscite in northern Sleswig was not held in Bismarck's lifetime;
but he was not to blame for this.

ment was no part of his policy—at any rate when the offence was against the king, not against himself. The lesser princes were a nuisance; therefore they should disappear. Prussia would be no stronger for a fragment of Austrian territory; therefore should claim none. He said to William: 'Austria was no more in the wrong in opposing our claims than we were in making them'—an even-handed judgement that will stand as the verdict of history, but not one likely to appeal to a simple-minded Hohenzollern.

The conflict raged for more than two days at Prussian headquarters. The generals, with their simple moral code, supported William. The crown prince, with a vision of a united Germany, supported Bismarck. There has never been a clearer dispute between the moral and the 'real' view of politics; the more fascinating in that William was advocating a more severe peace with Austria and a less severe peace with the princes—but both on moral grounds. Bismarck used all his most powerful weapons—tears, hysterics, the breaking of crockery, even the threat to jump from a high window. On 24 July the crown prince at last talked William round. The preliminary peace with Austria was signed two days later. Austria withdrew from Germany, consented to a new German confederation under Prussia, and surrendered Sleswig to her. Bismarck kept his word to Italy: he stipulated that she receive Venetia. But he did not go an inch beyond this; and when the Italians tried to conquer south Tyrol, he left Austria free to defeat them. She benefited already from a Prussian neutrality that might soon turn into active protection.

Schweinitz, one of Bismarck's assistants, said in 1870: 'You ask what we gave Austria. We gave her life.' But even Bismarck did not appreciate in 1866 that, by failing to carry the war to a revolutionary conclusion, he had committed himself to the maintenance of Austria as a Great Power. He wrote to his wife after the victory: 'There has never been such a decline in so short a time. And all this because Austria would not tolerate Prussia beside her as a Great Power!' Now he had got what he wanted, and therefore was prepared to leave her alone. But he still supposed that she was a power of the first rank. He believed in theory that national frontiers were the final solution; and he advocated them in Sleswig, with France, and later in the Balkans. Ultimately all Germany would be united; and this would mean the dismemberment of the Habsburg monarchy. But Bismarck had ceased to be the man in a hurry that he was at Frankfurt or even when he became prime minister in 1862. Then he had believed that the national reconstruction of Europe could be carried through in a year or two. Now he began to think that it would take generations. He did not even aspire to bring in the south German states. He insisted during the peace negotiations on the impossibility of including 'the German-Catholic-Bavarian element': and he wrote to his wife, with obvious sincerity: 'There is nothing more to do in our lifetime.' If south Germany was beyond his ambition, how much more then the Austrian empire. It would last his time; and he wanted its friendship. He said immediately after Sadova 'We shall need Austrian strength for ourselves later.' It was the mistake of his successors, and perhaps even of himself, to believe that they needed even her weakness.

Even Bismarck did not foresee all the consequences of his success. They were still more obscure to others. Not only had Austria ceased to be the dominant Power in Germany. France had ceased to be the dominant Power in Europe. She could no longer play off one German power against the other. One Frenchman, slightly more farsighted, said: 'It is we who were beaten at Sadova.' But France would have been beaten even more decisively if Austria had won. France could dominate central Europe only so long as the conflict between Prussia and Austria was not resolved. The French politicians did not understand this. They insisted that France would receive the primacy of Europe if she received compensations for Prussia's gains. Napoleon was once more dragged reluctantly forward. Bismarck had often talked before the war of surrendering territory on the

Rhine in exchange for French support. Whether he meant this seriously we cannot know, for Napoleon had evaded the bargain. France had remained neutral, and, after Sadova, an unfriendly neutral. Bismarck refused to sur-render any German territory. He turned the French demand to good purpose. He revealed it to the south German states; and they, lately the enemies of Prussia, concluded alliances with her, even agreeing to put their armies under Prussian command in time of war.[1] Bismarck remarked cynically: 'We shall need the national swindle later as protection against French demands.'

Though Napoleon did not know of these treaties, he drew back at the first sign of difficulties. Despite the warnings of his advisers, he had always wanted to be on friendly terms with national Germany, as he was with national Italy. In August the French envoy produced a proposal of a different nature. Napoleon would forget the gains of the past. Instead he offered an alliance, which should be a mutual-benefit society for the future. France should acquire Belgium; and Prussia should lay her hands on southern Germany. Bismarck had no objection in principle. He held that France should extend 'as far as French is spoken'. But he saw no reason to assist her, when he himself did not wish to move in south Germany and when Prussia certainly did not need French protection against either Austria or Russia. The negotiations ran away to nothing, leaving only a draft treaty which Bismarck was to use with devastating effect against France in 1870. But there was as yet no breach between France and Prussia. Napoleon thought that Prussia's aggrandisement and the division of Germany into three was a gain for France, despite the failure to get com-pensation; and Bismarck appreciated that Napoleon had

---

[1] It is often said that these alliances were a breach of the peace treaty with Austria, by which the south German states were to enjoy 'an international independent existence'. But this did not forbid their making alliances either with each other or with Prussia. Nor was Napoleon offended by the alliances when they were made public in 1867: he regarded them as primarily a guarantee against Austria, and he was more fearful of her than of Prussia in south Germany.

made things easy for him, despite occasional complaints.
Both were right. Bismarck had managed to defeat Austria
and remake northern Germany without offending either
France or Russia—a feat previously regarded as impossible. But he had done it only by a moderation in victory
which no other statesman has ever shown.

The victorious war also brought reconciliation at home.
A new Chamber had been elected on the very day of
Königgrätz; and Bismarck's opponents returned much
weakened. Even the most liberal regarded him as a national
hero—with some excuse. Bismarck came to meet them.
Even before the war he was putting all the blame for the
conflict on the king. He had needed the conflict with the
Chamber in order to keep a firm hold over William I and
to get his own way in foreign policy. Now the war was safely
past; and new difficulties on the way to building up a
strong national Germany were more likely to come from
William I than from the Prussian liberals. Bismarck was
quite ready to play the Chamber against the king. He said
publicly: 'Absolutism on the part of the Crown is just as
little defensible as absolutism on the part of parliamentary
majorities'; and, to the former opposition: '*In verbis simus
faciles.*'[1] He confessed that the expenditure of money
without parliamentary authorization had been illegal, and
asked for an indemnity. It was granted on 3 September by
230 votes to 75.

This vote is often described as the abdication of Prussian
liberalism; but it represented a genuine compromise and
even an assertion of constitutional legality. Perhaps Bismarck took the liberals prisoner, but he was also forced
into alliance with them. Some of his conservative associates
had been outraged by the war against Austria; the rest
were scandalized by the request for indemnity. Formerly
the Prussian reactionaries had cheered him on against the
liberals. Now the liberals helped him to ride over the
scruples of the reactionaries. He was not tied to either—
a lone hunter who followed no rules but his own. He had

[1] Kind words cost nothing.

set out to make Prussia the equal of Austria; and he had succeeded. Now his mind was turned to the north German confederation. The former advocate of great Prussia would soon be saying: 'Prussia needs Germanizing rather than Germany Borussianizing,' and he would describe Prussian particularism as 'the most powerful and dangerous enemy that we have to deal with'.

V

THE NORTH GERMAN CONFEDERATION

WHEN Bismarck took office in 1862 he found his policies
and his enemies ready-made. Austria and the Prussian
liberals did not need to be invented. They existed already;
and the assertion of Prussian equality in Germany was
the way to defeat both of them. Bismarck's policy had
been response to a challenge. His admirers have even
described it as defensive, though it certainly took an
aggressive form. There was no longer the same urgency
after the victorious war of 1866. Prussia still had enemies.
Francis Joseph might seek to undo the verdict of Sadova;
Napoleon III might be pushed by French opinion into
opposing any further advance towards the unification of
Germany. And there were domestic obstacles also to that
union. But the enemies were not active. Bismarck had
to take the initiative for the first time. The years between
Sadova and Sedan were for Bismarck years of transition
when he moved from defence to creation. He ceased to
be a Prussian and became a German. He almost became
a liberal. He did not admit this himself and marked
approvingly an article which described him as a revolutionary: 'Only chance decides whether conditions make
the same man a White or a Red.' In his case, chance
turned him into a moderate, holding back the extreme
current of events.

He had little idea of this when he returned to Berlin
from the Austrian campaign in September 1866. Indeed he
had no vision of future action; and it was as much this
as genuine nervous exhaustion which led to his retirement from affairs throughout the autumn. He buried
himself in the country, unable to read, hardly able to talk
coherently. Blue skies, green meadows brought him back

to life. By the end of October he was dictating to his wife scathing comments on his harassed colleagues. He returned to Berlin at the end of the year, seeking new worlds to conquer. He found this new world in the North German confederation. He had had no clear picture during the conflict with Austria of the Germany that would follow her defeat. Indeed, he had supposed that it would be much the same as before except that Austria and Prussia would somehow share the presidency and that Prussia would command the armed forces north of the Rhine. Now the old confederation had gone; and, though Prussia had annexed some of the north German states, there were enough left to make it necessary for her to organize a new one.

His first impulse was merely to perpetuate the old pattern: a federal diet of diplomatic representatives from the member states, with Prussia as the presiding power, and a parliament, elected by universal suffrage, to approve the legislation laid before it by the diet. Only gradually did he realize that times had changed, and he along with them. Previously he had been in opposition—fighting against Austria, against the Chamber, even against the king. No wonder that he wanted to cut down the power of others; it seemed the only way of preserving his own. Now he discovered that he was leading, and that the others were in opposition. He had to apply the spur, where previously he had put on the brake. A great national Germany led by Austria or even united by the liberals would have ruined Prussia—and Bismarck along with her. A national Germany made by Bismarck would bring him greater control of events. He had spoken contemptuously of German nationalism even after Sadova. By the beginning of 1867 he was talking as though he had taken out the patent for it. He got on well with the liberal politicians, who now appreciated his speeches and followed their arguments. He was impatient with the German princes and even with the King of Prussia. Of course, he did not capitulate to the liberals, though he made an alliance with them. His approach to politics was always that of a diplomat, balancing between the various forces and playing one off against another; and he aimed to be the dominant partner in any association. He never became identified with any cause, whether monarchy or German nationalism or, later, conservatism. This gave him freedom to manœuvre; but in the last resort the lack of any party of his own led to his fall.

When Bismarck returned to Berlin, the new federal constitution was still to be made. Immediately after the war, the member states had signed treaties with Prussia, agreeing that a new federation should come into existence. These little states would indeed have had to agree to anything that Prussia laid down; but Bismarck needed the appearance of a federal structure. Now in December 1866 he studied the Frankfurt constitution of 1849, and the constitution of the United States—the only important federal constitution then in being. Prussian experts made some early drafts. Then Bismarck tore them in pieces and produced a scheme which suited his plans. It was very much the old confederation except that the King of Prussia was firmly in control of the armed forces. The federal council, representing the princes, was to govern Germany and to initiate legislation; Prussia's representation gave her a veto on any changes of the constitution.[1] The parliament, elected by universal suffrage, was merely to approve the legislation which the Council laid before it.

Representatives of the states approved this draft early in 1867. It only seemed necessary for a constituent assembly to greet it with acclamation. But the liberal politicians felt the ground under their feet when it came to constitutional discussions. They held out firmly against political shams. There was an extraordinary and unexpected result. Having failed to trick the liberals, Bismarck went over to their side; and between February and April agreed with them on almost every decisive point. He accepted the secret ballot. He had intended to keep

---

[1] She got this by the simple device of adding to her former representation at the old diet the votes of the states just annexed.

universal suffrage a fraud, the peasants voting at the command of their landlords. The secret ballot ensured freedom
for the political parties. In return Bismarck secured a
concession which was in fact a blunder on his part. He
refused to allow payment of members in order to avoid a
class of professional politicians. He got something which
he liked even less. Despite universal suffrage, parliament
was long dominated by liberal intellectuals of independent
means—the very class most alien to Bismarck. This was a
relatively small issue. Greater concession soon followed
over the army. In every state power rests with the armed
forces; and whoever controls these forces controls, in the
last resort, the state itself. Bismarck had fought the conflict of 1862–66 in order to ensure that the king, and not
the Chamber, should determine the size of the Prussian
army. Yet his victory turned out to be barren. For now,
though the Prussian army continued to exist, it was merely
the largest contingent in the federal army of North Germany; and whoever controlled that army would have the
decisive power.

In his original draft Bismarck had written the federal
army into the constitution: the annual intake of recruits
was to be fixed on a percentage basis for good and all. The
liberals held out more successfully than they had done in
Prussia. There they had been tied by a constitution which
gave the king much power, the constitution of 1850. Now
the federal constitution could not come into being without
their agreement. Bismarck tried to shake them with the
argument, 'we cannot allow ourselves to fail'; but it was
an argument that worked even more strongly against
himself. After his repeated proposal of a German parliament
and his repeated claim to represent Germany, he could not
afford an open quarrel. Moreover he came gradually to see
that concessions to the liberals would strengthen his own
position, once he was in alliance with them. The states of
southern Germany would join the federation sooner or
later; and they would surrender their military autonomy
more willingly to a German parliament than to the King

of Prussia. The German princes were now Bismarck's
opponents, parliament became his ally. In his own words:
'A parliament without liberal backing would not exercise
an effective pressure on the reluctant governments.' He
therefore compromised with the politicians, as previously
he had compromised with Austria, and put off the decisive
struggle. He persuaded parliament to authorize the army-
establishment for four years, that is, until 1871. No doubt
he hoped that by then something would turn up which
would enable him to avoid further surrender. Nothing did.
Instead imperial Germany turned up, and liberal confidence
was stronger than ever. Once more there was postponement
until 1874. Only then did he agree that the military
establishment must be authorized by parliament once every
seven years. This was much the solution which Oliver
Cromwell, Bismarck's prototype, laid down in his constitution of 1653.

No doubt it was a poor thing by the standards of modern
democracy in Great Britain or France, where the service
estimates have to be approved every year.[1] Yet, in the
last resort, it came to much the same. The interval—
whether one year, seven years, or (as later in Germany
after Bismarck's fall) five years—was less important
than the principle; and that had been established. The
German army could not exist permanently without
parliamentary approval; and power therefore rested,
though at a longer interval than usual, with a parliamentary
majority. Nor was this all. Bismarck had not originally
projected a federal budget. Once the parliament had
approved federal expenditure, the federal council would
call on the member-states to provide the money in agreed
proportions; and as ninety per cent. of this expenditure
was military, the parliament would give its approval
rarely. The politicians, however, insisted that they must
give their approval each year; and once more Bismarck

---

[1] Even democracy can manage to evade its own standards. Atomic power
was developed in Great Britain for some years without the authorization and
even without the knowledge of parliament.

gave way—it would strengthen his hand against the princes. A true budget came into existence, even though the federal parliament did not devise the taxes to meet it;[1] and the federal government could not keep going unless it somehow secured the agreement of a parliamentary majority.

This was a most unexpected consequence. Bismarck had not intended that there should be a federal government at all. The federal council was to be the organ of government, as it had been in the confederation of Frankfurt; and the Prussian agent who presided would receive his orders from the Prussian foreign minister, though he enjoyed the title of chancellor. But once the chancellor had to persuade parliament to authorize the budget and the army establishment, he became the keystone of power; and the liberals only underlined this when they insisted that the chancellor should accept 'responsibility'. Bismarck had to take the post. He refused to allow a federal ministry, at any rate in theory; he alone was 'responsible'. But the revolution had been made. Henceforth his relations with the Prussian chamber counted for nothing; his relations with the federal parliament were all-important. Bismarck so forgot Prussia that he did nothing to reform the three-class franchise, though he himself said that 'a crazier, more contemptible electoral law had never been thought of in any country'. The titles of Prussian prime minister and foreign minister were eclipsed; Bismarck held on to them solely to ensure that Prussia obeyed Germany's will. He lives in history as chancellor. Henceforth he spoke for Germany. Maybe the king had imposed Bismarck on parliament; but the support of parliament enabled Bismarck to impose his will on the king.

Bismarck often sought to disguise this. He liked to make

---

[1] The primary income of the confederation, as later of the Reich, came from indirect taxation, most of it fixed permanently on grounds of economic policy. But this was never adequate for federal needs; and the deficit was made up by 'matricular contributions' from the member-states. The Reich never imposed direct taxation itself until just before the outbreak of the first World war.

out that he depended on no one—neither on the king
nor on the politicians. His very outward appearance
symbolized his independence. In the days when he had
been fighting the Prussian chamber for the sake of the
army he always wore a civilian frockcoat. Now, when he
had become a parliamentary statesman, he was never
seen except in a military tunic. Only in old age did he
explain, probably with some truth, that he had done it
to save tailors' bills. An old uniform was respectable;
a shabby tail-coat was not. But there was no escaping
the reality. Bismarck may have intended 'to ruin parliamentarianism by parliamentarianism', as he himself
boasted. In fact, he made Germany a constitutional
country. Not only was the franchise the widest in Europe,
with the only effective secret ballot. The parliament
possessed every essential function. It was the seat of
power. The King of Prussia, later called German emperor,
directed the executive; but so did, and does, the president
of the United States. And both president and emperor
were closely bound by the terms of a written constitution.
Bismarck was a parliamentary statesman exactly like Sir
Robert Walpole or the younger Pitt, even though, like
them, he depended on royal favour. A political party with
a stable majority in parliament would have ruled Germany;
and if no majority ever emerged the blame must lie as
much with the politicians as with Bismarck.

The parallel with eighteenth-century England can be
pushed further. Not only did the Hanoverian kings control
the executive and appoint their own ministers. They
commanded the army or handed it over to a commander-
in-chief on their own volition. The British parliament of
that age had only to authorize the military establishment
and to find the money for it. When contemporary observers, Voltaire or Montesquieu, praised the classical
constitution and called England a free country, they
meant that there was the rule of law, not at all that
parliament was supreme. Exactly the same was true of
the Germany that Bismarck had created. Imperial Ger-

many was a *Rechtstaat*, secure from arbitrary government. Bismarck spoke truthfully when he said during the constitutional debates: 'I too am convinced that it is the duty of any honest government always to strive for the greatest measure of popular and individual freedom which is compatible with the security and common welfare of the State.' He never claimed that the constitution of 1867 was perfect. It was simply the best they could do at the time; and only time would improve it. He hoped that it would grow 'as the British constitution has grown, not by the theoretical assertion of an ideal which must be aimed at without considering the obstacles in the way, but by organic development of what exists, taking every step forward that appears at the moment possible and harmless.' If the German politicians had known more English history and less political theory, if they had worked together more and criticized less, Bismarck's constitution would have opened the way to cabinet government and ultimately to parliamentary sovereignty. Perhaps 'organic development' was impossible by the middle of the nineteenth century. Everyone had become too conscious of the historical process, particularly in Germany. Bismarck, instead of ranking as a pioneer of constitutionalism, came later to be regarded as the precursor of a tyrannical demagogy which he of all men would have found abhorrent. All he had in common with Hitler was a determination to make his will prevail, but parliamentary statesmen, too, have not been free from this weakness—or strength. Certainly he meant to succeed as federal chancellor. It was his duty, he said, 'to develop the power of Germany and not that of a greater Prussia.'

We can imagine the difficulties that he would have made, if he had remained only Prussian prime minister and another had been chancellor. As it was, he brooked no opposition. His old Prussian friends dared to criticize him. He broke off relations with them and treated them as personal enemies. The Austrian war and its outcome turned the political situation upside down. Parties split

both on Left and Right. The majority of the liberals
formed the National Liberal party—still liberal in outlook,
but now willing to co-operate with the federal chancellor.
A minority of conservatives decided to follow Bismarck,
even if this meant swallowing liberal measures. Though
the Free Conservatives, as they called themselves, were
the more personal in their loyalty, this made them less
satisfactory as supporters: they never knew what they were
supposed to be advocating until Bismarck gave them the
signal. The National Liberals, on the other hand, had a
clear-cut legislative programme which happened to co-
incide with Bismarck's projects; and this gave a genuine
impression of co-operation between chancellor and parliament. They remained two independent authorities. Bismarck never became a member of the German parliament.
He sat aloof on the ministers' bench—the more aloof in
that he was for many years the sole German minister.
He never had social dealings with the politicians on their
own ground—in their clubs or homes, not even in the
smoking-room of the Reichstag. They had to come to him—
to the beer-evenings which he gave with the same conscious
condescension as is shown by a headmaster, entertaining
the senior boys. He never established relations of confidence
let alone of friendship, with any politician.

Still, Bismarck looked very like a liberal in the years
after Sadova. No doubt he sometimes lamented the past
days of feudal subordination, just as he had spoken
nostalgically of Metternich's system when he was moving
towards conflict with Austria. But he went to war with
Austria, despite his devotion to Metternich's principles;
and he became a reformer on a grand scale after 1866
despite his earlier conservatism. He claimed only to
understand foreign policy; and the post of president
of the chancellor's office was created for his technical
adviser, Delbrück. But Bismarck never relaxed his grasp
of responsibility; and perhaps his early training as a
Prussian administrator had left a deeper mark than he
liked to confess. He altered Delbrück's draft-laws to con-

form to a common pattern, and the new German *Rechtstaat* was largely of his making. In 1867 Germany did not exist except as a name on paper—her only common possession the commercial code which Bismarck had helped to carry through the federal diet. Now, under Bismarck's direction, Germany was given all the qualities of a great modern state. The civil and criminal codes were ready before the making of the Empire; a unified judicial system came into operation in 1873. In a curious, though trivial, gesture of decentralization, Bismarck allowed the High Court of Appeal to sit at Leipzig. Though he sometimes wearied of the legal technicalities, he enjoyed lecturing parliament on general principles. Perhaps he overreached himself when he argued that only those who believed in personal immortality could support capital punishment; this would seem to be a strong argument in favour of atheism. The new Germany was as much his work as modern France was the work of Napoleon; and Bismarck had to cajole more, could order less.

He never reconciled himself to the liberal demand for centralized administration. He paraded a countryman's distrust of bureaucrats—all the more from having been one himself; and used to claim that, unlike most of the deputies, he had been at the receiving end of government orders. He, as a landowner, was a taxpayer, belonging to the *misera contribuens plebs*; his liberal critics had 'no property, no trade, no industry'. In practice he did little to check the advancing march of bureaucracy. His economic ideas, too, were at this time little developed. He pushed on the establishment of a unified currency and of a unified financial system. Otherwise he accepted without much thought the Free Trade principles of his colleague, Delbrück. Yet he had qualms. He once proposed to subsidize the weavers of Silesia. When Delbrück answered that every industry would then ask for aid, and that therefore the state could do nothing, Bismarck commented: 'And therefore it is to help no one?—The state can do it!' As yet, no action followed.

In foreign affairs, even more than at home, Bismarck
had no clear aim after the victories of 1866. Previously
he had been determined to settle the problem of German
dualism. Now he asked only to be left alone; and his desire
seemed to challenge no one. He was content to leave the
south German states in their 'international independent
existence'. He said repeatedly: 'We have done enough
for our generation.' Austria was no doubt disgruntled; and
Francis Joseph showed his hope for revenge when he
appointed Beust, former prime minister of Saxony and
Bismarck's principal opponent among the German states,
as Austrian foreign minister. But the danger was remote.
The Austrian army was disorganized, her finances weak;
and every political force in the Habsburg monarchy pulled
against war. Bismarck understood this: 'The German
Austrians know that an Austrian victory would rob them
of their gains. The Hungarians know that a victorious
Austrian army would overthrow their constitution.' The
Prussian general staff never treated war against Austria
as a serious problem after the peace of Prague. The
German problem had been settled; and Bismarck now
counted that European controversies would arise elsewhere—at Rome or in the Near East—topics from which
Prussia and north Germany were profitably detached.

Of the other Powers, England was now moving towards
complete isolation from continental affairs. Bismarck foresaw in any case that she would soon elevate the new
Germany to the honorary position of 'natural ally' which
Austria had enjoyed since the congress of Vienna. Russia
and Prussia were on good terms, bound together not only
by family ties but also by common hostility to Polish
nationalism. Yet Bismarck recognized that they were not
as close as they had been. The course of events between
1848 and 1867 had moved Prussia spiritually westwards.
Before the revolutionary year Prussia had been an autocratic monarchy, dependent on Russian protection. Now
she had become the leader of a liberal confederation which
could protect itself. Much has been made of the French

claim to influence in southern Germany; but the Russian assumption of predominance at Berlin was much stronger. The tsar treated the King of Prussia as his satrap and showed resentment when he was disillusioned. Moreover, Bismarck was slowly coming to realize that, once Austria accepted Prussian hegemony in northern Germany, however unwillingly, she could claim the counterpart that Prussia had previously offered to her—a guarantee of her position against Italy and in the Near East. The Italian danger was no longer serious once Venetia had been lost; the Near East would become the central problem of Bismarck's diplomacy. He was as yet far from being willing to support Austria against Russia; but already he could not support Russia against Austria.

He wanted above all to avoid the choice. All his later diplomacy was devoted to this evasion. In 1867 an easy way of escape still seemed open to him. France and Prussia had no reason for conflict and much ground for agreement. If they came together, they could impose peace on Europe even in the Near East. Bismarck wrote in December 1866: 'I have always regarded this alliance as the natural expression of the lasting agreement of the interests of the two countries.' Napoleon III thought exactly the same. He welcomed the victory of the national principle in Germany, just as he had welcomed its victory in Italy; and he wanted to become the leader in an alliance of free national states, expressing in new form the civilization of western Europe. The obstacle came from the Bonapartist adventurers who demanded a revival of Imperial prestige. Bismarck diagnosed the problem: 'A king of Prussia can make mistakes, can suffer misfortune and even humiliation, but the old loyalty remains. The adventurer on the throne possesses no such heritage of confidence. He must always produce an effect. His safety depends on his personal prestige, and to enhance it sensations must follow each other in rapid succession. Napoleon III has recently lost more prestige than he can afford. To recover it he will start a dispute with us on some pretext or other. I do not believe he personally wishes war, indeed I think he wants to avoid it, but his insecurity will drive him on.'

Bismarck threshed around for some means of satisfying Napoleon's prestige without injuring German interests; and at the end of 1866 he thought he had found it. He had refused to cede any German territory—whether the Bavarian palatinate or even the 'frontiers of 1814' which would have given France the valley of the Saar. But there was a fragment left over from the old confederation which could not be fitted in to the new one. The grand duchy of Luxembourg was under the sovereignty of the King of Holland—the last remaining personal union. Its capital had been garrisoned by Prussian troops as a federal fortress. Here at last was a German 'Savoy'—territory which the French could acquire without offending against the national principle. The inhabitants did not regard themselves as Germans; the King of Holland would be glad to sell Luxembourg in order to pay his private debts; and, with the dissolution of the old confederation, the Prussian troops would in any case have to be withdrawn. Many writers, in the light of what followed, have accused Bismarck of setting a trap for France. This was not at all in keeping with his intentions in 1867, whatever it might have been three years later. For the moment, Bismarck wanted peace abroad so as to concentrate on making the new federal constitution at home; and the crisis over Luxembourg was most unwelcome to him. He cared nothing for Luxembourg itself: it had little value as a fortress, and its heavy industry was still undeveloped. Bismarck's anxiety, as usual, concerned the king. William I still lived in the atmosphere of the war of liberation against France in 1813. He would protest violently against the French acquiring Luxembourg. Therefore Bismarck wanted to take him by surprise: the French were to settle everything with the King of Holland and then present William I with a *fait accompli.*

The French procrastinated. They were perhaps a little

afraid of being tricked by Bismarck; but Napoleon III
had never matured his conspiracies in a hurry. The King
of Holland was not made ripe for cession until the end of
March 1867. By then a North German parliament was in
existence; and Bismarck needed to keep its favour in
order to carry the constitution. He was caught for the first
time by the national spirit that he evoked. Those who
argue that he often disregarded public opinion fail to see
that, whereas between 1862 and 1866 his political life
depended on his being on bad terms with the liberals,
now their support was essential for his political success.
Nothing is free in this world; and the crisis over Luxembourg was the price which Bismarck paid for the North
German confederation. He could perhaps have overruled
the king. He could not disregard the liberal clamour
against surrender of 'ancient Germanic lands'. Yet even
so, he did not mean to give way to it. He sought, as so
often, for a way out in which there should be 'neither
victors nor vanquished'.

The Prussian generals, and some politicians also, were
eager for war. Moltke wrote: 'Nothing could be more welcome to us than to have *now* the war that we must have.'
Bismarck set his face against it. War, he held, should be
fought only for essential interests, not for reasons of
sentiment or prestige; and he did not regard Luxembourg
as an essential interest for Germany. The experiences of
the Austrian war had not left him unmoved. He was a
civilian despite his military tunic and, what was more, a
father with growing sons. He said on the battlefield of
Sadova: 'It makes me sick at heart to think that Herbert
may be lying like this some day'; and later: 'No one who
has looked into the eyes of a man dying on the battlefield
will again go lightly into war.' Bismarck allowed the
German parliament to storm but he kept his hands free.
Bennigsen, the National Liberal leader, demanded that
Luxembourg should remain united with the rest of Germany, and that the Prussian garrison should not be
withdrawn. Bismarck asked the deputies to have con-

4*

fidence that he would defend Germany's national interests.
They did so. They were bewitched by his phrases and in
the outcome failed to notice that he had surrendered the
two points on which Bennigsen had insisted. Bismarck
settled the affair with the first of his many diplomatic
miracles—satisfying German public opinion and yet giving
the French all that they could reasonably claim.

In earlier years Bismarck had excluded the other Powers
from the German question when he had wanted to defeat
Austria. He called them in to the question of Luxembourg.
An international conference met on his initiative and
found a compromise which should have satisfied all parties.
Though Luxembourg remained an independent state, the
Prussian garrison was withdrawn; its fortifications were
razed, and its neutrality put under the collective guarantee of the Great Powers. All this was sheer gain for
France, yet achieved with German consent. Luxembourg
had long been called—with some exaggeration—'the
Gibraltar of the north'. Now this Gibraltar disappeared
and an ineffective guarantee took its place. Louis XIV
would have regarded this as a great triumph. The road
to invasion of Germany was more open than before to
the French if they cared to take it. The French generals
recognized this and, freed from the anxiety of a Prussian
force in Luxembourg, they planned more lightheartedly
the offensive strategy which, in fact, led them to disaster
in 1870. But French opinion wanted a symbolical triumph,
not a real one. Napoleon III was expected to show that
nothing could happen in Europe without gain for France.
Yet, one may ask, why should France acquire territory
merely because northern Germany had been united?
Unfortunately men do not reason in this way; and the
settlement of the Luxembourg question, though eminently
sensible, ruined good relations between France and Germany. Henceforth the French believed that they had been
tricked by Bismarck, and regarded every step forward
that he took as a step against them.

No one appreciated this at the time. Bismarck himself

feared the effect of the Luxembourg settlement on German, not on French opinion. His fears were not without foundation. One member of the North German parliament indeed protested against the compromise on grounds of national pride and appealed to the German people. This patriot was the Social Democrat, Bebel. War and an aggressive foreign policy were still the prerogative of the Left; love of peace still the most telling accusation that could be made against a man of the Right, and Bismarck showed his usual courage in facing the charge. His dealings with German liberalism were the exact counterpart to the implicit bargain which he had made with King William in 1862. Then he had defended the rights of the crown and had exacted the price in a foreign policy directed against Austria. Now he offered the Germans liberal institutions and imposed a pacific foreign policy in return. Many liberals would have liked to challenge France and to show that Germany had taken her place as *la grande nation*. Bismarck dreaded war with France, not from fear of defeat, but because of the consequences which victory would bring. He said during the Luxembourg crisis: 'I shall avoid this war as long as I can; for I know, that once started, it will never cease.' And later, to his friend Keyserling: 'Even if Prussia wins, where will it lead to? Even if we took Alsace, we should have to defend it, and in the end the French would find allies again, and then things could go badly!' The war against Austria had been fought for a practical purpose and with concrete aims; once these aims were achieved, peace could be made. War with France would be a test of strength without solid prizes; and the test would have to be repeated whenever the defeated party felt strong enough to challenge the verdict.

Bismarck knew that he could keep German feeling under restraint. He believed rightly that Napoleon III too was a man of peace; where he erred was in supposing that Napoleon controlled the French as firmly as he himself mastered the Germans. The second empire in France was slithering into decay; and Napoleon was constantly urged

to restore imperial prestige, if not for his own sake, then
for that of his son. Napoleon hated this line of policy.
He was a political conspirator, not a fighting man, by
nature and by experience. He disliked war and feared it;
he knew the gross defects of the French army; and he was
proud to have helped both Germany and Italy towards
national unification. Why should he regard the triumph
of his ideas as a blow against French prestige? When
Bismarck visited Paris in the summer of 1867, Napoleon
showed him all the old friendship of Biarritz. There
seemed no cloud between them. Only later did French
writers hit on the idea that Bismarck and Moltke had
come to Paris, not to see the great Exhibition, but to find
the best sites from which Paris could be bombarded. It
was not in regard to Prussia that the Paris exhibition
influenced international affairs. Alexander II and Gorchakov also came to Paris; and they hoped to revive the
entente with France which had been destroyed by the
quarrel over Poland in 1863. If they had succeeded, the
dynamic alliance of Bismarck's early years would have
been again in existence; and he might well have revived
the revolutionary plans which he had when he first took
office. The Habsburg empire might have been partitioned;
a greater Germany might have been created. Bismarck
was to win much credit from later observers for having
barred the way against greater Germany; but perhaps
the real credit should go to Alexander II and Napoleon III
for failing to hit it off during the exhibition.[1]

The Franco-Russian alliance seemed out of sight for
good. Some of Napoleon's advisers pushed him into a
futile search for some alternative combination. In August
1867 he and Francis Joseph met at Salzburg to demon-
strate an ineffective Franco-Austrian *entente*. Later they
attempted to negotiate a formal alliance, and in April

---

[1] The Paris exhibition had another, more trivial, influence on the future.
The Prussian crown prince was offended that his father, a mere king, took
second place behind the emperor of Russia; hence he became an enthusiastic
advocate of a revived German empire.

1869 Italy was drawn in as well. This grandiose Triple Alliance ended in empty talk. The new Austria-Hungary was concerned only to resist Russia in the Near East. Even Beust, Bismarck's old rival, admitted that the alliance could act in Germany only when it had showed its value in the eastern question. The Italians wanted to get the French out of Rome and knew that Prussian strength was their best guarantee against both Austria-Hungary and France. The French ministers wanted to push the two others against Prussia without going to war themselves; and Napoleon merely wanted to keep his name in the news. No negotiation was ever more barren or hopeless. Though Bismarck knew all about it, he never showed any anxiety. He called the talk of a Franco-Austrian alliance 'conjectural rubbish', and said of the Triple Alliance in 1869: 'I don't believe a word of it.' Some of his apologists have argued that the war of 1870 was launched by Bismarck to forestall a threatening alliance against Prussia. There is no contemporary evidence for this, and much against it. Bismarck did not fear this triple alliance; he did not favour preventive wars; besides he did not design the war of 1870—it took him by surprise and was most unwelcome to him. In later life he developed 'a nightmare of coalitions'. At this time he said: 'The day of permanent alliances is over. Alliances nowadays are made only for practical objects': and no power seemed to have a practical object for opposing Prussia.

Everything is relative in this world. Though Bismarck was later to display greater diplomatic activity than any other statesman in Europe, he was not a 'system-maker' in the sense that Metternich had been. Despite his conservatism, he was a man of the *laissez-faire* age, and was pushed into creative action against his will. Like all his contemporaries, he tended to assume that things would run themselves pretty well, once a few adjustments had been made. The political reformers, for example, in England as in Germany, always supposed that the spate of legislation would sooner or later come to an end when 'the liberal state' had been made; they never foresaw legislation as a continuous, endless process. Even the most radical Socialists, Marx and Engels themselves, imagined that politics would cease for ever once socialism had been created. Bismarck looked on foreign policy in much the same way. The international system had been unbalanced so long as Austria overshadowed Prussia in central Europe. Now this had been put right, and there was no more for Prussia to do. A natural order had been created, and it would maintain itself by its own weight. This was the liberal philosophy; and Bismarck shared it in his brief liberal period.

There were still, of course, practical problems in Europe, but Prussia was not concerned in them. The Polish question had been removed from the international stage after the failure of the revolt in 1863. The French claims for compensation from Prussia ceased with the Luxembourg crisis in 1867 and were never, in fact, renewed. Some French politicians planned to lay hands on Belgium. Bismarck had no objection to this, and it is silly to imagine that he encouraged these schemes in order to estrange England and France. Belgium was still an artificial state, not forty years old. If France had taken the French-speaking or Walloon districts of Belgium, Bismarck might have claimed the Flemish districts for Germany. Such a national division would have been in strict accord with his principles, as indeed with those of more liberal thinkers. It would have been a western equivalent to the partitions of Poland, on which the greatness of Prussia was based; and it might have cemented friendship between Prussia and France for a hundred years, just as the partitions of Poland cemented friendship between Prussia and Russia. It was not Bismarck's concern to overcome British objections—nor, however, to encourage them.

Apart from this, the only troublesome question in western Europe was Rome, still occupied by French troops, but claimed by Italy. Here again Bismarck's only aim was to keep out of the way. He would not join France in guaranteeing papal sovereignty; still less would he help the Italians to conquer Rome. The Eastern Question gave him more anxiety, and he drew there a faint preliminary sketch for his more elaborate diplomacy later on. During the Crimean war he had wanted to take advantage of Austria's difficulties; but Prussia could only lose by a new eastern conflict now that she was satisfied in Germany. His object was to keep Russia and Austria-Hungary at peace so far as he had a foreign policy at all; and the task was becoming more difficult. Russia was resuming her interest in the Near East after her defeat in the Crimean war; and the Austrians were turning to the Balkans now that they had been excluded both politically and economically from Germany. As early as 1868 Bismarck laid down that Prussia could not allow either empire to be again defeated; and he did something to ward off incipient dangers. For instance in 1868, when Rumanian irredentism disturbed Austria-Hungary, he prevailed on the Hohenzollern ruler of Rumania to silence the campaign. Again in 1869, when a revolt in Crete threatened to provoke war between Greece and Turkey and then to drag in the Great Powers, Bismarck acted for the first time as 'honest broker' and arranged an acceptable compromise in an international conference at Paris. These were isolated episodes, dealing with occasional alarms. For most of the time between 1867 and 1870, Bismarck—the greatest master of diplomacy in modern history—had no foreign policy except to be left alone.

Bismarck held the reins of power more loosely in his hands after the Luxembourg crisis and the making of the federal constitution. Indeed, he often talked of retiring from political life altogether. Between 1862 and 1866 he had lived only for public affairs, except for his trips to Biarritz with Kathi Orlov. Now he began to look after himself, though he never saw Kathi again. Politics were for him a duty, not a pleasure, at any rate consciously; and he was always assuming that their claims on him would one day come to an end. He never acquired a home of his own in Berlin. In 1862 he moved into the house of the Prussian foreign minister in the Wilhelm-strasse, where Barbarina—the platonic mistress of Frederick the Great—had once lived; and he stayed in these in-convenient old quarters for twenty-eight years, always giving visitors the impression that he was 'camping' there. His study gave directly off the entrance-hall. It was littered with books and bric-à-brac; a railway time-table, a Russian grammar, and costly presents from the tsar heaped up chaotically on tables and chairs. Paintings of crowned heads were piled against the walls—some of them remaining unhung for ten or twenty years. Upstairs some of the carpets were never laid. There were hardly any shelves for books and no separate library. The kitchen was inadequate for a public man; and the food had to be sent in from a restaurant on the one occasion in the year when Bismarck entertained the diplomatic corps to dinner. Only the cellars were properly stocked. When Bismarck left in 1890, 13,000 bottles of wine had to be cleared out in a couple of days. This is not surprising in view of his statement that he intended to consume 5,000 bottles of champagne in the course of his life—and this only as light refreshment after the table wines and brandy, to say nothing of beer. Bismarck built on a few office-rooms for his secretaries in the garden. Otherwise he made no attempt to provide the German chancellor with a suitable residence and met all expostulations with the remark: 'What does not belong to me does not interest me.'

In 1867, however, he got something to interest him. The grateful Prussian parliament voted him 400,000 thalers (say, £40,000) on his return from the Austrian war; and with them he bought the Junker estate of Varzin in Pomerania. This fulfilled all his youthful dreams. Though even Johanna found the house 'unbearably ugly', Bismarck was delighted. As he said: 'Whoever is interested in furnishing is not interested in food; the essential thing is to eat well.' He buried himself in Varzin for months at a time—five hours by slow train from Berlin, and then forty miles on bad roads. There were no visitors, and virtually no social life with the neighbouring gentry. The estate was covered with trees, indeed overburdened with them. It would have been sounder to clear the ground and cultivate it. But Bismarck said: 'If I wanted to see maize growing, I need not have left Schönhausen'; and he guarded every decaying tree as though his own life depended on it. There was something pathetic and yet absurd in this man of only fifty already identifying himself with an old weather-beaten oak. The sophisticated intellectual from Berlin was building up a legend even for his own benefit.

Not that Bismarck failed to turn Varzin into a money-making concern. He became an industrialist like many another Junker; he manufactured spirits for the market and ran a paper-factory, exploiting his political position to get favourable contracts from the Prussian and even from the Russian state. It was also characteristic that he got from William I a secret decree, exempting the entail of the property from stamp-duty. More than one Prussian official injured his career by claiming from Varzin the local rates for building schools or making roads. The old aristocratic politicians from the Duke of Newcastle to Metternich ruined themselves in the service of the state. Bismarck always saw to it that his accounts balanced, despite his ceaseless complaints of poverty. He lived at Varzin a patriarchal life, patronizing his peasants and even occasionally beating them. Yet the reality for which he lived was the daily arrival of the courier from Berlin. Nothing could be done without Bismarck. Internal affairs did not interest him, and he often delayed an answer for months at a time. But he poured out pencilled comments on foreign policy; and the North German confederation somehow kept going, though ambassadors complained that they never saw the man on whom policy depended.

Bismarck was already in search for new decisions. In 1866 he had grasped at what was within reach—the unification of Germany north of the Main. Now he was intoxicated with his success in wielding the weapons of liberalism; and he who had once sneered at the idea of uniting Germany by public opinion and moral appeal planned just this in regard to south Germany. The war of 1866 had dissolved the treaties of the Customs Union; and when Bismarck renewed them he introduced a customs-parliament, which was to be made by adding representatives of the southern German states to the existing federal parliament. The south Germans would be elected by universal suffrage, 'free from bureaucratic control'. In this way an all-German parliament would come into existence almost unperceived. The manœuvre was not a success. The Roman Catholic peasants of south Germany used their new franchise to bring a clericalist party, the Centre, into existence. Bavaria returned 26 clericals out of 48 members; all Germany south of the Main returned 50 particularists against 35 supporters of unification; and when the customs-parliament met in April 1868 the south Germans took care that it never strayed from the narrow path of tariffs. Bismarck preached patience: 'An arbitrary interference in history brings only the gathering of unripe fruit; and it is obvious to me that German unity is not a ripe fruit at this moment.' He took the members of the customs-parliament on a trip to Kiel, to see German warships actually afloat, and to Hamburg, where they saw the beginnings of Germany's world trade. There was a strange symbolism in this echo of the Frankfurt parliament of 1848 with its abortive plans for a German navy; but it made little appeal to the suspicious clericals from the south.

Thereafter Bismarck's hopes for German unity ran backwards. Later sessions of the customs-parliament proved increasingly obstructive. The national enthusiasm of 1866 and 1867 began to die away. The southern states complained more and more against the burdens which their military treaties with Prussia imposed upon them. The Bavarians in particular would have liked to go over to a militia on the Swiss model—a system which it would have been impossible to amalgamate with the Prussian army in time of war; and early in 1870 the Bavarian prime minister Hohenlohe, who favoured co-operation with the North German confederation, was overthrown by a particularist and clerical majority. Bismarck continued patient: 'We can put on our watches, but time doesn't go any faster for it.' On the other hand, he saw approaching for the first time the problem that was later to shape his policy again and again. Parliamentary authorization for the federal army would run out in 1871. Its renewal would be more difficult now that the excitement of the Austrian war lay far away. Bismarck needed to give Germany a new 'dose' of national enthusiasm. He thought early in 1870 of proclaiming the King of Prussia as German emperor; but the plan came to nothing. He seemed at a loss for a policy when he retired to Varzin in the spring of 1870 with an attack of jaundice. No one could have supposed that another great surge of German unification was just round the corner.

Did he foresee it himself? Of all questions in Bismarck's career this is the most difficult to answer. He was always emphatic that he could not make events. He said once: 'Politics are not a science based on logic; they are the capacity of always choosing at each instant, in constantly changing situations, the least harmful, the most useful.' And again, in more devout terms: 'A statesman cannot create anything himself. He must wait and listen until he hears the steps of God sounding through events; then leap up and grasp the hem of his garment.' When someone praised his direction of events between 1862 and 1871, he pointed to many mistakes he had made and said: 'I wanted it like this, and everything happened quite differently. I'm content when I see where the Lord wishes to go and can stumble after Him.' Was this false modesty? Did he in fact manœuvre the Lord's will just as he manœuvred William I? Perhaps he did, though not so much as his enemies and later historians have alleged.

Certainly there is not a scrap of evidence that he worked

deliberately for a war with France, still less that he timed
it precisely for the summer of 1870. He was always too
impatient and highly-strung to let a crisis mature behind
his back; and if he had really anticipated an explosion
in July 1870, he would have remained in Berlin, controlling
events. In fact he was at Varzin from April until 12 July,
except for a few days at the end of May when he appeared
in parliament and two days early in June when he and the
king met Tsar Alexander II at Ems. At this meeting there
was no hint of the coming war—no request for Russian
support on the one side, no pledge of Russian support or
even of neutrality on the other. Indeed, France was not
mentioned—only Rumania and the affairs of south Germany. It is likely indeed that Bismarck planned some
national stroke in south Germany quite soon to smooth
the way for the military discussions in the federal parliament; and it is probable, too, that he anticipated protests
from both France and Austria. But they would not
necessarily lead to war. German-Austrian and Magyar
opinion would oppose a war against Prussia; and together
they dominated Habsburg councils. Napoleon III was
becoming increasingly pacific; and 'the liberal empire'
which he established early in 1870 was a further guarantee
of peace.

Bismarck on his side had shown no sign of increasing
hostility towards France. On the contrary, he made repeated gestures of friendship towards Napoleon. He
pressed hard for a plebiscite in north Sleswig where the
Danes were in a majority. This would please Napoleon's
nationalist principles; and Bismarck favoured it also.
He said: 'It is harmful that a hostile nationality should
live in the same community with the Germans.' Opposition
came from King William, who could not bring himself
to renounce territory once he had conquered it. Bismarck
even tried to get round the king's resistance by asking
the Danes to invoke the assistance of the tsar—perhaps
William would listen to him. The manœuvre was put into
operation. Alexander II wrote to his uncle, reminding him

of his promise for a plebiscite. William was furious, and Bismarck had hard work preventing an angry answer. The episode, though trivial, is a reminder that Bismarck had real difficulties with the king, which he could not always overcome; and he was not always responsible for German policy. At least the goodwill to improve relations with France was clear, though unsuccessful.

In May, 1870, there was a danger-signal from the French side. Napoleon quarrelled with his pacific foreign minister, Daru; and Gramont, the new man, was an extreme clerical who believed fervently in the Austrian alliance. He intended to humble Prussia at the first opportunity. Yet neither Gramont nor Bismarck foresaw the crisis that blew up in July 1870, when it suddenly became known that Prince Leopold of Hohenzollern was about to be elected King of Spain. This affair had a long and obscure history which has given rise to even more than the usual dogmatism always associated with 'war-origins'. In 1868 the dissolute Queen Isabella had been turned off the throne of Spain; and ever since the vacant throne had been hawked around Europe. The French were busy in Madrid, intriguing for one candidate after another, as though Spain was their private property; and early in 1869 Bismarck urged Prince Leopold to become a candidate also. Leopold was a Roman Catholic, but not a clerical; he was married to a daughter of the former King of Portugal and also closely related to the Bonapartist house of Murat; and his younger brother had become Prince of Rumania—on French nomination. It is impossible to decide with any confidence why Bismarck involved Germany in Spanish affairs; usually he tried to keep out of such remote questions. Perhaps he wanted the Hohenzollerns to think of themselves as rulers of a Great Power, and no longer obscure princes in north Germany. He may have had an eye on Spanish trade. There were two more practical motives. Firstly, Bismarck was not a Lutheran for nothing. He regarded Roman Catholicism as his enemy, particularly in the obscurantist form it was taking under the direction of Pius IX. The clericals were already Bismarck's principal opponents in Germany, and the *Kulturkampf* against them was just round the corner. It would be a great stroke against clericalism, as well as against radical republicanism, if Spain acquired a liberal Catholic king; and one highly pleasing to Protestant German liberals.

There was also a motive in foreign policy. Leopold's candidature was a precaution against the projected Franco-Austrian alliance. Bismarck launched it in April 1869, when the negotiations between Paris and Vienna were at their height, and renewed it in May 1870, when Gramont, the advocate of this alliance, became French foreign minister. The alliance, if it had ever come to anything, would not have operated in the first place against Prussia; it would have operated against Russia in the Near East. But Russia would then have turned to Prussia for support, and this would have revived all the embarrassments of the Crimean war. Spain under a German prince might deter France from an active Eastern policy—at any rate it was worth trying. Bismarck had no immediate plans so far as southern Germany was concerned; but here, too, Leopold would act as a brake on France. She would, he claimed, have to keep two army-corps on the Spanish frontier, and would therefore be unable to act on the Rhine. In short, the Hohenzollern candidature, far from being designed to provoke a war with France which would complete the unification of Germany, was intended rather to make German unification possible without a war.

Bismarck did not make much headway with Prince Leopold for some time. The Spanish leaders were eager—nothing could suit them better than a Catholic prince who was not a clerical. Leopold was unwilling; he preferred a quiet life. King William, too, was reluctant to consent—not from fear of France, but from dislike of his family's being involved in the turbulent politics of Spain. In May 1870 both at last gave way, William 'with a heavy, a very heavy heart'. There followed a fantastic accident which changed the course of world-history. On 19 June Salazar, the Spanish representative in Berlin, telegraphed to Madrid that he would be back within a week with Leopold's consent in his pocket. The Spanish cortes was in session, and Leopold could be elected King before anyone knew what was happening. A cipher clerk at the Prussian legation in Madrid blundered; he passed on the message that Salazar would return in the middle of July. Prim, the Spanish dictator, dared not keep the Cortes hanging about; on 23 June he prorogued it until the autumn. When Salazar returned on 26 June he found Madrid deserted. Prim agreed to recall the Cortes, but he had to reveal why it was being summoned. On 2 July the news that Leopold was to be elected King of Spain reached Paris. This was Gramont's opportunity. He wanted to restore the prestige of the Napoleonic empire and to show that he was a more forceful foreign minister than his predecessors. Had he wished merely to bar Leopold from the Spanish throne, he should have protested in Madrid, and the Spaniards would have given way, as they did a fortnight later. But Gramont wanted to humiliate Prussia and to restore French primacy in Europe. He said on 6 July: 'We have unanimously agreed to march. We have carried the Chamber with us, we shall carry the nation also.'

Gramont had chosen his ground well. The Austrian ambassador in Paris said to him: 'You have seized the chance of either scoring a diplomatic success or of fighting a war on a subject where no German national feeling can oppose you.' And Gramont replied: 'You put it exactly.' The states of southern Germany resolved one after another not to be involved in the dynastic affairs of the house of Hohenzollern. But the Hohenzollern dynasty had no wish to be involved itself. Leopold was eager to give way, and King William encouraged him. On 12 July Leopold announced his withdrawal or, to be precise, his father announced it for him. The French success was complete. Bismarck had recognized the dangerous ground he was on from the first moment that Leopold's candidature had become known. Had he intended to provoke a war with

France, he would have hurried to join the king at Ems,
just as he never quitted William's side during the crisis
which preceded the war with Austria. Instead he remained
buried at Varzin, even failing to answer the king's agonized
requests for advice until too late. He was indignant when
William listened to the French complaints; but he would
have been equally angry if William had rejected them.
His overriding consideration was not some high issue of
foreign policy: it was to shift on to William the responis-
bility for any failure and yet to grasp for himself the credit
for any success.

On 12 July Bismarck at last left Varzin. When he reached
Berlin, he learnt of Leopold's withdrawal and of William's
hope that the crisis was now over. Bismarck's first thought
was to resign. He soon improved on this, and proposed to
demand the summoning of the North German parliament,
under threat of resignation if William refused. It was a
beautiful combination. Bismarck would appear as the
defender of German honour, either by resigning in protest
or by delivering a flaming, though tardy defiance to France
from the tribune of parliament: William would be dis-
credited as the blundering spokesman of an outworn
dynasticism. This policy showed little loyalty to the house
of Hohenzollern, but Bismarck was often ready to risk the
king's position when his own power or popularity were at
stake. This time it turned out to be unnecessary. While
Bismarck sat in Berlin intriguing against the king,
Napoleon III and Gramont fired a new shot from Paris.
They made further, more extreme demands—demands
which would either display the humiliation of Prussia or
force war upon her. William must endorse Leopold's withdrawal; he must apologize for the candidature and promise
that it should never be renewed. If not, war would follow.
These demands were presented to William I at Ems on
13 July. He still did not understand what was at stake.
Though he rejected the new French demands, he repeated
the announcement of Leopold's withdrawal and supposed
that he had made a fine stroke for peace.

When William's report of these doings reached Berlin, Bismarck saw his chance at last. He cut out William's conciliatory phrases and emphasized the real issue. The French had made certain demands under threat of war; and William had refused them. This was no forgery; it was a clear statement of the facts. There is curious evidence of this, which is often overlooked. After Bismarck had issued his edited version of 'the Ems telegram', a second message from William reached Berlin. He had refused to see the French representative and had said: 'If what you have to say concerns the Spanish candidature, I have nothing to add.' Bismarck did not forge the king's message; he anticipated it. But, just as he had intended to blame William for any failure, now he would not allow him credit for any success. The edited 'Ems telegram' was to be presented henceforth as the cause of the war. What is more, Bismarck was now eager to snatch the initiative from the French. This is the key to all his subsequent explanations. He had neither planned the war nor even foreseen it. But he claimed it as his own once it became inevitable. He wished to present himself as the creator of Germany, not as a man who had been mastered by events. Moreover, attention had to be diverted from his carelessness in giving France an opportunity to humiliate Prussia and from his discreditable manœuvres to shift the responsibility for this on to the king. Therefore, against all his previous statements,[1] the war with France had to appear necessary and inevitable, long-planned by the master-statesman. Bucher, his closest associate, was soon calling Leopold's candidature 'a trap for France'; and Bismarck himself claimed to have provoked the war by the Ems telegram. Probably he came to believe his own story and spoke in all

---

[1] Bismarck betrayed his inner thoughts, when shortly after the outbreak of war he justified it by the example of Cavour who launched a European war to achieve the unification of Italy. But this is exactly what Cavour did not do. The Italian war against Austria in 1859 was the equivalent of Bismarck's war against her in 1866. In 1860 Cavour won southern Italy without an international war ; and no doubt Bismarck had planned to do the same with southern Germany.

sincerity on 30 July 1892, when he declared: 'We could
not have set up the German *Reich* in the middle of Europe
without having defeated France. . . . The war with France
was a necessary conclusion.' Yet Germany had no reason
for a war against France; and its gains proved a perpetual
embarrassment. France had more reason for attempting
to prevent German unification; and if the war had gone well
for France, every French statesman would have been eager
to take the credit for it. In truth, the French blundered
into a war which was not unwelcome to them; and Bismarck, though taken by surprise, turned their blunder to
his advantage. His contemporary verdict was far from his
later claims to foresighted policy. On 15 July, when war
was already certain, he underlined in his private book of
devotion a sentence from Luther: 'In this affair no sword
can advise or help, God alone must create here, without
human thought and action.'

VI

THE GERMAN EMPIRE IN THE DAYS OF LIBERALISM

THE war against France certainly achieved the unification of Germany, whether it was designed to do so or not. It was a very different affair from the war of 1866. That had been a Cabinet war, brought on by secret diplomacy and with no popular enthusiasm on either side—least of all in Prussia. The king had decided on war, however reluctantly; and the people of Prussia had to obey his orders. In 1870 William I was almost the last man to realize that war was about to break out. He still thought that he had handled things peacefully at Ems. Only when he read Bismarck's version of the Ems telegram, did he understand what had really happened; and soon he was complaining of the French insults which he had not noticed at the time. The feeling against France was irresistible throughout Germany. Even Bismarck's most radical opponents supported the war at any rate until the fall of Napoleon. The rulers of south Germany were driven to make common cause with Prussia much against their will. The Bavarian chamber voted for war against the advice of the government; and the King of Württemberg said farewell to the French envoy with tears in his eyes, still asserting his friendship with Napoleon III.

Bismarck did not, perhaps, appreciate fully the strength of feeling in southern Germany. At any rate, desire to whip up this feeling still further drove him to a fateful step. He announced that Germany would claim Strasbourg and Metz as security against a new French invasion. Strasbourg, of course, had been a radical demand in 1848; and the Romantic conservatives who dreamt of restoring the glories of the Holy Roman Empire also endorsed it.

The Prussian generals, too, were delighted that this time they would not win a war without taking territory from their defeated opponent. Bismarck did not usually sympathize with any of these emotions. His principle of sorting people out into their linguistic 'tribes' perhaps justified the claim to German-speaking Alsace; but Metz lay far in French-speaking territory, and even Alsace, with its Roman Catholic population, was unwelcome to him. Besides, it is a fundamental condition of good diplomacy not to lay down rigid conditions in advance; and the claim to Strasbourg and Metz caused Bismarck endless difficulties when he came to negotiate with the French. He was trapped by his own impetuosity, the prisoner of German public opinion, as he had been over Luxembourg in 1867. Later on he often lamented the blunder that he had made in taking Metz; but the blunder was of his own designing.

The difficulties that he had thus created soon became clear. The king, the generals, and public opinion might want to crush France for ever. Bismarck, as usual, wanted a quick victory and then a peace of reconciliation. The quick victory was achieved; the peace of reconciliation was beyond his reach. The French armies, which had planned to invade southern Germany, were beaten in the battles of the frontiers during August. On 2 September, Napoleon III and the bulk of the French army were surrounded and driven to capitulate at Sedan. Bismarck received the fallen Emperor in a peasant's cottage; it was a far cry from their last meeting at the Tuileries in 1867. The German press attacked Bismarck's courtesy to Napoleon. He answered German opinion in much the same terms as he had used to William I in 1866. 'The politician has to leave the punishment of princes and peoples for their offences against the moral law to Divine providence'; and again, with more worldly wisdom: 'The politician has not to revenge what has happened but to ensure that it does not happen again.' But Bismarck's politeness to Napoleon had no practical result. Napoleon, as a prisoner, refused to speak for France. On 4 September a provisional government was set up in Paris; and Jules Favre, its foreign minister, at once announced: 'We will not surrender an inch of our territory or a stone of our fortresses.' A meeting between Favre and Bismarck proved barren. Bismarck had to demand Strasbourg and Metz, whether he would or no; and Favre could not surrender them. Henceforth France was fighting for her national integrity, not for imperial prestige or for influence across the Rhine; and the Germans were fighting a war of aggression and conquest. The war took on a new character—French partisans on the one side, ruthless oppression (by the standards of the time) on the other. Gambetta tried to inspire French opinion and to create fresh armies; Bismarck sought to make the French war-weary, and became war-weary himself.

When Bismarck joined the king at military headquarters, he imagined that he would be back at Berlin within a month. As it was, though the German armies swept through northern France, they were held all winter at the siege of Paris; and Bismarck, too, had to settle down at Versailles, which he left only on 6 March 1871. It was a strange system by which the sole responsible minister of a great state remained for six months in a foreign town; but Bismarck knew that he was powerful only so long as he was in personal contact with the king, though even then he was not always successful. At Versailles he had three tasks—to influence the conduct of the war; to prevent European intervention between France and Germany; and to create the German *Reich*. Of the three, the first was probably the most difficult, certainly the most exasperating for him. The Prussian generals were determined not to repeat their mistake of 1866, when Bismarck had snatched the fruits of victory from them almost before the fighting had started. This time they would allow no civilian, not even Bismarck, to interfere with their war. Though Bismarck was now a major-general,[1] he was excluded from the

---

[1] He was made a full general on 18 January, 1871, the day when William I became German Emperor.

councils of war; and he was reduced to learning the progress of the campaign from the Berlin newspapers. He
replied by speaking contemptuously of 'the demi-gods' of
the general staff and declared: 'None of them except the
good old Moltke could stand up to critical scrutiny.' It
was indeed fantastic that he should be kept ignorant of
military developments; but, with perhaps less justification,
he also wished to dictate them. Ever fearful of European
intervention, he was impatient to force a French surrender
and demanded that Paris be bombarded instead of being
reduced by hunger. There may have been sound military
reasons against this course. But Bismarck, as always,
detected a 'conspiracy' against himself—perhaps by the
crown prince, perhaps by his English wife, perhaps by
Queen Augusta, in any case by someone. The demi-gods,
he insisted, regarded Paris as the centre of modern civilization instead of as the modern Sodom. In the end he got his
way and Paris was ineffectually bombarded, though it
was hunger that brought surrender. The estrangement
between Bismarck and the generals was never overcome;
and nothing could be more false than to suppose that he
favoured military rule in Germany. The only general he
wished to see in power was General Count Bismarck.

The danger of European intervention was never serious.
Neither Russia nor Great Britain regretted the defeat of
France. Russia hoped for a freer hand in the Near East;
Great Britain was relieved of her anxieties in regard to
Belgium. Italy was content to have occupied Rome on
20 September and was already looking to Germany as her
new patron. Only Austria-Hungary might have entered
the war against Prussia and then only if France had won
the first battles. She was saved from disaster by her usual
policy of delay. By October Francis Joseph was saying to
the Prussian ambassador: 'You cannot expect me to like
what has happened. But I shall agree to anything; I shall
do nothing.' The myth grew up later that Austria-Hungary
had been kept out of the war by a threat of Russian intervention against her; and the Russians made great play

with this myth during the great Eastern crisis of 1876–78. There was no truth in it. The Russians gave no promises to Prussia, made no threats to Austria-Hungary; more important, they made no military preparations. The Austrians kept out of the war solely from a well-founded reluctance not to tie themselves to a country that was already defeated. When Thiers, the veteran French statesman, toured Europe in an effort to provoke some intervention or at any rate mediation, he received only empty words. The British were busy building a 'league of neutrals', all pledged to stand aside. Beust said sadly to Thiers: 'I do not see Europe any more'; and the Russians told him that they would welcome an alliance with France —when the war was over. France had to do what she could on her own.

Bismarck had grown up when the Concert of Europe was a reality, and it was difficult for him to appreciate that it no longer existed. He was driven desperate by the fear of European intervention, while the demi-gods of the general staff fumbled on with the siege of Paris. He had a further alarm at the end of October when the Russians denounced the clauses of the treaty of Paris (1856), neutralizing the Black Sea. For, though Bismarck cared nothing about the Black Sea one way or the other, the clauses concerning it could only be undone by an international conference; and at this meeting the French might at last discover the Europe which had hitherto evaded them. Once more Bismarck acted as honest broker, as he had done over Crete in 1869, though this time to keep the other Powers out of his own war rather than at peace with each other. He persuaded the Russians to accept a conference on the understanding that it would free them in the Black Sea; and he persuaded the British to annul the clauses of the treaty of Paris on condition this was done by an international conference. In return both Powers gratefully accepted Bismarck's condition that the conference should limit itself strictly to the Black Sea and that the Franco-German war should not be mentioned.

Here again a myth grew up that Bismarck gave the Russians what they wanted in the Black Sea in exchange for their support against Austria-Hungary. In reality, Bismarck was angry with the Russians for raising the question at this time; and far from supporting them, he balanced between Great Britain and Russia, as he was to continue to do for the rest of his life. The Russians accused him of being pro-British, the British of being pro-Russian. He was neither. He considered only the interests of his own country—always the worst offence that a statesman can commit in the eyes of foreigners.

In much the same way, he was indifferent to the form of government in France. What he wanted was to make peace as soon as possible—of course, on his own terms. If the provisional government in Paris had agreed to surrender Strasbourg and Metz, he would have recognized it without a qualm. When it tried to evoke a patriotic revival, he developed constitutional scruples and announced that the Empire was still the legitimate government of France. But again all that mattered to him was a quick peace. He negotiated with the Empress Eugenie, who was in exile in London, and with Bazaine who held out for a time in Metz; Napoleon III refused to exercise any political activity while remaining a prisoner. None of the Bonapartist spokesmen would agree to the surrender of territory; and Bismarck soon dropped them, despite his suggestion that an Empire, restored by German arms, would be the most pacific form of French government in the future. Certainly he talked of the social dangers which would follow a long war; but the ghost was evoked to frighten others, not himself. For the time being he failed to shake French resolution, either among the Bonapartists or in the provisional government; and he resigned himself to the fact that no peace was possible until Paris had fallen.

During this long delay Bismarck feared that German resolution would break down sooner than the French. The unanimous enthusiasm of the first victories did not survive Sedan. Some radicals and Social Democrats took the line of high principle that Germany was now fighting a war of aggression; and anti-war agitators were imprisoned even in East Prussia. The princes and politicians of south Germany were more concerned to preserve their independence. On 23 September Lewis II of Bavaria, though still effervescing with German enthusiasm, said: 'But we are not going to enter the North German confederation, eh?' Even Bismarck had not intended any such thing when the war broke out. The military treaties had provided adequate unity on the battlefield; and he still had a deep Protestant distrust against organic unity with the Roman Catholics of south Germany. He wrote on 23 July, just after the outbreak of war: 'We shall let the measure of our mutual co-operation depend entirely on the free decision of our south German allies.' This was enough for the first victories; it would not last—or so he feared—for a long war. He pushed the south German states into the Reich not at all with a vision of a distant future, but solely to keep them in the war. They could make a separate peace so long as they remained independent states; they would have to hold on with north Germany once the empire was made. This anxiety explains the haste with which he drove the negotiations for unity forward. It explains the concessions which he made particularly to Bavaria.

Liberal critics later discovered in these concessions a deep and sinister design. Bismarck, it was said, kept the south German princes in existence in order to prevent Germany from becoming a democratic state. In fact, Bismarck thought always of the needs of the present, not of a speculative future; and the present need was to keep the south German states in the war. He welcomed the campaign of national propaganda which Lasker and other liberals conducted in south Germany; but he doubted whether popular feeling was enough to overcome the reluctance of the princes. He could, no doubt, have engineered disturbances and even revolts; but he could not afford a civil war in Germany with the German armies pinned down in front of Paris. Far from using the war in

5

order to promote unification, he sought unification in
order to continue the war. Besides, he always preferred
conciliation to force. When the crown prince said in his
National Liberal way: 'We have got them in our power!'
Bismarck replied: 'Your Royal Highness, a prince can
perhaps act in that way, a gentleman like me cannot.'

There was, too, a deeper calculation behind this high
sentiment. The force of public opinion might sweep away
the south German princes. It would not work with
William I, who was most reluctant to submerge the title
of King of Prussia in that of German Emperor. He was
even less ready to 'pick up a crown from the gutter' than
Frederick William IV had been in 1849. He would have
refused the imperial crown if it had been offered to him
by a German parliament; he accepted it grudgingly from
the princes. Bismarck needed these princes in order to
force William I on the path which it seemed necessary to
follow. Of course, he threatened that German unity would
be made against the princes if they held back; but he also
held out the prospect that they could be its makers. With
his usual adaptability, he first played national enthusiasm
against the princes and then played the King of Bavaria
against William I. The negotiations were more difficult
than those which preceded the North German federation in
1867. Then all the states had been trivial except Saxony;
and she had already agreed to federation as the penalty
for defeat in the war of 1866. Now, though only three
states had to be won over—Bavaria, Baden, Württemberg
—they had some real existence, two of them (Bavaria
and Württemberg) actually kingdoms.[1] The Grand Duke of
Baden was eager for unification, had indeed to be restrained
so as not to get out of step with the two others. The King
of Bavaria was obstinate for independence; the King of
Württemberg scarcely less so. Bismarck negotiated with

[1] Strictly there were three and a half states to be won. Hesse-Darmstadt
was a member of the North German federation for its territory north, and
independent for that south, of the Main. But clearly no new decision of
principle was needed here.

them separately, scaring each in turn with the story that the other two had given way.

He made some real concessions. Bavaria retained lighter duties on beer, her national industry; she issued her own postage-stamps, kept her own railways and even, in peace-time, her own army. A committee of the Imperial Council under Bavarian chairmanship was to consider German foreign policy. There would be full autonomy in domestic affairs. But the great cause was won. Germany became a united nation for foreign policy and for war. German power existed whatever the separate states might still claim. The south German princes and politicians did not foresee that the federal element in the Reich would be weakened with the passing of the years or that national sentiment would turn the states into empty symbols. Berlin would over-shadow Munich, Stuttgart, and Dresden. But Bismarck did not cheat them over this. He did not foresee it himself, and regretted it when it happened.

The treaties with the south German states were con-cluded in November. The greatest hurdle had still to be overcome—William I, the last independent German prince. Bismarck appealed to the romanticism of Lewis II and even evoked the time when the Bismarcks had been feudal vassals of the Wittelsbach house—a characteris-tically bizarre allusion, in that the estate for which they owed service was the one of which they had been deprived by the Hohenzollerns. Bismarck said: 'Such idiocies have their effect on the king.' It was probably more effective that he promised Lewis II a secret pension of some £20,000 a year out of the sequestered fortune of the deposed King of Hanover. Romantic flattery and bribery together did the trick. Lewis II wrote at Bismarck's dictation a letter offering the imperial crown to William I. The German people were also allowed their humble say. A deputation from the North German parliament requested William I to accept the crown when the princes offered it to him. The leader of the deputation had also headed the deputation from Frankfurt which made the offer to

Frederick William IV in 1849. This time Frederick William's condition was fulfilled—the effective offer was made by the German princes.

There were difficulties to the last moment. William I wished to be called 'Emperor of Germany'—a territorial title. Bismarck would only allow 'German Emperor'—a glorified presidency. He regarded this as trivial nonsense: '*Nescio quid mihi magis farcimentum esset*'[1], but he insisted as usual on getting his way. William felt more deeply about this question than about any of the great conflicts he had with Bismarck. He could forgive the making of peace with Austria in 1866 or later the alliance with her in 1879; he could not forgive being saddled with the wrong title. And this was natural. All men care most about the tools of their own trade; and kings are concerned with titles or orders just as a writer is offended by bad grammar or a cricketer by bad sportsmanship. Kings can determine the cut of a tunic or the precedence in a ballroom. They can do little to change the fate of the world—and they do not often try. Bismarck was impatient with the rigmarole. He wrote to his wife: 'The imperial delivery was a difficult one and kings—like women—have strange longings at such time, before they bring into the world what they cannot keep to themselves all the same.' The ceremony of acknowledging William I took place in the great gallery of the palace of Versailles on 18 January 1871. William I tried to cheat at the last moment. He told the Grand Duke of Baden to lead the cheers for 'the Emperor of Germany'. Bismarck intercepted the grand duke on his way upstairs, and suggested a safe compromise: cheers simply for 'Emperor William'. William was furious at the trick; and he ignored Bismarck's outstretched hand as he stepped off the Imperial dais.

Bismarck soon had other negotiations on his hands, this time with the French. Paris capitulated on 28 January; and an armistice followed, providing for a French national

---

[1] 'I don't know what could be a matter of more indifference to me'; or, in modern idiom, 'I couldn't care less.'

assembly, which should agree to the peace-terms. Bismarck now paid the penalty for his rashness at the beginning of the war. Though he was determined to claim Strasbourg, he wanted to give way about Metz: 'I don't like so many Frenchmen in our house, who do not want to be there.' He thought that the French would be resentful at their defeat in any case and wrote: 'This bitterness will be just as great even if they come out of the war without loss of territory.' But now it would have been a great stroke of conciliation if Metz had remained French after all the German talk. Bismarck failed to get his way. Moltke and the generals insisted in Metz; and after fierce debate William I supported them. Bismarck lamented that he would have done things very differently if he had had supreme power like Frederick the Great or Napoleon I. As it was, he had to set his hand to a peace which, he knew, would not be a peace of reconciliation. Still, he met the French on many points. He reduced the indemnity from six to five milliard francs,[1] and he allowed them to retain Belfort, despite Moltke's protests, discovering an easy compensation in a victory-march of the German army through the streets of Paris.

What was more important, he won the trust and even affection of Thiers, the principal French negotiator. Thiers had been prime minister of France when Bismarck was still a schoolboy; and Bismarck treated him with genuine respect. Once, finding the old man asleep in the ante-room, he covered him with his military cloak; and he did everything he could to make Thiers's task in governing France easier. When Bismarck in later years supported French republicanism, there was in this sentiment as well as policy—a sentiment of affection for the greatest French statesman of the day. The preliminary peace was concluded on 28 February. Bismarck marked in his devotional book the verse from Psalm 44: 'For they got not the land in possession by their own sword, neither did their own arm save them; but Thy right hand, and Thine arm, and

---

[1] This figure was calculated, on the basis of population, as the precise equivalent of the indemnity which Napoleon I imposed on Prussia in 1807.

the light of Thy countenance, because Thou hadst a favour unto them'—a curious judgement on the Franco-German war. The following day he took part in the march through Paris. On 6 March he at last left Versailles, taking with him the table from his lodgings on which the peace had been signed. Apparently he did not pay for it or even ask his landlady's permission.

Bismarck never saw France again, indeed never again left German soil.[1] National hatreds affected the private lives of statesmen for the first time in modern history. He would not have been safe from insult in France. Perhaps even Bismarck, too, was growing more nationalistic in character, though he said sadly that the peace-treaty should have contained a clause, authorizing him to visit Biarritz each year. Perhaps the absence of Kathi Orlov from Biarritz and her death a few years later deprived foreign travel of its charm so far as Bismarck was concerned—all that remained of the romance was a god-child at Biarritz, much persecuted during the Franco-German war. But there were consolations, some of them valued by Bismarck. On 28 March William I created him a prince of the German empire. He was not impressed: 'I was a rich Junker and I have become a poor prince.' He alleged that his fellow-Junkers envied him, and he even attributed their later opposition to this envy. Honours and decorations never meant much to him. When William I gave him the Grand Cross of the Hohenzollern Order in diamonds, he said: 'I'd sooner have had a horse or a barrel of good Rhenish wine.' He received also a reward more to his taste. William I granted him a princely domain at Friedrichsruh in the duchy of Lauenburg—Prussia's first acquisition under Bismarck's rule. This was an estate ten times as big as Varzin, and Bismarck added to it by purchase.

Bismarck was now one of the greatest landowners in Germany, particularly in timber. At Friedrichsruh he

---

[1] The phrase is deliberately chosen so as to cover his visits to Bad Gastein and Vienna.

showed the same exaggerated love of old trees as at Varzin
and planted new ones as well. In 1887 he sent to Gladstone
the malicious message: 'Tell him that, while he is chopping
trees down, I am busy planting them.' He developed, too,
a love of animals and soon carried no weapon except a
pair of field-glasses. At Friedrichsruh and Varzin he wore
glasses so as to observe Nature. When asked why he did
not wear them in Berlin, he answered that he found
nothing to interest him there. This was not quite true.
He used to survey the Reichstag through an old-fashioned
lorgnette—perhaps, however, more to overawe the deputies
than to see what was going on. Bismarck took some time
to get used to Friedrichsruh. He visited it little in the first
decade when he was Imperial chancellor. Later, he settled
there more and more. It was more accessible, only two
hours by train from Berlin; and Hamburg lay near at hand.
The acquaintance with Hamburg which Bismarck made
from Friedrichsruh helped to develop his interest in
colonies; and the leading Hamburg newspaper became his
mouthpiece after his fall. The traditions of the Hanseatic
league came to mean something to him, as those of the
Holy Roman Empire never did.

The house at Friedrichsruh was even uglier than the one
at Varzin. The original mansion had long disappeared, and
its place had been taken by an hotel for week-enders from
Hamburg. Bismarck did not even trouble to remove the
numbers from the hotel-bedrooms. He did not instal
electric light, managing with oil-lamps to the day of his
death; and he stored in the cellar the countless books
which were given to him but which he did not read. He
knew nothing of contemporary literature, either German
or foreign. He condemned Sybel, his own official historian,
as one who muddied the waters of history. He never even
read Clausewitz, to whom he once referred as 'a distinguished general'. Ranke had always been his favourite
historian; and he made a revealing exception later for
Taine. He continued to soak himself in the Bible and
Shakespeare; and he developed a consuming passion for

the novels of Dumas. Otherwise his tastes remained those of his Romantic boyhood. He ignored altogether contemporary developments in philosophy, science, and economics; despised all artists; and dismissed Wagner, the greatest musician of the day, as 'a monkey'—perhaps because the wife of Schleinitz, his predecessor as foreign minister and now the confidential adviser of Queen Augusta, was a Wagnerian enthusiast. He attended the Opera in 1889 during the tsar's visit to Berlin; it was his first appearance there since he became chancellor. Indeed, though he now held the greatest position in Europe, he made no attempt to fulfil the representational side of his office. He never appeared at funerals, even at those of royal princes; and he ignored visiting foreign celebrities unless they had something interesting to say. He attended the court balls when he was first chancellor and danced with almost boyish zest. William I said that such dancing was too frivolous for an Imperial chancellor and forbade it; Bismarck did not appear at court balls again. He entertained the diplomatic corps once a year, otherwise hardly saw them. He never dined out. When the King of Saxony called at the Chancellery one morning, he was told by the porter to go away and make an appointment. A grand duke who was expected at 9 p.m. arrived a little late. He was greeted by Bismarck wearing an old coat and with the words: 'I had given up hoping for the honour of a visit from Your Royal Highness; it is 9.20.' Even the crown prince often failed to encounter Bismarck for months at a time.

Bismarck made an exception only for William I whom he saw every afternoon when they were both in Berlin. He established over the emperor an ascendancy that was great but never complete. The crown prince said shortly after the war of 1866: 'If Bismarck proposed an alliance with Garibaldi—well, he's at least a general. But if he proposed an alliance with Mazzini the king would at first walk up and down the room in distress and would exclaim: "Bismarck, Bismarck, what are you turning me into?" Then he would stop in the middle of the room and say: "But if you believe that it is absolutely necessary in the interests of the state, there's nothing more to be said".' Things did not really go as easily as this. For one thing, the old gentleman (whom Bismarck accused of always sleeping heavily) would complain of a restless night just when Bismarck meant to describe his own insomnia. He called the Emperor heartless and liked to repeat the saying: 'There are white men, there are black men, and there are monarchs.' Once, returning from an interview, he exclaimed: 'I cannot be the servant of princes.' William I lamented on his side: 'It is not easy to be emperor under such a chancellor.'

Bismarck suffered much ill-health during his first decade as Imperial chancellor. This was largely due to the nervous irritation which grew on him all the time. But he also smoked too many cigars (at one time fourteen a day) and ate and drank too much, worst of all a gigantic supper before going to bed. Then he would lie awake piling up grievances. He once announced: 'I have spent *the whole night hating*'; and when he had no immediate object for his hate he would go back over the injuries of twenty or thirty years before. 'I often forget, I never forgive;' only the second part of the statement was true. He suffered much also from toothache, but refused to see a dentist; and the pain brought on a nervous cramp of his cheeks. Between 1878 and 1883 this twitching became so bad that he grew a beard again to hide it. Though the twitch disappeared when the teeth were finally drawn, Bismarck never admitted the connexion—the blame had always to be put on his opponents or, still more, on his friends. Most of his ailments were probably imaginary, except for indigestion; but, of course, that did not make them any less painful. He looked and acted like an old man when he became Imperial chancellor—and a shaky old man at that. Yet he was only fifty-six with more than a quarter of a century of full activity before him. The one thing which really laid Bismarck low was boredom. He could always rise to an emergency and work with a penetration and efficiency that few men have shown. But he needed to live in a crisis all the time.

Like many men with deep family affections, he cared little or nothing for public causes in themselves. These were, as he once said frankly, 'luxuries'. What mattered to him was to make the instrument he controlled—first Prussia and then Germany—as strong as possible and therewith to increase his own power. He expounded this ruthlessly to the Reichstag in 1881: 'I have often acted hastily and without reflection, but when I had time to think I have always asked: what is useful, effective, right, for my fatherland, for my dynasty—so long as I was merely in Prussia—and now for the German nation? I have never been a doctrinaire. . . Liberal, reactionary, conservative— those I confess seem to me luxuries. . . . Give me a strong German state, and then ask me whether it should have more or less liberal furnishings, and you'll find that I answer: Yes, I've no fixed opinions, make proposals, and you won't meet any objections of principle from me. Many roads lead to Rome. Sometimes one must rule liberally, and sometimes dictatorially, there are no eternal rules. . . . My aim from the first moment of my public activity has been the creation and consolidation of Germany, and if you can show a single moment when I deviated from that magnetic needle, you may perhaps prove that I went wrong, but never that I lost sight of the national aim for a moment.' He cared as little for persons as for causes, and had few personal loyalties. He wrote once: 'The capacity of admiring men is only moderately developed in me, and it is rather a defect of my eye that it is sharper for weaknesses than good qualities.' He paraded an exception in favour of William I, but this exception operated only so long as the king agreed with him; and he gave his devotion free rein only when the emperor was safely dead.

Bismarck said to some politicians in 1874: 'I am bored; the great things are done. The German *Reich* is made.' So indeed it turned out. The period of making was over;

that of conserving had begun. Definitive peace between France and Germany was signed at Frankfurt on 10 May, 1871—twenty years to the day since Bismarck first took train to Frankfurt as Prussian representative at the federal diet. There were no further wars between the Great Powers in his lifetime; no frontier in Europe was changed outside the Balkans; the German constitution itself remained unaltered until 1918. These forty years of stability became in retrospect 'Bismarck's system'; and he was credited with profound foresight where there had been only a quick instinctive response to events. Bismarck had had a conscious plan when he became prime minister in 1862, though he failed to operate it—the plan of a revolutionary remodelling of Europe in co-operation with France and Russia. He had intentions of a less definite nature up to 1866: he wanted somehow to make Prussia stronger in north Germany. He never meant to carry his power south of the Main. All his political and religious outlook was against it. Lutheranism was his deepest principle. He regarded the south Germans as corrupted by Roman Catholicism and French liberalism, moreover beyond the reach of Prussian militarism. Schweinitz once said to him: 'This expansion must cease where the supply of Prussian officers gives out,' and he replied: 'I do not say so, but it is the basis of my policy.' The military treaties with the southern states were then all he wanted. He was driven to go further first by the accident of the war with France and then by its prolongation. He made 'little Germany' without ever intending to do so.

Could this 'little Germany' be permanent? Could German nationalism be arrested at the Austrian frontier? When the 'little German' programne was devised in 1848, it was not proposed as an alternative to the 'greater Germany' which should include the German-Austrians, but as a practical first step made simply because the greater programme was unattainable. Every 'little German' at that time expected 'greater Germany' sooner or later. The only real alternative to greater Germany was

to divide Germany at the Main with Austria; and this is
what Bismarck had tried to do until 1866. The independence of the south German states was another, though
inferior, version of the same idea. It had now broken down.
The German *Reich* was unmistakably a national state,
despite its federalism; and it was bound to exercise an
increasing attraction on the Germans still outside it in the
non-national Habsburg monarchy. Bismarck had not only
done enough for his generation; he had done too much
when, however inevitably, he overstepped the line of the
Main.

He recognized this himself. No man was more convinced
that Europe would never be settled until national reconstruction was complete or, as he put it, until the peoples
were sorted out into their 'tribes'. Yet after 1871 he did
everything to stave off the consequences of his own work.
He tried to make out that his Germany was still an
exclusively Protestant state with no interests in the valley
of the Danube or in the Near East. There was no 'philosophy' behind this. Bismarck did not believe that his
negations could be permanent; he merely shrank from
further trouble and upheaval. 'When we have arrived in
a good harbour, we should be content and cultivate and
hold what we have won.' He constantly told the German-
Austrians that they should lose their national character
and develop loyalty to the Habsburgs; but the only reality
he recognized in the Habsburg monarchy was the Hungarian gentry—the nearest equivalent in central Europe
to the Prussian Junkers. Time often gives to things a
sanctity which they did not possess at the start; and the
frontier which Bismarck drew in 1871 between the
Austrians and other Germans is now perhaps a genuine
dividing-line. If this is so, Bismarck made 'little Germany'
by accident; that he should have believed in it himself
is to credit him with a foresight which he did not and
could not possess.

It was the same in his relations with the other Powers.
Metternich had perhaps planned a system of perpetual

peace. Bismarck was content to avoid the troubles of the moment. He did not expect them to present much difficulty after the peace with France. She was too weak to challenge the settlement by herself; and no other Power was likely to aid her in doing so. He is often said to have aimed at the isolation of France. But this was unnecessary: the French did it for themselves. They too wished to avoid new troubles. Certainly Bismarck supported the republican form of government in France and even justified this by arguing that republicanism disqualified her as the ally of any monarchist Power. This was window-dressing for his emperor. His real concern was that a royalist or Bonapartist government in France—caring more for prestige and less for the French people—might turn to a grandiose foreign policy, as Gramont had done in 1870, and provoke a new war, disastrous for both France and Germany. Of course, the temptation might be irresistible even to the republicans if other Powers actively sought a French alliance. But they would do this only if they had themselves causes for quarrel with Germany; and these did not appear to exist. Bismarck had no colonial ambitions—it did not even occur to him to claim any French colony in 1871. Hence England and Germany were friends, if not 'natural allies', as England and Austria had been earlier. Austria-Hungary was reconciled to national Germany. Even Beust met Bismarck with every evidence of friendship in August 1871; and it was henceforth Bismarck's anxiety to avoid Austria-Hungary's alliance, not her enmity.

Nor did the rise of Germany seem to threaten a conflict with Russia. Bismarck, and indeed most Germans, remained hostile to Polish nationalism after 1871 as they had been before it. He repudiated any interest in the German 'Baltic barons', despite their ties of class with the Junkers. 'They have got into the ogre's cave, and we cannot help them. If I wanted to conduct a purely Machiavellian policy, I should even wish that they would be Russified as soon as possible; for as long as they remain German,

they form an element of strength and energy.' Germany
had no practical conflicts with any of the Powers. Therefore
he still assumed, as he had done between 1866 and 1870,
that she could follow a line of pacific detachment, friendly
to all, allied with none. He was never chary of kind words.
He emphasized to England their common character of
industrial progress and liberal monarchy; to France the
common need for a settled frontier. With Austria-Hungary
and Russia he revived the cause of monarchical solidarity,
and sometimes spoke as though it were his dearest wish
that the old Holy Alliance should return to life. He never
took this very seriously. He knew quite well that Francis
Joseph was no longer a despotic monarch and that even
Alexander II had to consider Russian opinion. When a
party of German officers visited St. Petersburg at the end
of 1871, the tsar said to one of them: 'You don't know
how I love you; I daren't even show it to you here.'

Bismarck himself was far from Metternich's position.
He was the chief minister of a constitutional state, ruling
in close co-operation with a great liberal party. Perhaps
he emphasized the conservative nature of his foreign
policy for that very reason. It is often said that home
and foreign policy should go hand in hand, each reflecting
the other. With Bismarck the opposite was the case. He
was always most revolutionary abroad when reactionary
at home; liberal at home when conservative abroad. He
had preached revolutionary nationalism between 1862
and 1866, when he was in conflict with the Prussian liberals;
he was pacific between 1867 and 1870, when making liberal
Germany. Later he abandoned the Holy Alliance just when
he broke with the liberal party in parliament. He liked to
make policy himself, not to have it dictated to him either
by politicians or by the emperor; and he practised in this
as in everything else a policy of balance—taking away
with one hand what he gave with the other. Though he
frightened the tsar and the Austrian emperor with talk
of 'the social peril', he did nothing against the Social
Democrats in Germany until after the Holy Alliance had

disappeared. Having one of Marx's friends among his own associates, he knew that the Marxist International was dying; yet he used its ghost as excuse for the League of the Three Emperors.

This League had nothing in common with Bismarck's later alliances. It was founded on sentiment, not on interests; and it had no precise terms. In 1872 the three emperors met in Berlin without making a written agreement of any kind. Later in the year Moltke drafted a convention with the Russian chief-of-staff, providing for military co-operation in time of war. Bismarck refused to confirm this convention, and it was never invoked later. In 1873, when Alexander II was in Vienna, Austria-Hungary and Russia at last got something down on paper. The essential clause was a promise that, if they quarrelled in the Near East, they would subordinate their differences there to the general interests of monarchical solidarity. Bismarck gave a vague approval to this agreement. He could hardly 'accede' to it in any real sense, having no stake of his own in the Near East. The League was not designed to isolate France—Bismarck had other means of doing this. Its object, so far as it had one, was to prevent a conflict between Austria-Hungary and Russia in the Eastern question—a conflict in which Germany could only lose. Like most associations based on sentiment from the Holy Alliance to the League of Nations, it turned out to be ineffective. It was a fair-weather system. The League of the Three Emperors was supposed to secure the peace of Europe. It survived only so long as the peace of Europe was secure. Monarchical solidarity was a luxury which was blown to the winds as soon as Russia and Austria-Hungary saw their eastern interests in danger.

Bismarck knew this from the start. No man had denounced alliances of sentiment more fiercely or more accurately. The League did no harm, though little good. It pleased William I, and, therefore, perhaps made it easier for Bismarck to continue the liberal line in home affairs which he had been following since 1867. His interest in foreign policy was at its lowest. He hardly troubled to do anything except record the successive payments of the French indemnity and, of course, to quarrel with his ambassadors. His legislative activity, on the other hand, was at its height, pushing through to a wider conclusion the liberal measures that had been prepared between 1867 and 1870. These measures were indistinguishable from those of Gladstone's contemporary ministry in England, except that they were more sweeping and more effective. The National Liberals regarded themselves as the government party. Bismarck consulted their leaders on the parliamentary work of the session; and their candidates were treated as Bismarck's men. Only a few conservatives supported Bismarck, and that grudgingly. A political conflict in 1872 showed how far Bismarck had travelled since the days when he was the Junker enemy of liberalism and the defender of Prussia against Germany. He brought forward in the Prussian parliament proposals for a modest element of self-government in local affairs—an attack on the Junker monopoly of local office. The liberals of the Prussian Chamber supported his proposals. The Upper House, on which he had once relied, rejected them; and William I had actually to create twenty-five peers to force the government measure through.

Nor was this all. Bismarck resigned his position as prime minister of Prussia, remaining only foreign minister and Imperial chancellor. It was not his affair, he said, to protect the interests of his former friends, and he was exhausted by contending with them. Even the Prussian ministers were too reactionary and timid for his taste. Roon, who had proposed Bismarck as prime minister ten years before, had now to repay the debt and become prime minister himself. The experiment was not a success. When Bismarck had planned the German constitution so that the chancellor was subordinate to the Prussian prime minister and the mouthpiece of the Prussian ministry, he was himself prime minister. Now he was furious to discover that the Prussian prime minister was not subordinate to the Imperial chancellor. Of course, neither Roon nor any other minister attempted to issue orders to the chancellor, as the Prussian ministry was entitled to do. But this was not enough. Bismarck insisted on issuing orders to them. He complained that legislative proposals were being made in Prussia without his knowledge. Prussia, he added, must now conform to a German pattern. Bismarck had resigned as being too liberal; Roon had taken his place as more conservative. But it soon turned out that Bismarck would not allow Roon to act on his conservative principles. His function, in Bismarck's eyes, was to exploit his reputation as a conservative in order to force through Bismarck's liberal measures with less fuss—above all with less nervous irritation for the great man. Roon would not play this part. He resigned within a few months, and Bismarck resumed the post of Prussian prime minister for the rest of his active life.

A further episode soon showed again how far Bismarck had moved from his original position of 1862. The German military establishment was still on a temporary basis. Parliament had authorized it in 1871 immediately after unification, for three years only. The general staff and the military cabinet of the emperor now tried to make it permanent. They submitted their proposal to the Reichstag without consulting Bismarck or asking his advice. The politicians resisted. They would authorize the establishment for the lifetime of a single parliament (three years) or, as a gesture of conciliation, for four years; they would not agree to the 'eternat'. Bismarck told the National Liberal leaders: 'The proposal is not my work. You can discuss it freely.' They took his hint and threw it out. William I announced that the conflict of 1862 had begun again and that he would fight it through once more. Bismarck, far from showing fight, first took to his bed and then offered to resign. The emperor gave way; and the politicians, threatened with a dissolution, gave way also. Bismarck imposed authorization for seven years—a compromise acceptable only to himself. The politicians did not get authorization by each Reichstag; the emperor did not get eternity. Bismarck had proved himself the master of both elements in the constitution, the agent of neither.

He often claimed to be educating Germany into parliamentary government. Nothing was more frequent than his call for a steady majority which should work hand-in-hand with the government of the day. He said in private: 'I am no absolutist. There should be only two parties, for and against the government. If the ministry is overthrown, the opposition party must be forced to form a new ministry.' He referred enviously to the example of England where there was 'a parliament with a strong majority, homogeneously organized, under a leadership such as was provided by the two Pitts or Canning, or even Palmerston, Peel.'[1] Such a parliament, he said, would soon reduce the king and the Upper House to a very little space and tie them down. He blamed the Germans for having 'eight or ten factions, with no constant majority, no united, recognized leadership'. And it was true that the Reichstag never knew a single majority-party. The National Liberals, even at their most powerful, could provide a majority only by associating themselves with the Bismarckian Conservatives on the one side or with the Progressives on the other; and they were themselves divided into a Left under Lasker and a centre under Bennigsen.

Yet it is difficult to put all the blame on the politicians. Though Bismarck called for a parliamentary majority, he disliked its consequences. His theories led him one way, his personality another. There is an exact analogy in his

[1] The existence of a two-party system in England ever since the Glorious Revolution was a received dogma of the time. If Bismarck had understood English history as we do now, he would have held up these statesmen as a warning, not an example. The elder Pitt never had any party support ; the younger Pitt had to juggle a number of groups, relying mainly on the support of the Crown. Canning was put in office by royal favour, against the will of the majority of the House of Commons. The Liberal party on which Palmerston relied was in fact a collection of differing factions. Only Peel had the support of a compact party—much to his discomfiture in 1846.

relations with William I. Bismarck said to Roon in 1872: 'I don't know why, I don't manage to please the king. As a gentleman and a soldier, I only want to obey him.' Roon, who knew his Bismarck, answered: 'Certainly you want to, but you don't do it.' It was the same with the Reichstag. He wanted a majority, but it had to be one which followed his lead unquestioningly. 'I have often spoken to English members of parliament, and they said to me in reference to some measure: I regard this measure as foolish, dangerous, and mistaken, but the minister who leads the party, the leader of the party wants it, he must accept the responsibility for it—I think he is making a mistake.' But what if instead the majority tried to impose its will upon Bismarck? He rejected the idea with violence. 'The crown prince wants me to obey the majority. That demands a suppleness of character and conviction that I do not possess.' And again: 'The foreign policy of a great country cannot be put at the disposal of a parliamentary majority without getting on to a false track.' Yet Bismarck can be defended by the English example to which he himself appealed. Sir Robert Peel was the first man to see that parliamentary government demanded a stable majority. He built up such a majority for the Conservative party and used it to force himself upon an unwilling queen in 1841. But when it came to the repeal of the Corn Laws, he repudiated his responsibility to the Conservative party and rejected its claims in words which Bismarck might have used: 'I am not under an obligation to any man or to any body of men. . . . I have served four Sovereigns and there was but one reward which I desired—namely, the simple acknowledgement, on their part, that I had been to them a loyal and faithful minister.'

It is surprising, indeed, that Bismarck co-operated with the National Liberals for so long or that he did not run earlier into a crisis such as brought Peel down. The breach was postponed by a great political struggle, in which Bismarck and the National Liberals seemed to be on the same side—the *Kulturkampf*, or conflict of civilizations between

national Germany and the Roman church. This conflict
had many deep causes. The Church itself was in combative
mood against every modern idea. In 1864 Pius IX denounced the mortal error that 'the Pope can and must
compromise and be reconciled with progress, liberalism,
and modern culture'; and in 1870 the Oecumenical council
at the Vatican proclaimed the Infallibility of the Pope
just when his territorial supremacy was being destroyed.
It is easy to see now that this infallibility was asserted only
in matters of doctrine. It seemed at the time that the
papacy was claiming again the right to excommunicate
and depose temporal rulers which it had tried to exercise
in the Middle Ages. The papacy had identified itself with
the defeated Powers in the war of 1866 and 1870. Antonelli,
the papal secretary of state, exclaimed on the news of
Sadova: 'the world is falling to pieces!', and Windthorst,
the Roman Catholic leader in Germany, said that the
Kulturkampf began on the day of Sadova. Similarly,
Napoleon III had been the protector of the papacy, and
Rome fell to the Italians as a direct consequence of Sedan.
Bismarck had some grounds for thinking that his work
could be undone only by a clericalist conspiracy, linking up
Paris, Vienna, and Rome. On the other hand, the decree
of infallibility seemed to have opened a chink in the
clericalist armour. It was opposed by the leading German
theologians, and every German bishop at the Vatican
council voted against it.

The aggression was not all on one side. Bismarck and the
Reichstag were making liberal Germany; and the modern
liberal state came everywhere into conflict with the Church.
Education, for instance, could be a matter for compromise
so long as it was limited to a few. It was bound to cause
bitter dispute as soon as it became universal; and after
1871 universal elementary education was everywhere the
order of the day. Disputes over religious education dominated the politics of every European country in the last
thirty years of the nineteenth century—not merely Germany, but England, France, Belgium, and Austria-

Hungary, to name a few at random; and Germany, in fact, got by with a less fierce conflict than the others. What made the conflict seem sharper in Germany while it lasted was in part Bismarck's own ruthlessness of expression and still more the political associations of the Roman Catholics. Germany had been divided religiously for three hundred years, each state possessing a defined religious character of its own. In some states the Roman Catholics were a secure majority, in others a barely tolerated minority; and this made them infinitely adaptable. Prussia had long had peculiar difficulties. By tradition a purely Protestant state, she acquired a large Roman Catholic population on the Rhine in 1815; and there had been a full-dress rehearsal for the *Kulturkampf* (this time over mixed marriages) between 1836 and 1840, with priests and bishops in prison, churches standing empty, and the state impotent against a religious opposition. In 1840 the Romantic enthusiasm of Frederick William IV had led to a compromise, with the king actually attending celebrations at the Roman Catholic cathedral of Cologne in 1844. The conflict was postponed for a generation. Bismarck's victories renewed it in acuter form. The North German confederation was still predominantly Protestant; but the unification of 1871 created a state in which the Roman Catholics were a formidable minority.

Moreover, they were a minority clearly identified with the defeated cause. The clericals of Bavaria opposed unification to the last; and when the Roman Catholics created their own political party, the Centre, this won support from all those who disliked the Bismarckian *Reich*. The Poles and Alsatians who co-operated with the Centre were Roman Catholics; but Hanoverian separatists also voted solidly for it, though they were Protestants, just as on the other side Roman Catholic nationalists urged Bismarck on. It was, for instance, Hohenlohe, former prime minister of Bavaria and a Roman Catholic, who proposed the attack on the Jesuits in 1872. Bismarck emphasized the anti-national aspect of the conflict and even attributed it all to the Poles: 'I got involved in the struggle through the Polish side of the affair.' This was an exaggeration. The conflict would have happened even without Poland. The Centre was rather the rallying-point for those who, though German patriots, had a different German ideal—'greater Germany', a resurrection of the Holy Roman Empire, ruled perhaps from Vienna, perhaps from Frankfurt, but certainly not from Berlin. Bismarck expressed this when he called the Centrists *Reichsfeinde*, enemies of the empire. Windthorst answered: 'The prime minister is not the state and no minister has yet dared to call *his* opponents opponents of *the state*.' This was a telling reply: Bismarck easily identified himself with the state and did so increasingly as time went on. Yet the accusation was true. The Centrists were enemies of Bismarck's Germany, though not of Germany itself, and enemies above all of the state's claim to regulate all temporal affairs.

Bismarck was exasperated and driven forward against the Centre by his realization that he had himself put power into their hands. The Centre was the creation of universal suffrage and could not have existed without it. Bismarck, as so often, had got out of one difficulty only to find himself in a greater. He had carried universal suffrage in order to ruin the liberals, his opponents of the eighteen-sixties. His calculation proved correct. Middle-class liberalism had little appeal to a mass-electorate; and it fell to pieces in Germany as in every other country within a generation of the establishment of universal suffrage. But this did not strengthen Bismarck. Indeed, his parliamentary position would have been stronger if a compact liberal party had survived, and its backing would have enabled him to defy William II in 1890. When he introduced universal suffrage, he seems lightly to have assumed that the masses would vote dumbly for Conservatives and that these would give unquestioning, even unreasoning support to the Imperial chancellor. He had played the national appeal successfully against the king and against the liberal politicians; he supposed that he could play it just as easily against any rivals for the support of the masses. He did not realize that the free peasants of western Germany and the industrial workers had a very different character from the Prussian peasants whom alone he knew at first-hand. These masses had a national consciousness, but they expressed it by voting for democratic leaders, not for their landlords or their employers. Bismarck's Reich had two opponents—first the Centre, then the Social Democrats. Both owed their power, if not their existence, to Bismarck's own actions; and against them he had to rely on the National Liberals, whose decline he had irrevocably decreed.

The *Kulturkampf* was an effort to arrest this development at its start, to strangle the Centre in the cradle. And, of course, Bismarck always held that struggle against a common enemy was the simplest method for attaining political unity. It made it easier for him to carry the budget or the army-law when he could claim that he and the National Liberals were allies against the Roman church. The alliance was artificial. The National Liberals insisted that two philosophies of life were in conflict—clericalism against the modern spirit of secularism. Bismarck disliked both philosophies. He was defending the rights of the state, and he traced the struggle back to Agamemnon, contending with the priests at Aulis, or to the struggle between emperors and popes in the Middle Ages. He raised the old banner of Luther and declared: 'If I follow the pope, I shall lose my eternal salvation.' This Lutheran appeal, though it rested on genuine conviction, had also a political motive. Bismarck wished to escape from dependence on the National Liberals by enlisting the Conservatives, too, on his side. This manœuvre did not work. The Prussian conservatives, though Lutheran, disliked the attack on religion more than they liked the attack on Roman Catholicism. They acquiesced in 1872 when Bismarck proposed that all school inspectors should be appointed by the state; they jibbed when he added that henceforth they could be laymen. The rift grew wider in 1873. The Conservatives could swallow the 'May-laws', Bismarck's great engine against the Roman Catholics, by which the training and even the licensing of priests required state approval. They were outraged by civil marriage, an inevitable consequence of the struggle, but one which Bismarck had bitterly opposed in 1849. Even William I disliked the trend of policy: baptism, he thought, would go next.

Bismarck warned the Conservatives that they would be ruined if they went against him: 'You were elected under my name; if I withdraw my hand from you, you will not come back.' And so it proved. The Conservatives suffered disaster at the general election of 1874. But this did not help Bismarck. Gains went to the Left wing of the National Liberals and, much worse, to the Centre. It sprang from 61 to 95, and, allied with the Poles, the Alsatians, and the Danes (from north Sleswig) could command 120 votes— almost as many as the combined National Liberals. Repression, far from weakening the Centre, strengthened the Roman Catholic cause. It forced back on to the clericalist side nearly all those who had opposed the decree of infallibility in 1870. Priests and bishops were imprisoned; sees remained vacant; passions on both sides grew more bitter. On 13 July a young Roman Catholic attempted to assassinate Bismarck. He replied by saddling the Centre with responsibility for the attempt: 'Push the man away as much as you like. He still clings to your coat-tails.' From the Centrist benches came a cry of 'Pfui!'—one of the strongest German expressions. Onlookers expected Bismarck to strike the deputy or to reach in his pocket for a pistol. He stood at the tribune, rocked with rage; then mastered himself and said coldly: ' "Pfui" is an expression of loathing and contempt. Do not think that these feelings are far from me; I am only too polite to express them.' No public man knew better how to provoke others and how to control himself.

Though he could not control the Conservatives and quarrelled with his few remaining Junker friends, he could still control William I. When the emperor hinted his doubts, Bismarck answered in December 1874 by offering to resign. William I was contrite, even swallowed criticism of his wife, and Bismarck swept tumultuously on his way. He said in the Reichstag—if the pope triumphs, 'we non-Catholics must either become Catholics or emigrate or our property would be confiscated, as is usual with heretics.' There was something old-world in this frenzy. He tried to switch the conflict on to a field where he had always been a master—foreign policy. From the beginning his gravest charge against the Centre had been its international character. Yet he was prepared to exploit this international loyalty. He tried repeatedly to negotiate with the pope behind the backs of the Centre leaders, and offered to drop the May-laws if the pope would order the Centre to give him unquestioning support in the Reichstag on everything else. A bargain of this kind ended the *Kulturkampf* later. It was impossible so long as Pius IX remained pope; and he survived until 1878. Since Bismarck could not dominate the Centre by its international association, he tried to discredit them by the same means. He accused them not merely of subservience to the pope, but of collaboration with Roman bishops and clericalists in other countries. Bismarck never found it easier to tolerate criticism from abroad than at home. In 1874 he tried to insist on a press-law against clerical writers in Belgium. In the spring of 1875 he made the same move on a greater scale and saw in France the heart of a great clericalist conspiracy.

France had certainly recovered miraculously from the defeat of 1871. Moreover, Thiers and the pacific republicans had been overthrown. The royalists had elected MacMahon as temporary president, and they aspired to increase their prestige by a challenging foreign policy. Bismarck accepted their challenge. He even allowed his associates to talk of a preventive war; and Moltke talked of it also, without waiting for the chancellor's permission. It is inconceivable that Bismarck meant this talk seriously. A man cannot go against the habits of a lifetime, however much he may change his ways of expressing them; and Bismarck never wavered in his dislike of war except as a last resort. Besides, he had always insisted that war must bring practical gains. What gain could victory over France have brought him in 1875 ? Only more discontented French voters, to strengthen the Centre in the *Reichstag*. But talk of war, or of the French danger, might discredit the Centre; it might even weaken the French clericals and bring a sensible republican government to power—or so Bismarck, in his bullying way, too easily assumed. On 5 April the *Kölnische Zeitung* asked, 'Is war in sight ?', perhaps not at Bismarck's instigation, but certainly with his encouragement. It was the signal for a crisis which did not work out to Bismarck's advantage.

Though the French government were alarmed, they did not respond, as Bismarck had hoped, with apologies or with a reduction of their armament-programme. Decazes, the French foreign minister, revealed the German talk of preventive war to *The Times*—a stroke as telling as Bismarck's publication of the French designs on Belgium in 1870; and he appealed to the European powers, this time more successfully than Thiers had done during the Franco-German war. Andrássy, the Austro-Hungarian foreign minister, alone did not respond. He was bidding for an alliance with Germany, not for the alliance with France which had escaped Beust even before the war of 1870. Indeed, Andrássy saw estrangement between Russia and Germany in the offing, and expressed his joy by three hand-stands on the table that had once been Metternich's. The British and Russian governments both expostulated seriously in Berlin—the British through their ambassador, the Russians personally on the occasion of a visit by Alexander II and Gorchakov. Bismarck gave way with the masterly grace which he knew how to use when necessary. The crisis turned out to be a false alarm, even helped to improve Franco-German relations. It left only a lasting estrangement between Bismarck and Gorchakov. Bismarck did not forgive the Russian interference and alleged that

Gorchakov had announced to his ambassadors: 'Peace is now assured'.[1] Gorchakov on his side was not sorry to humiliate the man who had once described himself as Gorchakov's admiring pupil; and he said in private: 'Bismarck is ill because he eats too much and drinks too much and works too much.' Though this was true, Gorchakov like others would have done well to remember that Bismarck, even when ill (or perhaps most when ill) was more formidable than most men when well.

The 'war-in-sight' crisis was a casual episode in Bismarck's policy, and it seemed to leave no mark on domestic affairs. The *Kulturkampf* was waged as fiercely as ever; Bismarck's alliance with the National Liberals grew closer. In February 1876 he openly denounced the *Kreuzzeitung*, the paper of the extreme right which he had helped to found in the bitter days of 1848. More than a hundred Junkers, including all the famous names of Prussia, answered with a declaration of loyalty to their paper and of defiance to Bismarck. He published the names in the official gazette and went over the offences of his former friends in many a sleepless night. Yet there were warning signs that his confidence in the National Liberals was on the wane. It left perhaps only a passing mark when in 1875 they defeated his attempt to smuggle into the criminal code provisions against stirring up class-hatred and civil disobedience which would have enabled him to prosecute the Social Democrats. It was more significant when Bismarck proposed later in the year the nationalization of the German railways—not in itself an illiberal measure, for Gladstone had favoured it in England, but an indication all the same that Bismarck was losing faith in Free Trade and *laissez-faire*. One of Bismarck's closest associates took the hint. In April 1876 Delbrück resigned. The most competent of officials and a convinced Free Trader, he would not follow Bismarck, yet shrank from conflict with

---

[1] The text of Gorchakov's message was in fact: 'The tsar leaves Berlin perfectly convinced of the conciliatory dispositions which reign there and which assure the maintenance of peace.'

him. At just the same time, Bismarck said of the National Liberals: 'They always want to wash the fur without making it wet and so always turn in shame from any naked idea.'

Even Bismarck took some time to look facts in the face. The German protective tariffs would expire on 1 January 1877. Thereafter Germany would become a Free Trade country. In England Free Trade had been followed by almost thirty years of uninterrupted prosperity. Germany was going into Free Trade just when the boom after the Franco-German war was ending and when trading conditions were becoming more difficult. Bismarck might have told German industrialists to face these difficulties if Free Trade had been an intrinsic part of his political thought, and if industry alone had been threatened. But the Prussian landowners were also encountering the competition of cheap Russian grain—first result of the new Russian railways; and a prosperous agriculture was always essential in Bismarck's outlook. It would be unfair to ascribe his conversion solely, or even mainly, to his private interest as a great landowner. He had allowed others to introduce Free Trade, without much thought or leadership of his own. There had always been a doubt beneath the surface. Bismarck was never liberal in thought, though sometimes in action. For him the state, not the individual, was the mainspring of political action; and he did not accept the 'night-watchman' theory of the state which was common to all liberals. He held that the state could lead in economic affairs, just as he had tried to take the initiative in foreign policy and not wait upon events.

There was a second consideration. The *Reich* was not financially self-supporting; it depended upon contributions from the individual states for the bulk of its income. A new tariff-system would both protect German industry and give to the *Reich* a secure revenue of its own. No doubt there were cruder political calculations. Tariffs might win back the support of the Conservatives; they might ruin the more doctrinaire National Liberals; in any case they would supply a new national appeal to take the place of the *Kulturkampf*. The steps of God could again be heard sounding through history. It took Bismarck some time to grasp the hem of God's garment. He said as early as 1875: 'To give the German *Reich* a powerful, unshakable financial foundation, which provides it with a dominating position and brings it into organic union with every public interest in state, province, district, and commune—that would be a great and worthy task, which could tempt me to devote to it the last scrap of my failing strength.' But he added: 'The task is difficult. I am not an expert in this field, and my advisers have no creative ideas.' Bismarck might have found a target nearer home for the taunt which he discharged against Francis Joseph: 'The emperor of Austria has many ministers, but when he wants anything done he has to do it himself.' Bismarck was already Imperial chancellor, prime minister of Prussia, and foreign minister. When he turned to economics, he had to become also Prussian minister of trade; and he held all four posts until he left office in 1890.

His delays, his hesitation, his planlessness throughout 1876 were not surprising. He saw new tasks ahead, tasks for which he had no training or experience. His health grew worse. He had become enormously fat. His teeth were rotting. His list of ailments included jaundice, varicose veins, perforated stomach, gastric ulcers, gall-stones, shingles. He told his wife he was 'weary of life'. In March 1877 he again asked to resign. William I almost took him at his word, much to Bismarck's alarm. He withdrew his resignation and compromised on a prolonged leave of absence. On 15 April 1877 he retired to Friedrichsruh; in the summer to Varzin. He returned to Berlin only on 14 February 1878. During this absence he turned his ideas upside down. His return brought an upheaval in every aspect of economic, political and foreign affairs. The liberal Bismarck disappeared. A more universal Bismarck —more conservative but also more constructive—took his place.

VII

THE CHANGE OF COURSE

BISMARCK claimed a consistency of policy and purpose. His speeches treated forty years of political activity as a single theme; and the memoirs which he wrote after his fall were designed to show that he had always pursued the same long-term aims. He boasted of being an opportunist only in the sense that his means and methods changed with the times. He said in 1887: 'What is an opportunist? He is a man who uses the most favourable opportunity to carry through what he regards as useful and appropriate.' And it is, of course, true that Bismarck remained unmistakably the same throughout his career—always more concerned to get his own way than to lay down in advance what that way should be. He loved both combat and success. It was a sad contradiction to him that one excluded the other: by winning a combat, he also brought it to an end. He was devoted to his instruments—the Hohenzollern dynasty or the German nation—so long as they served his will; but ultimately it was the triumph of his will, a mastery of the external world, that mattered to him.

Yet, on a more practical plane, there were two occasions when he changed his outlook on life and public affairs so profoundly that we can speak of a real change of course, even of a change in himself. One man disappeared; and a different man took his place. No doubt the new man was equally determined to get his way, but the way went in quite a different direction. The first of these occasions was shortly after Bismarck went to Frankfurt in 1851; the second during his long absence from Berlin in 1877. When Bismarck went as Prussian representative to the Frankfurt diet, he was a 'reactionary', as he had been consistently since he entered serious politics in 1847. He wanted to suppress the revolution by force, indeed to resist every liberal idea. His foreign policy rested on a devout belief in the Holy Alliance; and he regarded it as his practical task to build up again Prussia's alliance with Austria. We cannot say what experience shook his faith in conservatism—perhaps it was no experience in particular. But within a few months, even a few weeks, of arriving in Frankfurt, he changed course. He abandoned resistance and went instead with 'the current of the times'—meaning no doubt to master and control it, but steering with events instead of against them all the same. He advocated conflict with Austria, sought alliance with revolutionary France, even with German nationalism.

Every step which Bismarck took for the next twenty-six years followed logically from this conversion of 1851. The champion of Olomouc co-operated with Hungarian revolutionaries, German radicals, and national Italy; the 'pure Prussian' unified Germany; the former reactionary gave her a liberal constitution, based on universal suffrage. The line did not change with the establishment of the Empire. Far from defending the old order, Bismarck took the modern ideas of others and gave them practical form— in codes of laws or in economic and social policy. Germany under his guidance became a *Rechtstaat*, fought the Roman Catholic church, and went over to Free Trade. He was too great, too domineering, too skilful, to be controlled by a parliamentary majority; but it began to look as though a liberal majority would control the government when he went. *Laissez-faire* ruled in foreign affairs as at home. Bismarck made alliances solely as the prelude to wars; and he made wars to settle immediate practical dangers. He assumed until 1878 that the balance would work itself once it had been set right by his wars against Austria and France; and he relied, like any liberal statesman, on the natural community of interests between states to give Germany peace and security. Bismarck's foreign policy between 1871 and 1878 was indistinguishable from Gladstone's between 1868 and 1874. Both avoided alliances and kept their hands free; giving offence to none, they both assumed that no one would give offence to them.

It was difficult to say between 1871 and 1877 whether Bismarck or the National Liberals determined the character of German policy. Certainly the Liberals owed part of their strength to the fact that Bismarck favoured them. But equally Bismarck got his way because they supported him. At the beginning of 1877 this alliance still seemed secure. A general election returned the National Liberals in undiminished number. The Centre was unshaken, and there were a few more Social Democrats; but the National Liberals and the loyal Conservatives still provided a secure Bismarckian majority. The campaign against the Roman Church was still being pursued; Free Trade had been reached; Bismarck made no attempt to go over to an active foreign policy despite the growing clouds in the Near East. His alliance with the National Liberals seemed to be on the point of growing even closer. He invited Bennigsen, the National Liberal leader, to Varzin and offered him the post of Prussian minister of the interior. This would have been a dramatic step—the first time that a parliamentarian had joined the government. Bennigsen was willing. He only stipulated that two other National Liberals should join the Prussian government at the same time. Bismarck raised no objection. He foresaw difficulties from the emperor, but expected as usual to overcome them. The two men met again in December. Bennigsen repeated his condition; Bismarck left it unanswered. The National Liberal leaders began to practise their manners as Prussian ministers.

The negotiations ended with explosive violence when the Reichstag met in February 1878. Camphausen, the Prussian minister of finance, proposed a tax on tobacco, but added that this was not the prelude to a tobacco-monopoly, which the National Liberals opposed on general economic principles. Bismarck rose from the chancellor's seat and

announced: 'I am working for the monopoly and accept
the proposal in this sense as a first step.' It was the moment
of decision. Bennigsen broke off the negotiations with Bismarck, and the National Liberals ceased to co-operate
with the government. What had happened? The tobacco-
monopoly was a symbol, though no trivial one—it was the
weapon of centralized governments both in Austria and in
France. Bismarck described it as 'the feather which suddenly turns the scales'; and the scales certainly turned
against liberalism, towards a wider, more constructive
conservatism than any known before. Even the negotiations
with Bennigsen may have been a preparation for this.
Bennigsen certainly intended to make Bismarck the
prisoner of parliamentary government; perhaps Bismarck
intended to make Bennigsen a prisoner of a different sort.
He often suggested that parties should take the helm in
order to carry out the policy which they opposed and
held up the example, which he claimed with some exaggeration to have found in England: 'If reactionary measures
are to be carried, the Liberal party takes the rudder, from
the correct assumption that it will not overstep the necessary limits; if liberal measures are to be carried, the
Conservative party takes office in its turn from the same
consideration.'

It would be foolish to suggest that Bismarck's breach
with the National Liberals was a personal whim. Old-
fashioned liberalism was dying everywhere. It ended in
Italy in 1876, in Austria in 1879. Gladstone was so conscious of its being played out that he resigned from the
leadership of the British Liberal party after the general
election of 1874. Legal and administrative reform was
exhausted; social improvement would take its place.
Bismarck declared: 'Political parties and groups based on
high policy and political programmes are finished. The
parties will be compelled to concern themselves with
economic questions and to follow a policy of interests. . . .
They will melt like ice and snow. Voters with the same
interests will co-operate and will prefer to be represented

6

by people of their own instead of believing that the best
orators are also the most skilful and most loyal representatives of their interests.' In the same spirit he told the
Prussian ministers that he wanted to see 'moderate
Conservatives who would offer the people material benefits
in place of those who thought only of formal guarantees.'
No doubt he wished to defend his independent power from
the encroachment of the National Liberal party; no doubt
he was alarmed at the rise of the Social Democrats; and
no doubt the effects of Free Trade heightened his general
turn against *Laissez-faire*. But his concern for social welfare
was genuine and of long standing. He had defended
Silesian weavers against their employers in 1865; he always
avowed his belief in 'the right to work'—the most revolutionary demand of 1848; and he wrote as early as 1871:
'The action of the state is the only means of arresting the
Socialist movement. We must carry out what seems justified in the Socialist programme and can be realized within
the present framework of state and society.' He apologized
in 1872 to an academic advocate of social welfare: 'I too
am a Socialist, but I cannot fight two campaigns at the
same time.' There was nothing surprising or unprincipled
in his breach with the National Liberals. The surprise was
rather that it had been so long delayed.

There were other factors, some of a more temporary
nature. He had already proposed an exceptional law against
Social Democratic propagandists in 1875; he was anxious
to renew this proposal in the Reichstag session of 1878,
and knew that he must quarrel with the National Liberals
over this, if over nothing else. There seems to have been
no urgent cause for his anxiety. Indeed the 'social peril' was
rather a spectre which Bismarck raised against the
National Liberals than one which disturbed his own sleep—
but of course he always took care to experience genuine
alarm at the ghosts with which he frightened others. One
of his greatest gifts was to believe in his own spooks and
legends so long as these suited his purpose. On the other
hand, he cared less about the conflict with the Roman

church. It had been going on too long; and Bismarck no more favoured siege-operations against the Roman Catholics than against Paris in 1870. Quick victories, followed by reconciliation, were always his ideal; and, as a first step, he was already propagating the legend that the *Kulturkampf* was none of his doing. It was a bit of luck for this legend that he had been temporarily out of office as Prussian prime minister just when the 'May-laws' were passed in 1873; and he impudently claimed that he had been too busy to read them. Roon was indignant at this excuse; and even Bismarck contradicted it in private: 'I carried on the struggle against the papal claims more energetically than any of my colleagues, including Falk [the minister actually responsible for the May-laws].' The legend did as a starting-point when a prospect of agreement showed itself. And this happened in 1878. Pius IX died. Leo XIII, his conciliatory and worldly-wise successor, was elected two days before Bismarck took the tobacco-monopoly under his wing in the Reichstag. Though he could not foresee all Leo's moderation and diplomatic skill, he already had in his pocket a letter to William I from the new pope, hoping for an improvement in relations. It would make it easier for Bismarck to end the *Kulturkampf* if he quarrelled with the National Liberals and posed as a Conservative. And, to put it the other way round, he could shake himself free of the National Liberals if he ended the *Kulturkampf*. Apart from these tactical considerations, the Centre, as the party of the small man, favoured social welfare; it was, in fact, a perfect 'interest-group' such as Bismarck now advocated. And as the champion of dogmatic Christianity, it might also favour legal measures against the Marxists—at any rate it had no objections of liberal principle.

Bismarck always loved to balance. He never committed himself irrevocably to any course. In foreign policy his alliances often led to wars; and his wars were the prelude to alliances. Alliance with Austria in 1864 led to war against her in 1866; and that war produced in time the

alliance with Austria-Hungary in 1879. That alliance in
its turn might have been broken if he had remained
longer in power. The near-alliance with France of 1866
was followed by the war of 1870; and it was not Bismarck's
fault that the war did not lead to a renewed alliance in 1877
or later between 1883 and 1885—with again a new period of
hostility in 1886. Italy was the only ally with whom he did
not go to war; and that was merely from lack of opportunity—his phrases were often hostile enough. It was the
same in home affairs. Bismarck straddled between king
and parliament, later between emperor and Reichstag,
and played them off against each other. He was always
ready to tell the Reichstag that his only responsibility was
to the emperor—'my only constituent'; and he warned
the politicians that they could not even cut his salary—
it was guaranteed by the constitution, and he would go to
law for it. Things were very different when he went to
court. Then he insisted that the emperor must agree to the
Reichstag's wishes, whatever Bismarck interpreted them
to be.

Bismarck had an easy time with the Reichstag between
1871 and 1878, a difficult time with the emperor. The old
gentleman did not like the successive doses of liberalism,
and still less the measures against the Roman church.
Bismarck spoke of William with increasing contempt.
'The emperor does not smoke, reads no newspapers, only
documents and dispatches; it would be more useful if he
played patience.' He described William to the palace
gardener as 'an officer who does his duty, well-mannered
with ladies'; and on another occasion said that William
was 'cold, hard as a stone'. He made no secret of his feelings: 'I took office with a great fund of royalist sentiments,
and veneration for the king; to my sorrow I find this fund
more and more depleted.' His special grievance was that
William listened to the empress when his back was turned,
and that she always opposed him: 'Either marriage or
monarchy; both together are impossible!' His weapon
against the emperor was the threat to resign; and he used

it repeatedly in these years—in 1869, twice in 1874, in May 1875, in April 1877. Though his excuse on each occasion was the state of his health—once he even threatened to go mad like Frederick William IV—the real reason was always that William I had criticized or opposed him. It is significant that at this time he never threatened the Reichstag. Each Reichstag ran its full course; and there were regular elections in 1871, 1874, 1877.

Now he decided to play things the other way. There was only one more threat of resignation—in September 1879, and that was for a special purpose. Its object was to force on William I the alliance with Austria-Hungary, not some legislative programme. After September 1879, the threat was never repeated. On the other hand the Reichstag was ceaselessly bludgeoned. There were forced elections in 1878 and 1886. Bismarck considered more extreme measures. In 1878 he proposed 'a legal *coup d'état*'. The princes, who had made the empire, should be summoned and should suspend parliamentary government. In 1881 on the eve of a general election, he again proposed that the Reichstag should be abolished; and in 1884, at the next general election, he wanted to return to open voting. His swing to conservatism made it easier for him to get on with the emperor, though it would be an exaggeration to say that their relations were ever perfect or that Augusta ever ceased to criticize him. There was a more important consideration. William I was now over eighty— he had been born in 1797. He could not last much longer. His successor, the Crown Prince Frederick, was liberal in outlook, though not always in practice. Bismarck had needed a liberal Reichstag so long as he was faced with a conservative emperor. He began to prepare a Reichstag of conservatives and clericals when a liberal emperor was in the offing. Still, this was not urgent. In 1877 William seemed as fit as ever. Bismarck got the final push to his change of course from the two attempts to assassinate William in 1878—the second of which he seemed unlikely to survive. Perhaps Bismarck would have remained longer on the liberal side if he could have foreseen that the emperor would live another ten years.

It is impossible to say which of these factors was decisive. Even Bismarck did not pretend to know which feather turned the scale. He often gave the impression that personal resentments determined his actions; but they did so only when they fitted in with the needs of more general policy. He would have swallowed his dislike of the National Liberals and his apprehensions of the crown prince, if Pius IX had remained as pope; he would not have been reconciled with the Centre, if he had not wanted to carry protective tariffs; he would have postponed social welfare, if he had not been alarmed at the increase of the Socialist vote; and he felt this alarm principally because he wanted a rallying cry at a new general election. Accidents, such as the election of Leo XIII or the attempted assassination of William I, were simply the signal for Bismarck to do what he had long decided to do; yet he might not have done it without them. He would certainly have done these things at some time, though perhaps not in that order. He was again bored, as he had confessed to being in 1874. It was a contradiction of his nature that he aimed always at peace and security and then was discontented when he got them. He said in 1877: 'I have been hunting since daybreak; it is late, I am tired, and I will leave it to others to shoot at hares and partridges. But if you have seen the slot of a wild boar, that is another story.' The wild boar in Bismarck's life could only be the chance to turn upside down everything which he had accomplished and to set out on new tasks.

A piece is missing in this jigsaw puzzle, though the fact that it completes the picture does not necessarily make it more important than the others. An upheaval in foreign policy as well as in home affairs followed Bismarck's return to Berlin in February 1878; and probably one could not have happened without the other. The upheaval in this case was certainly not of Bismarck's making. In his great formative years he had welcomed quarrels between other

Powers, so that Prussia could herself make easy gains. He had wanted to exploit the Crimean war; he had reaped enormous advantage from Austria's difficulties in Italy; and it had been a great misfortune for him that the Eastern question had remained obstinately quiet before 1866. But once Germany was satisfied, he wanted every other Power to be peaceful too. The nearest he came to activity in foreign policy after 1871 was to keep Russia and Austria-Hungary on friendly terms. But he could not dictate to the subjects of Turkey in the Balkans. There was a rising in Bosnia in 1875; and a worse rising in 1876 which provoked the Turks to the Bulgarian horrors. Russian opinion was outraged by the sufferings of the fellow-Slavs; the Habsburg monarchy was concerned to preserve another 'ramshackle empire'. Bismarck cared nothing for the Eastern question one way or the other. When Gorchakov urged that this was not a German or a Russian, but a European question, he replied: 'I have always found the word Europe on the lips of those politicians who wanted something from other Powers which they dared not demand in their own names.' Of course, he added, 'as Christians we ought to have sympathy for suffering humanity everywhere and especially for suffering Christians in foreign lands.' But this sympathy did not oblige him to risk 'Germany's power, her peace and her European relations'.

In December 1876 Bismarck first used a famous phrase that he often repeated later. Germany, he said, had no interest in the Eastern question 'that was worth the healthy bones of a Pomeranian musketeer'.[1] The phrase was more revealing than he perhaps intended. In his more expansive moments, he would show sympathy for Austria's 'German mission' down the Danube and in south-eastern Europe, just as he once called Trieste (an Austrian port) 'Germany's outlet on the southern seas'. But when he wanted to define Germany, it was Pomerania on the Baltic, not the Rhine-

[1] The more familiar grenadier took the musketeer's place in a speech of 1888.

land, Bavaria, or Austria which came into his mind. And certainly, Pomerania was remote from the Eastern question, however much this affected the German communities of Transylvania, Constantinople, or Salonica. The other Great Powers had vital interests in the Near East. Bismarck's Germany stood aloof, as though in a different continent.

Bismarck tried, therefore, to adopt an attitude of amicable detachment during the discussions which went on between Russia and Austria-Hungary. He despised the Turks with a true Lutheran contempt; and he believed, as in other cases, that a partition of the Balkans on national lines would be the safest and most sensible solution. But since his two friends could not agree on this, he joined with them in advocating futile programmes of reform. He welcomed Andrássy's initiative in recommending reforms for the Ottoman empire in December 1875; and when these failed, he invited Andrássy and Gorchakov to Berlin in May 1876 for a further effort. England and France were excluded from the Berlin meeting but not from malice or monarchical prejudice. Bismarck took trouble over Russia and Austria-Hungary solely because they seemed the two likely to quarrel. Nor did he insist on being a party to their agreements so long as they agreed. In July 1876 Gorchakov and Andrássy met at Reichstadt and agreed, or so they thought, on what they would tolerate in the Balkans, if the Ottoman empire collapsed. Unfortunately it failed to do so. Quite the reverse, the Turks suppressed the risings and defeated the semi-independent Slav state of Serbia. Pan-Slav enthusiasm in Russia could no longer be restrained. The tsar was captured by it and resolved on war against Turkey. But the example of the Crimean war made him hesitate. Gorchakov was always insisting that Russia must not fall again into the isolation that had then led to disaster.

Alexander II, free at Livadia from Gorchakov's control, thought that he would pull off a great stroke on his own. He would invoke the traditional friendship between Russia and

Prussia and would ask William I to keep Austria-Hungary neutral by threats as he now genuinely imagined that Russia had done in 1870. It was a typical bit of old-style diplomacy between crowned heads that might have once worked. Now Bismarck stood in the way, even though Gorchakov might be evaded. Alexander II made his inquiry of William I in October 1876. The old German emperor had long lost all independence of action in foreign affairs. Bismarck snatched the question out of the monarchs' hands. He replied to Gorchakov, not to Alexander: Germany was friendly to both Russia and Austria-Hungary, and she could not allow 'any of the factors on which she counted in the Balance of Power to fall out of it'. There was nothing new in this answer—it was no different from the line that Prussia had taken during the Crimean war, though then to brush off Austrian, not Russian, demands for support. It was not an 'option' for Austria-Hungary; it was a refusal to take sides, a hope that the balance would still work of itself. Gorchakov was not surprised or offended; more probably, he welcomed the snub to Alexander II's amateur diplomacy. He knew that Russia could not go to war against Turkey without the permission of Austria-Hungary; and he obtained this permission in a convention negotiated at Budapest in January 1877.

One new question was raised in Bismarck's answer, though not with much serious purpose. He suggested that Germany might support Russia if she received in return a Russian guarantee of Alsace and Lorraine. A little later he took a similar line with the British government, which was preparing to resist Russia for the sake of the Ottoman empire; an Anglo-German alliance against Russia was possible only if it was also directed against France. Bismarck knew perfectly well that neither Russia nor Great Britain would commit themselves in this way. Both courted France—the Russians to prevent 'the Crimean coalition', the British to resurrect it. Nor did Bismarck want their support—war against France was far from his thoughts, and he could not bind the future. Gorchakov said truly:

6*

'This guarantee would be of little use to you, treaties have
very little value nowadays.' Bismarck's answer was a
friendly evasion, no more, and was so accepted by all
parties. A myth grew up later, encouraged by Bismarck,
that in October 1876 he had offered to go with Russia
'through thick and thin' and that decisive estrangement
followed Russia's refusal. In fact, Bismarck had simply
kept out of the Eastern question, as his predecessors had
done before him. Russia bought Austria-Hungary's neutrality; went to war with Turkey in April 1877; and was
bitterly engaged throughout the year. Bismarck at Varzin
and Friedrichsruh ignored foreign affairs and brooded on
his domestic problems.

The Eastern question took a new turn in February 1878.
The Russians had defeated Turkey; their troops were at the
gates of Constantinople. The British government determined to preserve the remains of the Ottoman empire. The
British fleet passed the Straits. War between Russia and
Great Britain seemed imminent—a war in which Austria-
Hungary was likely to be involved. Bismarck decided that
he could no longer stand aside. He was indifferent to the
fate of the Balkans; he could not be indifferent to the
Balance of Power. Germany had nothing to gain from a
general war, and much to lose; therefore she must act as
peace-maker. On 19 February Bismarck announced in the
Reichstag that Germany came forward not as arbitrator
but 'as an honest broker'. Bleichroeder, Bismarck's man of
business, commented: 'There are no honest brokers.' But
in this case Bismarck was really concerned to settle the
affair, not to earn a percentage. His action, far from being
hostile to Russia, helped to save her from a disastrous war.
The Russians imposed the treaty of San Stefano on the
Turkish empire in March. Then, urged on partly by Bismarck's mediation but more by their own fear and weakness, they agreed to submit the treaty to a European
congress. Bismarck tried to dodge further responsibility.
He suggested that the congress should meet in Paris; and
when this was rejected, offered the chairmanship of the

congress to Waddington, the French representative. Bismarck's efforts were in vain. He had made Berlin the capital of Germany, and Germany the centre of Europe. Now he had to pay the price for his success.

By the spring of 1878 Bismarck had cast off from his old moorings. He was not yet running with full sails before a fresh wind. Doubtful of the old course, he could not yet see the new. The first storm signals of February 1878 were followed by some months of calm. At home, the alarm over the tobacco-monopoly was forgotten—the monopoly never in fact achieved. The National Liberals continued to assume that they were Bismarck's allies, even though he had not admitted them to the government. At most they thought to make him more amenable by a little harmless obstruction. Bismarck, on his side, found reconciliation with the Roman Catholic Centre more difficult than he had at first supposed on the death of Pius IX. Leo XIII was a match even for Bismarck. Though he wanted a settlement, he was prepared to wait for it. In April he demanded the repeal of the May-laws and the restoration of the legal privileges which the Roman church had enjoyed in Germany, before he would advise the Centre to compromise itself politically. These were terms of unconditional surrender; and Bismarck would not 'go to Canossa' even for the sake of protective tariffs and social welfare. He broke off negotiations with Leo XIII and waited in his turn. In foreign affairs equally, Bismarck did not admit that a new era had begun. The approaching congress was a nuisance; but he still imagined that it would settle the differences between the Great Powers and that the natural order of peace and security would then reassert itself. He had some thought of a grandiose initiative, proposing a partition of the Ottoman empire—Egypt to England, Bulgaria to Russia, Bosnia to Austria-Hungary, Tunis or Syria to France. But even this was far from a policy of permanent alliances. Foreign affairs in his eyes were something that could be dealt with and finished, a book to be closed. In April he retired again to Friedrichsruh.

Two unforeseeable accidents pushed him again into action. On 11 May a crazy youth attempted, ineffectively, to assassinate the emperor. Bismarck at once answered by laying before the Reichstag the 'exceptional law' against the Social Democrats which he had failed to carry in 1875. He was not concerned with public order—the police themselves did not want the law. His object was to ruin the National Liberals. They still had liberal principles, though they supported Bismarck's legislative programme; and some of them at any rate would oppose exceptional measures against the Socialists. On the other hand, refusal to take an anti-Socialist line would estrange their respectable voters. When it came to a vote in the Reichstag, the National Liberal party stuck unitedly to liberalism. Indeed, every party except the Conservatives voted against the exceptional law on 24 May. Bismarck, who had remained quietly at Friedrichsruh, affected to treat the bill as solely the work of his ministerial colleagues; and merely remarked that they were unfortunate in their dealings with the Reichstag.

Then came a further accident, so providential for Bismarck that he might almost have arranged it. On 2 June another crazy anarchist shot at William I, and this time wounded him severely. When the news reached Bismarck, he exclaimed: 'Now we'll dissolve the Reichstag!' He did not stop to inquire whether the criminal was a Social Democrat. He almost forgot to ask about the Emperor's condition. He saw decision and victory before him, as he had seen it on 13 July 1870, when his pencil remodelled the telegram from Ems. By a curious irony, William I not only survived the attempted assassination, but benefited from it. The shock acted as a stimulus to his aged frame and freed him from the fainting fits which previously afflicted him. He often said truly in the following years: 'Nobiling [the assassin] was the best physician I ever had!'

Bismarck often emphasized in later years that 2 June 1878 had marked for him the beginning of a new course, though he was less frank about its meaning. He said in

1882: 'I thought in 1877 that I was entitled to resign. But after I had seen my lord and king lying in his blood, I felt that I could never desert this lord, who had sacrificed body and life for his duty to God and men, against his will.' The picture is less moving when one reflects that Bismarck did not see 'his lord and king' for nearly a week after the attempt. By then William was out of danger, and the political consequences were well in train. Bismarck gave a rather different version in private. 'Now I've got the scoundrels!'—'Your Highness means the Social Democrats?'—'No, the National Liberals'—and it was a matter of indifference to him that most National Liberals, after the second attempted assassination, supported the exceptional law. The Reichstag was dissolved without being given a chance to reverse its previous decision. The important thing for Bismarck was not to pass the exceptional law, but to impress the electors. Previously he had waited for the results of general elections and then made the best of them; now he tried to dominate the electoral campaign.

He did this in a curious way—by his absence. Western democracies expect the political leader, whether president or prime minister, to be the centre of public agitation. General elections are themselves a form of running debate. But Bismarck never argued or took part in the cut-and-thrust of debate. He rhapsodized in the Reichstag, standing ostensibly above the parties; and he would slip into his speeches some general philosophic reflection from which the voters were expected to divine the correct party-moral. Once an election began, he alone of all Germans was condemned to silence. Every politician had a platform, literally and metaphorically. Bismarck had none. He never identified himself with a party or laid down a precise programme; he never addressed a public meeting until after his fall. A tongue-tied leader of a country with universal suffrage seems strange, though not so strange then as now. In every constitutional country, but particularly in Germany, the deputies were supposed to be 'independent' of the government, both in policy and in origin. Even British members of parliament made out that they followed the dictates of the party-whip purely by accident. The electors also were expected to reason things out for themselves. Bribery had ended; mob oratory by respectable politicians had not begun. No British prime minister, or even former prime minister, addressed a public meeting until Gladstone broke the ban over 'the Bulgarian horrors'. Bismarck was not likely to follow this example. He knew that he could be talked down, and therefore appealed from words to facts. From 1878 onwards he always started the election campaign with some explosion which, he hoped, would muffle the oratory of the politicians. 'The social peril' which he invoked after the attempted assassination of the Emperor on 2 June was his first experiment in this method. It was meant to ensure that the voters would lose their heads and hence the use of their ears.

Bismarck used one weapon to influence public opinion which brought down on him much high-minded disapproval. He issued directives to the press and employed his own men, Busch and Bucher, to write leading articles which were then widely distributed. More than this, he drew on the sequestered funds of the ex-King of Hanover to bribe the press directly. This was the 'reptile fund' which received as much notoriety in Bismarckian Germany as the secret service fund had done in eighteenth-century England. The parallel supplies a useful warning. Our historians now regard the secret service fund as more of a myth than a reality; and the 'reptile fund' was much the same. Newspapers with a wide circulation, solidly buttressed by advertisements, did not need subsidies, as *The Times* was the first to discover. Newspapers with a small circulation needed financial support either from private persons or from the government; and most German papers were still in this condition. Why should Bismarck alone be without a journalistic voice? As a matter of fact, the 'reptile fund' was used mainly as the secret service money had been—to do things that were better not talked about. Elderly servants of the state were saved from penury; the indiscreet from the penalty of their mistakes. Of course, Bismarck—like Walpole or the Duke of Newcastle—expected loyalty in return for his financial assistance; but, like them, he was often disappointed.

The Reichstag was dissolved on 11 June, much against the will of Crown Prince Frederick, who was acting as his father's representative[1] and who foresaw the ruin of his liberal friends. Bismarck sent out instructions to all government officials, much after the fashion of eighteenth-century England: the object of the election was to split the National Liberal party, and it was to be fought with the two cries of the social peril and tariff reform. Once this circular had been dispatched, there was little more that Bismarck could do. A general election was for him a time of leisure, not of political activity; and he conveniently fitted the congress of Berlin in before the poll on 30 July. The congress was a grandiose episode in Bismarck's life rather than a vital event in his policy. It still sprang from the hope that all international rivalries between the Powers could be finally settled and that foreign affairs would then look after themselves. It was the last great effort of *laissez-faire* in foreign politics, not the prelude to a more conscious system. Indeed, it was mainly significant, so far as Bismarck was concerned, for what it left out, not for what it discussed or settled. Statesmen of the earlier nineteenth century, or even Napoleon III, would have been astonished at a European congress where the questions of Poland, Germany, and Italy were not mentioned. All these questions had received an answer in previous years, largely according to Bismarck's wishes, but without any intervention by the Concert of Europe. The Congress of Berlin dealt only with the Eastern question, and even with that in a limited sense —the French made their attendance conditional on the exclusion of Syria, Egypt, and North Africa from the

[1] In 1857 Bismarck had urged Prince William to revolt against being merely his brother's representative and to insist on becoming regent. In 1878 Bismarck silenced the crown prince's claim to the regency by an imperial Order which the emperor had been too weak to sign.

agenda, and Bismarck seconded them. The European order which Bismarck had created did not receive even formal approval. It rested, and continued to rest, on German strength, not on the agreement of the Great Powers.

The congress of Berlin confined itself to the settlement of the Balkans and its task was little more than to register the private agreements which had already been reached between Russia and England and between Russia and Austria-Hungary. In fact, Bismarck regarded the congress as a device for saving the face of the Russians. They could make to European opinion the concessions which would seem humiliating if made to British and Austro-Hungarian threats. Bismarck tried to win Russian favour by taking their side over the details which remained in dispute. But this did not satisfy them. He hoped to please the Russians by mitigating the effects of their defeat; they thought that he ought to have prevented the defeat itself. Their grievance was justified. It would have been small consolation to Bismarck in 1866 or 1870 if the Great Powers had intervened to impose a settlement and if Russia had then thrown to Prussia a few trivial concessions. He had settled with Austria and France in isolation; and this is what the Russians had wanted to do with Turkey. No polite phrases could conceal the fact that they had failed to repeat Bismarck's success, though more from their own blunders than from any maliciousness of his.

The congress was a show-piece for Bismarck's personality. It was the only international gathering over which he presided; and no one ever presided in the same manner. He gave the great statesmen of Europe a taste of the rough jovial manner with which he entertained German politicians at his 'beer-evenings'. He even appeared at the early sessions in a beard, and shaved it off only for the composite portrait which concluded the congress. The exuberant joy with which he disregarded aristocratic conventions revealed his nature—half-country squire, half-revolutionary. He bustled through the formal sessions,

commenting audibly if the Turkish delegate or even Lord
Salisbury dared to raise a new point, and scribbling during
Gorchakov's opening speech: 'pompos, pompo, pomp, po'.
Protocol was ignored; everything subordinated to punctual
and enormous meals. Bismarck was to be seen, stuffing
shrimps into his mouth with one hand, cherries with the
other, and insisting—not surprisingly—that he must leave
soon for a cure at Kissingen. Any real difficulty was settled
by Bismarck privately behind the scenes, and to great
effect. Gorchakov, who could remember the congresses of
Ljubljana and Verona, was horrified at this brusque
procedure. But the congress was a model for all time in its
way of doing business and reaching results, even if less in
the results themselves. Bismarck was not interested in
these or in the fate of 'the people down there'. 'We are not
here to consider the happiness of the Bulgarians but to
secure the peace of Europe.' He wanted to get everything
settled and to start getting his weight down at Kissingen.

Bismarck had often met Gorchakov and Andrássy
before. He was now on cold terms with Gorchakov, whom
he found vain and senile; and he did not care for Andrássy's
grand Magyar ways. Nor, despite political courtesy, did he
find any common ground with Waddington, the French
delegate—a man distinguished as the only prime minister
(French or British) to row in the university boat-race.
Bismarck at this time disliked Salisbury, the second British
delegate, whom he described as 'a lay preacher' and as
'wood painted to look like iron'. Perhaps Bismarck sensed
that Salisbury had gone one better than himself and that
he could combine equal cynicism in policy with a genuine
moral earnestness. Bismarck estranged the ethically-
minded politicians of the time when he appealed to 'blood
and iron'. Salisbury could rest his policy on 'the right of
conquest because it is the simplest and most effective' and
yet retain the admiration of English Nonconformists—
even of Gladstone.

The real hit of the congress was the personal tie between
Bismarck and Beaconsfield. No doubt Bismarck flattered

'the old Jew' in order to extract concessions for Russia's benefit. But the mutual affection was genuine. The two men recognized their common qualities. When they had last met in 1862, Disraeli was the struggling leader of the Conservative opposition, Bismarck merely Prussian minister at Paris. Now both had arrived. Bismarck was a prince Disraeli was Lord Beaconsfield and soon to receive the Garter. Each admired the actor in the other, and characteristically each noted the beauty of the other's voice. Both had the brooding melancholy of the Romantic movement in its Byronic phase; both had broken into the charmed circle of privilege—Bismarck as a boorish Junker, Disraeli as a Jew; both had a profound contempt for political moralizing. Was it Disraeli or Bismarck who said of himself: 'My temperament is dreamy and sentimental. People who paint me all make the mistake of giving me a violent expression'? Was it Disraeli or Bismarck who said on becoming prime minister: 'Well, I've climbed to the top of the greasy pole'? In politics both men had used universal suffrage to ruin liberalism or, in the English phrase, 'to dish the Whigs'. Both genuinely advocated social reform; Disraeli had once defended protective tariffs. Both used foreign success to strengthen their position at home. When Bismarck was told of the British occupation of Cyprus, he exclaimed: 'This is progress! It will be popular: a nation loves progress!' Beaconsfield was annoyed at having the words taken out of his mouth and commented sourly: 'His idea of progress obviously consists in taking something from somebody else'—an idea which Beaconsfield had made the basis of Tory policy. When they dined together Bismarck played for sympathy in his usual manner by abusing others and told Beaconsfield: 'Don't imagine that my illness is the result of the French war; its cause is the horrible conduct of my king.' Beaconsfield was a match for him: 'I have not seen any of this two-facedness in the monarch whom I serve; she is frank and upright, and all her ministers love her.' At least this is the reply which he recorded for the benefit of Queen Victoria. The conversa-

tion has an added piquancy from its date. It took place on
17 June, barely a fortnight after Bismarck had seen
William I weltering in his blood (at any rate in imagination)
and when the German election campaign was ringing with
the cry of monarchical loyalty.

The congress ended on 13 July, settling the Eastern crisis,
though not the Eastern question. Bismarck went off to
Kissingen, where the waters failed to counteract the effects
of his gluttony. He had there a further failure. He met the
papal nuncio from Munich and tried again to strike a
bargain. The pope should order the Centre to support
Bismarck; then the Imperial government would gradually
cease to apply the May-laws. Leo XIII, though conciliatory,
was still obdurate: he insisted on the ending of the *Kulturkampf* before he would intervene in German politics. After
this Bismarck could not be altogether content with the
results of the general election on 30 July. The National
Liberals were certainly weakened, losing some thirty seats;
and their successful candidates were all pledged to support
the anti-Socialist law. The two Conservative groups (one
loyal to Bismarck, one more independent) took the place
of the National Liberals as the strongest single party. But
the *Reichsfeinde*, the enemies of the Empire, were unshaken: the Social Democrats lost only three out of twelve
seats, the Centre came back stronger than before. Bismarck's impulsiveness had, as so often, rebounded against
himself. Disillusioned with liberal policy, perhaps irritated
at the liberal claims to office, he had set out to ruin the
National Liberal party; and he had succeeded—the party
was weakened and soon split. But this success did Bismarck
little good. The mass-electorate turned against liberalism,
as Bismarck told them to, but they did not turn towards
conservatism. They voted in increasing numbers for the
two mass-parties, the Socialists and the clericals. Bismarck
realized too late that liberalism was a barrier against the
two causes that he feared, though also a barrier against
himself.

Bismarck resurrected his alliance with the National

Liberals when the Reichstag met in the autumn, if only as a temporary expedient. He described the National Liberals and the two Conservative factions as 'regiments of one and the same garrison'; and this garrison gave him his anti-Socialist law—though on National Liberal insistence only for three years. The renewal of the law at triennial intervals gave Bismarck a further problem to add to the septennial crisis over the army-law—and the problem finally brought about his downfall in 1890. He was angry at this compromise which had been forced upon him and again determined to escape from National Liberal control or interference. Tactics might force him on to their side; fundamentally he hated a party which rested, however feebly, on principle instead of on material interest. He gave a sign that the breach with them would soon be renewed. The National Liberals were still hoping for a parliamentary ministry. Bismarck now promoted a law, by which the Imperial secretaries of state (hitherto merely administrative subordinates) could act as 'substitutes' for the chancellor. The secretaries were made Prussian ministers without portfolio and were thus qualified as the Prussian representatives at the Imperial Council. But the chancellor remained the sole 'responsible' minister for Germany. Bismarck continued to insist that cabinet or committee government was impossible in Germany. He never gave any reason; and indeed the only reason was that he could not stomach colleagues. Imperial Germany continued to be ruled by one man—a man who was sometimes restrained or obstructed, but never controlled, by parliament. There was another curious point. Though there were now secretaries of state for foreign affairs, for the navy, for justice, for finance, later for the colonies, there was no secretary for the army. That remained the exclusive concern of the emperor and of the chief-of-staff—an arrangement which Bismarck, considering his open hostility to the generals, tolerated rather than welcomed.

The last step in Bismarck's change of course came during the winter of 1878–79. It was a masterstroke of improvisation. His projected time-table since the death of Pius IX had clearly been, first to end the *Kulturkampf*, then to carry protective tariffs with the support of the Centre. This had not worked out: the *Kulturkampf* had not been ended. But in October 1878 the Centre came out in favour of protective tariffs. At once Bismarck reversed his order of tactics. He would first propose fiscal reform and thus compel the Centre to support him, even before the *Kulturkampf* had been brought to an end. The new economic order in Germany was Bismarck's own work as much as the legal and constitutional order had been. He studied political economy, saying: 'I am ashamed to understand so little of this subject', and drafted all the principal tariffs. Having once abandoned Free Trade, he now wanted thorough-going Protection, and stirred the sectional interests to bid against each other. The Conservative agrarians, for instance—most of them aristocrats—agreed to the tariff on iron and steel only in exchange for a high tariff on grain. As in every auction, Bismarck the auctioneer collected his percentage. The groups were all tied to him, though hostile to each other.

This fiscal revolution produced its political effect. Bismarck's anticipations were realized. On 3 May 1879, Windthorst, the leader of the Centre, appeared at Bismarck's beer-evening, and remarked as he left: '*extra centrum nulla salus*'—'no salvation without the Centre'. Bismarck responded by attacking in the Reichstag the intellectual politicians of the National Liberal party, 'who neither sow nor reap, weave nor spin . . . these gentlemen whom our sun does not warm, whom our rain does not make wet, unless they happen to go out without an umbrella!' Bismarck always made great play with his practical activity as a cultivator of the soil. But he had gained his estates by being the most intellectual politician of his time and was no more a farmer than our present-day company directors who go in for agriculture to offset their liability to surtax. Joseph Chamberlain, the English radical, turned the same phrase—'they toil not neither do they spin'—to a more appropriate use a few years later, when he fired it against the great landed aristocracy, the class to which Bismarck now belonged. On each occasion the phrase infuriated the other side. The alliance between Bismarck and the National Liberals, which had lasted twelve years, tumbled down in a few weeks. Falk, the leading fighter of the *Kulturkampf*, resigned in July; Bennigsen soon withdrew altogether from politics; the National Liberals dissolved into fragments—one group merging with the Progressives who had opposed Bismarck since 1862; another constituting itself the mouthpiece of heavy industry; and a third drifting disconsolately in the hope that a liberal Bismarck would one day re-appear.

The Centre was caught, as Bismarck had expected: its social basis made it support protective tariffs even though the May-laws were still on the statute book. But the Centre claimed a price, though of a different sort. Bismarck had two objects in mind when he introduced tariff reform: one was to protect German industry, the other was to end the dependence of the *Reich* on the matricular contributions from the separate states. Most of the National Liberals were ready to swallow tariffs for the second reason, if not for the first; but they insisted on voting these tariffs annually, so as to strengthen the budgetary control of the Reichstag. The Centre were prepared to vote for permanent tariffs, but not for the profit of the central authority. They insisted in their turn that the yield from customs-dues, above a limited amount, should be shared out among the member-states in the same proportions as their matricular contributions. In this curious way an artificial deficit was created in the Imperial budget, which the states would be called upon to fill. Bismarck could make his choice between parliamentary liberalism and federalism. He did not hesitate a moment. Though he had often urged the Reichstag to develop its authority and had dismissed the states as contemptibly unreal, he chose the concession to federalism —perhaps for this very reason.

This financial jugglery between the *Reich* and the states completed the ruin of German liberalism. Bismarck had insisted, when the federal constitution was made, that the central authority should levy only indirect taxes—customs and excise. Direct taxation remained the prerogative of the member-states. This was perhaps reasonable so long as the new *Reich* was not expected to be any more powerful or effective than the old German confederation. It soon appeared that Bismarck's *Reich* was the real centre of power; and the National Liberals claimed that a *Reich*, which maintained the greatest army in Europe and challenged the Roman church, should also raise its own direct taxes. Protection defeated this claim. What is more, by providing further revenue for the member-states, it actually lessened their direct taxation also. The political and social consequences were profound. Indirect taxation falls equally on all members of the community, rich and poor; indeed, when a tariff on grain is included, it falls more heavily on the poor than on the rich. Direct taxation, even when not progressive, is proportioned to the means of the taxpayer; and when it is made progressively heavier, it becomes of itself an engine of social revolution. Gladstonian finance was the decisive step towards making England a social democracy, or something like it. Bismarckian finance, as it operated after 1879, made the rich richer, even if the economic expansion of Germany prevented the poor from becoming poorer. In England the rich paid the taxes and therefore worked to keep them down; in Germany the rich profited from the expenditure of the *Reich* and therefore worked to increase it. So far as men of liberal principle still existed, they entered politics in the separate states, where alone direct taxation was possible. The politicians of the *Reich* promoted the economic interests of sectional groups, and their own into the bargain. High principle disappeared; horse-trading took its place. The German Junkers were saved just when the English landowners were ruined, though they had to take the great industrialists into partnership. Bismarck had been more concerned to ruin liberalism than to save the Junkers; but he saved them all the same.

By the summer of 1879 Bismarck's change of course in home affairs was virtually complete. Protection had been established; the anti-Socialist law was in operation; he was only waiting for a favourable opportunity to compromise over the *Kulturkampf*; and social welfare was just round the corner. In September 1879 he took an equally decisive step in foreign affairs by making a defensive alliance with Austria-Hungary. The policy of detached friendships ended; and a complicated system of alliances took its place. It is hard to establish a formal, let alone a conscious, connexion between the changes in home and foreign affairs. Of course, agrarian protection in Germany was directed principally against Russian grain and therefore, perhaps, weakened the traditional sympathy between Prussian and Russian landowners. But men did not act on such simple economic motives even in the nineteenth century; and there were still many factors, from class-solidarity to anti-Polish feeling, which held Prussian and Russian nobles together. It is more to the point that abandoning Free Trade meant a shift of emphasis from the Hanseatic towns, Hamburg and Bremen, with their essentially maritime and 'little German' attitude, to the heavy industry of the Rhineland, where the traditions of the Holy Roman Empire were still strong, and where the Habsburg monarchy was still regarded as German.

The real connexion lay deeper. The changes in home and foreign affairs both sprang from Bismarck's abandonment of the liberal belief that all things would work together for good if only they were left alone. He ceased to believe that peace and prosperity were natural; he took thought for the morrow and secured them by conscious effort. Protection, as the name implied, involved the deliberate fostering of German industry and agriculture against the dictates of 'economic law'; just as the anti-Socialist laws were an attempt to direct men's thoughts. Bismarck's alliances were also a form of protection, imposing a conscious design on international relations instead of waiting upon events. He was not alone in this change of outlook. At the very moment when Bismarck was concluding an alliance with Austria-Hungary, Gladstone—greatest of liberals—left his old line of moral detachment and preached in the Midlothian speeches a creative foreign policy, based on the Concert of Europe. Bismarck and Gladstone reached no doubt very different conclusions, but they both started from the same point—the loss of faith in *laissez-faire*.

It would be easier to explain Bismarck's new foreign policy if he had not explained it so much himself. His explanations were not made for the benefit of posterity, a subject which never interested him. They were advocacy, directed to the person with whom he was arguing. William I had to be frightened by the story that Germany was in danger of immediate attack from Russia or even—being a very old man—by echoes from the Seven Years' war. More hard-headed diplomatists had to be told that Bismarck wished to revive the 'organic union' of all Germans which he had destroyed in 1866. The French were assured that his object was to prevent the dismemberment of the Habsburg monarchy—a cause in which they also were deeply interested. The British were told that the alliance would create an unbreakable barrier against Russia; the Russians that it would sever Austria-Hungary from Great Britain— 'I wanted to dig a ditch between her and the western Powers.' No doubt there was some truth in all these stories. It was part of Bismarck's strength that he always believed what he said, at any rate while he was saying it. Only one story was pure legend, created in after years. In 1870 Bismarck was taken by surprise and improvised a war at the last moment. It suited him better later on to make out that he had planned the war against France for many years. Exactly the opposite was true in 1879. He deliberately planned the alliance with Austria-Hungary; but when its consequences appeared inconvenient for him, he made out that he had been bustled into it by events. Yet even in this there is a fragment of truth. His nervous illness and his

toothache were at their worst; and he might not have acted
so swiftly and decisively if he had been in better control
of himself.

The alliance was caused by the diplomatic events which
followed the congress of Berlin rather than by the congress
itself. Bismarck had hoped that the congress would really
end the eastern crisis: it would enshrine a reasonable
compromise and save Russia from humiliation. It did this
at first so far as Russia was concerned. Her strength was
exhausted; the Russians, like most liberators, were on bad
terms with the people whom they had liberated; and they
asked only to be rid of their Balkan worries. The discontent
was on the other side. The Austro-Hungarian, and still
more the British, government now regretted the opportunity of defeating Russia of which Bismarck seemed to
have deprived them; and they tried to make up for lost
time. Their representatives in the Balkans sought not a
settlement, but to eject Russia altogether. Russia, it
seemed, would be pressed to the wall; and she would respond by the most violent expedients of diplomacy, as she
had done after the Crimean war. Then she had offered her
friendship to any Power who would help her to overthrow
the treaty-settlement, and she had made a 'revisionist'
alliance with France—an alliance which Bismarck, in his
revolutionary days, had been eager to join. Now he was
conservative, anxious to preserve the European order that
he had created. The dangers which he feared were perhaps
imaginary. Russian ambitions were turning to central Asia
and away from the Near East; the republic in France, now
consolidated, was resolutely pacific; and the statesmen at
Vienna had abandoned any hope of recovering the old
Habsburg position in Germany. But even the greatest men
cannot foresee the future; they can only expect it to repeat
the pattern of the past, and Bismarck was now warding
off the dangers that had followed the congress of Paris,
not the dangers of 1879. He had argued long ago that
Prussia should not remain isolated, should not miss her
chance: she should join the revolutionary alliance of France

and Russia. His own position being now reversed, he reversed the conclusion also and insisted on a conservative alliance with Austria-Hungary. He was determined not to repeat the former mistake. There could be no more dangerous course: what was mistaken twenty years before is often the wisest policy in the present. Great disasters are caused by trying to learn from history and to correct past mistakes. Men being what they are, it is probably better to think about the present, not about the past—or the future. As Bismarck said to Napoleon at Biarritz: 'One must not make events; one must wait for them to happen.'

Now, for whatever reason, he was determined to guard against future dangers, not present ones. The great improviser built a system against the improvisation of others. Early in 1879 he resolved on alliance with Austria-Hungary. There was no obstacle on the Austrian side. Beust had proposed an alliance as early as August 1871; Andrássy had sought German backing throughout the eastern crisis. The difficulty came from William I, as it had often done before. His aged mind was choked with sentimental attachments; and he had to be jockeyed into alliance with Austria-Hungary, as he had once been jockeyed into war against her. Russia had to be provoked; and her response seemed to justify Bismarck's precautions. The German representatives on the Balkan commissions opposed Russia instead of supporting her; irritating restrictions were put on her trade with Germany; the new tariffs played a useful part. Most provocative of all, Bismarck published an agreement by which Austria-Hungary released him from the obligation, incurred in the treaty of Prague, to hold a plebiscite in northern Sleswig.[1] The honest broker seemed to have collected his percentage after all. Alexander II was bewildered by this unaccustomed German hostility. He supposed that there must be some misunderstanding, and

[1] Actually the agreement was made on 13 April 1878, before the congress of Berlin, when Austria–Hungary was still in difficulties and had to acquiesce in any German demand. Now Bismarck antedated it only to 11 October 1878. It therefore looked like an Austrian payment for services rendered, whereas it was in fact more like buying off a blackmailer.

he tried to remove it by writing privately to William I on
15 August. Being a tsar, he expressed himself in arrogant
terms, and Bismarck professed to see in the letter a threat
of war. William I saw nothing of the kind. He was as
bewildered as Alexander II, and bustled off to see him at
Alexandrovo on 3 September. He returned, confident that
all difficulties had been removed. Bismarck behaved very
differently. He proposed a meeting with Andrássy even
before Alexander II dispatched his letter; negotiated with
Andrássy before the meeting at Alexandrovo; and went
on to Vienna, where he signed a treaty against William I's
express instructions.

There followed a battle to extract approval from the
old emperor—the last of many battles between him and
Bismarck. William I brought out all Bismarck's old arguments—the traditional friendship with Russia on which
Hohenzollern success had been based; the danger of driving
Russia into the arms of France; the repeated warnings
against 'alliances which bind our hands'. Once more he
threatened to abdicate. Bismarck answered with a torrent
of arguments on his side, but his real weapon was a threat
to resign and to carry the whole Prussian ministry with him.
The pledge never to desert his noble master had not lasted
long. William I confessed: 'Bismarck is more necessary
than I am.' Besides, the threat to abdicate was pointless;
William knew that the crown prince would favour alliance
with Austria-Hungary, however much he differed from
Bismarck in other questions. On 3 October William I gave
way: 'My whole moral strength is broken.' This was true,
and not only in regard to the Austro-German alliance.
William I never opposed Bismarck again or tried to
influence policy.

The alliance was ratified on 5 October. Formally it
contained nothing which had not been said a dozen times
before. Each ally would aid the other, if attacked by
Russia; in any other war, in which one ally was involved,
the other would remain neutral. During the negotiations
Bismarck tried to get a pledge of Austro-Hungarian aid

against France, but he gave way readily. Andrássy des-
cribes how he said threateningly: 'You must accept my
terms. If not——,' and he rose dramatically from the table:
'——then I must accept yours.' In fact, Bismarck made the
demand only to please his emperor. He was quite content
with Austro-Hungarian neutrality, and even made out
that it would undo the verdict of 1866 if a Habsburg army
again mounted guard on the Rhine. The essential part of the
treaty was Germany's pledge to support Austria-Hungary
against Russia. Bismarck had already warned Russia in
October 1876 that he would not allow an attack against
Austria-Hungary; but it was one thing to warn Russia,
quite another to give a pledge to Austria-Hungary. The
alliance did not increase German security in the least.
On the contrary it brought her nearer to war; for there
was no danger of a Russian attack on Germany except as a
consequence of the pledge to Austria-Hungary. The alliance
was a liability for Germany, not an asset. Bismarck never
explained why he thought it a necessary liability.

Bismarck rushed into the Austro-German alliance without considering the remote consequences. He was always
impulsive; and the alliance seemed a quick way of ending
the tension in the Balkans. Austria-Hungary would feel
secure; she would no longer co-operate with Great Britain;
and Russia, therefore, would escape further humiliation.
Frederick William IV had made an alliance with Austria
(against Bismarck's advice) for much the same reasons at
the outbreak of the Crimean war. Probably Bismarck
assumed that this alliance would fade away as his earlier
alliances had done. But there was a fundamental difference.
The alliance with Austria in 1864 or with Italy in 1866 had
been alliances for more or less immediate war. They ended
when the war was fought and won. The alliance of 1879 was
an alliance to prevent war and therefore endured as long as
peace lasted. Whoever tries to secure peace becomes a
system-maker, and Bismarck did not escape this despised
fate. Henceforth he was, like Metternich, a philosophic
statesman. He had to make out that the dismemberment

of the Habsburg monarchy would make Russia too powerful; or that the national principle, which he advocated
elsewhere, would not produce a stable order in eastern
Europe. These were merely rationalizations. The truth was
simpler. He had come to desire peace for its own sake. In
earlier days he would have faced the reconstruction of
eastern Europe, as he had faced the reconstruction of the
west. Now he shrank from the turmoil that this reconstruction would involve. Security and tranquillity had
become his watchwords. He had done enough reconstruct-
ing. All he wanted was a quiet life.

Once he had been ready to stake everything on fortune's
wheel. Now he tried to stop it from spinning. How contemptuous he had been of the old Prussian statesmen who
had helped to prop up 'Metternich's system'. How strenu-
ously he had warned against tying Prussia's trim, seaworthy frigate to Austria's worm-eaten galleon. Now he
did everything that he had condemned in his predecessors.
Prussia's frigate had become the great German man-of-
war: Austria's galleon was more worm-eaten by twenty-five
years. Yet Bismarck tied them together for the rest of their
existence. The alliance of 1879 only recognized existing
facts; but, by recognizing, it sought to perpetuate them.
In 1866 Bismarck failed to carry through the thorough-
going national reconstruction of Europe which he had
advocated earlier. He allowed the Habsburg monarchy to
survive. Now he went further and committed Germany to
its survival. No more events must be allowed to happen.
The keeper of the Elbe dike had resumed his old employment.

No sooner had he taken this decisive step than he tried
to belittle it. He always reacted violently against arguments
that were put before him. One of his colleagues said:
'Beware of opposing Bismarck immediately if you disagree
with him. If you do, he—being so excitable—finds such
crushing arguments for his opinion and becomes so obstinate that no power on earth can move him from it.'
William's opposition during the negotiations had made

Bismarck behave as though the alliance was the be-all and end-all of German policy. Once he had got his way, he reacted against his own tumultuous arguments; and soon became as distrustful of the Austro-Hungarian alliance as he had once been enthusiastic, until at the end of his life he was almost its only critic and opponent in Germany. The alliance was to last only for five years, though then automatically renewed unless denounced. Bismarck always refused to make it permanent and left obscure hints to his successors that they should shake it off as he had shaken off the earlier alliance with Austria in 1866. During the negotiations he had put the Pomeranian grenadier on half-pay and had declared in romantic terms: 'According to a thousand-year-old tradition the German fatherland is also to be found on the Danube, in Styria, and in Tyrol.' Once the alliance was signed, he claimed that the most important thing in it was what it left out; it asserted by a significant silence that Germany would not support Austria-Hungary in the Balkans. She would be supported against a direct Russian attack. If she wanted to pursue Balkan ambitions, she must find other allies.

What is more, he did his best to ensure that she should not find these allies. The Austrians had been opposing Russia in Bulgaria with the help of Great Britain; and they hoped to add Germany to this combination. Even Bismarck approached the British government during his negotiations with Andrássy and talked of an Anglo-German alliance. He broke off abruptly as soon as the Austro-German alliance was made; and the Austrians were soon complaining that the principal effect of the alliance, so far as they were concerned, was to thwart their Balkan policy. As early as September 1879 Bismarck was assuring a Russian emissary that Austria-Hungary was now safely under control and that Russia would meet with no further obstacles in the Near East: 'The Crimean coalition is dissolved.' He decked this out with much talk of monarchical solidarity against the 'socialist' countries of western Europe; but this was window-dressing—Bismarck could always discover sentimental ties with any country whom he happened to favour. His real aim was to perform a gigantic conjuring-trick. He would satisfy Russia by concessions in the Near East and compel Austria-Hungary to acquiesce by insisting that her security depended on the alliance with Germany, not on Balkan predominance or gains.

This might have worked if he had limited himself in 1879 to a simple declaration of policy, as he had done in October 1876 or on many previous occasions. As it was, he became the prisoner of his own act. The treaty with Austria-Hungary was the first formal alliance between two Great Powers concluded in peace-time since the outbreak of the French revolution and the end of the *ancien régime*. The Powers might have sentimental attachments, such as the so-called 'Holy Alliance'. They signed treaties of alliance only before a war or on its outbreak; and these alliances ended when the war was over. So it had been with the Anglo-French alliance of the Crimean war; the Austro-Prussian alliance in 1864; and the alliance between Prussia and Italy which preceded the war of 1866. The written alliance with Austria-Hungary which Bismarck now made set a rigid pattern which shaped international relations until the first World war. Bismarck might say that every treaty contained an unwritten clause, *rebus sic stantibus*.[1] The solemn recital of full powers and the seals ponderously affixed were among the things that remained the same. Though no treaty can bind the future, a formal treaty influences the future by its very existence. Bismarck never gave the slightest hint why he had recorded Austro-German friendship in this formal way. His haste and dogmatic insistence almost justify the conclusion that he genuinely believed in the danger of attack from Russia in August 1879. But there were surely limits even to what Bismarck could make himself believe. The explanation is presumably to be found, as on many earlier occasions, in the effect on William I. Only a formal alliance would convince the Austrians that William I had really turned

1 'So long as things remain the same.'

against Russia; and William could be turned only by talk of immediate war.

Whatever the explanation, the effect was unmistakable. The alliance with Austria-Hungary overshadowed Germany's foreign policy; and in time it even came to be felt that countries could not be on friendly terms unless they had a written alliance. Bismarck sometimes argued that formal alliances were made necessary by democracy and the growth of public opinion. The masses could not understand diplomatic gestures; they had to be tied by precise words. But the statesmen were tied as much as the masses. The signature of the Austro-German alliance, though not its terms, was announced at once; and German national feeling was enthusiastic. 'Greater Germany' seemed to have been achieved in a roundabout way. Bennigsen said truly: 'For the first time the Chancellor has made an act of foreign policy, to which all interests, all parties, yes all Germany, joyfully agree.' Bismarck was embarrassed by this enthusiasm, but he could not repudiate it just when he was preaching the 'national' cause in economics and social welfare. He had prepared a strange fate for himself. He, the greatest and most successful enemy of the Habsburg monarchy, the man who had destroyed its predominance in Germany and ended it in Italy, became henceforth its guarantor and protector. He did not relish the part; and every subsequent step in his foreign policy aimed at escaping the inevitable consequences of what he had done in October 1879.

VIII

THE CONSERVATIVE CHANCELLOR

THE end of the year 1879 opened a new epoch in Bismarck's life. Gone were the days when he had unified Germany on the basis of universal suffrage and given her modern institutions with the help of a great liberal party; gone the days when he welcomed conflicts between the other Great Powers and profited from them. Now he echoed Metternich and became 'a rock of order'. The change has given him another cycle of posthumous fame. Fifty years ago Bismarck was admired as the great nationalist and revolutionary; now he is held up as the man who sought to preserve Europe's traditional civilization. Both pictures are true, though of different times. All revolutionaries become conservative once they are in power; and Bismarck had always longed for tranquillity even when he was a revolutionary.

Personally, Bismarck enjoyed more absolute power than ever before. The old emperor became a figurehead; even Augusta ceased to criticize, especially when the *Kulturkampf* was relaxed. His only fear now was of what would happen when the crown prince came to the throne; and Bismarck pursued with destructive hatred any political figure who he imagined might be the head of a so-called 'Gladstone ministry'. This was a spook of his own creation. The crown prince was too weary and too ineffective to have any clear plans. It was characteristic of Bismarck that whereas he had constantly expressed weariness of office when he was regarded as indispensable he now clung to it with frenzied determination. He said in 1888: 'I shall refuse to sign any letter of resignation. I shall cling to my chair and not go even if they try to throw me out.' Previously he had had colleagues of some independence and ability. Now he had underlings to carry out his orders. He distrusted even them and felt secure only in 1885 when he made his son Herbert secretary of state. He meant to found a Bismarck-dynasty and remarked complacently: 'Louis XIV said, *L'état, c'est moi*. I say, *Moi, je suis l'état*.' He cared for his son more than for any ruler or any public cause; yet he crushed this son with all his ruthless energy at the first sign of independence. Herbert fell in love with a divorced princess and proposed to marry her. Divorce was no handicap in Lutheran Germany—a few years later Bülow became chancellor, though married to a divorced woman, when this would have debarred him from the lowest ministerial post in England. But Herbert's lady was related to Schleinitz, Bismarck's old enemy. Bismarck used every weapon. He threatened to dismiss Herbert from the public service; announced that he would kill himself if the marriage took place; and got William I to exclude from the entail on Friedrichsruh and Varzin anyone who married a divorced woman. Herbert gave way and worked off on others the impatient brutality that had been no match for his father.

Bismarck did not reveal his thoughts even to Herbert, but he trusted him to execute orders. He trusted no one else. Suspicion grew with power; and he broke ministers and ambassadors who showed any sign of independence. He still pursued with unrelaxed hatred supposed opponents who had been dead for many years. His old friend Keyserling was amazed to discover in 1891 that Bismarck remembered petty slights which he had suffered during their student-days. When Lasker, the National Liberal politician, died during a visit to the United States, Bismarck forbade the Reichstag to accept a message of condolence from Congress. Lasker had given invaluable aid in 1870 in winning south Germany for unification; but, according to Bismarck, he had prevented Bennigsen from becoming a minister in 1878. The charge was quite untrue—Bennigsen was capable of making up his own mind; and Lasker's real offence was to have kept his independence of judgement. Bismarck's hostility was not confined to politicians. Though he could

flatter foreigners, such as Jules Ferry or Salisbury, when it
suited his purpose, it maddened him that they were out of
his reach. His greatest contempt was reserved for 'professor'
Gladstone, perhaps because he recognized there his only
equal.

This irritability and petty spite could earlier be excused
by Bismarck's nervous temperament and his constant ill-
health. It had less excuse in his last decade of power. He no
longer needed to worry about his tenure of office; he was
secure for William I's lifetime and could retire to Friedrichsruh or Varzin without risk of intrigue against him at court.
In 1883 a startling change took place in his health. A new
medical attendant, Schweninger, at last imposed moderation on the genius who had imposed it on others, but never
on himself. At their first meeting, Bismarck said roughly:
'I don't like being asked questions.' Schweninger replied:
'Then get a vet. He doesn't question his patients.' The
battle was won in a single round. Bismarck ate and drank
less, kept more regular hours. When Schweninger was
present, he even kept his temper. He underwent a slimming
diet, which consisted exclusively of herrings. However
curious this seems by contemporary standards, it did the
trick. Bismarck's weight went down from eighteen to
fourteen stone; he slept long and peacefully; his eyes
became clear, his skin fresh and almost youthful. The full
beard came off in 1884, not to reappear again until extreme
old age. He took up horse-riding after a ten-year interval;
and recovered a capacity for steady, sustained work which
he had not known since his days at Frankfurt. He still
sobbed easily; but there was no more nervous collapse even
at the time of his fall. Schweninger got his reward. He had
been guilty years before of a moral offence,[1] all the graver,
says one of Bismarck's biographers, from being committed
in a churchyard. Bismarck compelled the university of
Berlin to make Schweninger a professor, despite the outraged protests of the medical faculty. An appropriate ex-

[1] Rape? sodomy? bestiality? It is more interesting not to inquire.

change: Bismarck got fifteen years of life, Schweninger a university chair.

Every observer noted the change in Bismarck; and it can be seen in his photographs. In 1877 he is bloated, choleric, bursting at the seams; in 1883, before Schweninger took over, a bearded old man, bewildered at life and hardly able to control his twitchings long enough to face the camera. In 1885 he is fresh, clean-shaven, chin upright, face finely drawn, master of himself, seventy years old no doubt, but a man with long life before him. His talk and writing gave further evidence of renewed health. It was more serene, relaxed and patient, though still full of cunning, always with a calculated effect. Bismarck was never spontaneous, even with himself. His speeches and instructions now had an air of inner communing, which only the old can have, as though he were more interested in eternity than in events. It was a hard task to be one of Bismarck's ambassadors. He never learnt to give precise instructions, just as he never learnt at Frankfurt to write accurate reports. He would always explore remote aspects of a topic and turned easily aside to by-ways of historical allusion of personal reminiscence. The wise ambassadors kept quiet; when they acted on their instructions, they usually acted wrongly. For instance, in May 1884 Bismarck wrote to Münster, his ambassador in London, that the British government must be more sympathetic to German needs if they wanted to keep German backing in the Egyptian question, and in particular they should consider ceding Heligoland; he also remarked, in a casual aside, that Great Britain should show consideration for German trading interests in Africa. But Münster was only told to raise the question of Heligoland. He had long advocated Anglo-German co-operation and was delighted; he began to ask for Heligoland at once. A fortnight later Bismarck told him to drop the question. The following year Bismarck rebuked Münster in a Reichstag speech for not complaining about British obstruction over colonies—a question that Münster had never been told to raise; and the British government were also attacked for ignoring complaints that had never been made. Münster was lucky to escape only with the penalty of being moved to Paris. His offence was to have carried out instructions that he had received and for failing to carry out instructions that he had not.

Bismarck's speeches in the Reichstag also took on this character of grandiose obscurity. He spoke often—indeed, since he did nearly all the work of government, more often than ever before. When he had something to promote in the Reichstag—whether the army-law or social insurance—he attended every day and spoke to every amendment. But he no longer tried to identify himself with a party, as he had identified himself with National Liberal policy between 1867 and 1877. He seemed to stand aloof from the Reichstag and above its members, meditating aloud, sometimes striking out a dramatic phrase, more often wrestling for words exactly in the manner of Oliver Cromwell. He would wander from his notes, remain silent for a minute on end, and then break off to drink brandy-and-water—an observer once counted eighteen tumblerfuls in a single speech. The members would cough, laugh, and talk among themselves, until Bismarck, beside himself with rage, would shake his fist or stare them down through his lorgnette. His final resort was to exclaim: 'I am no orator . . . I am a minister, a diplomat, a statesman and I should be offended to be called an orator.' His speeches are among the greatest literary compositions in the German language, despite their repetitions and their clumsy, fragmentary phrases. But their historical allusions to the revolutions of 1848, to Metternich, or even to the Frankfurt diet, must have seemed remote to members who could hardly remember the founding of the North German confederation, let alone the Crimean war. Yet in the end Bismarck's personality forced itself through; and he usually got his way even in a Reichstag composed mainly of his opponents.

The basic argument of Bismarck's speeches in this last decade was always that he alone spoke for the nation, for Germany. This Germany existed only in his imagination.

He knew little or nothing of contemporary German life. He read no new books, knew none of the leading thinkers, never went out even in Berlin. Though he boasted that, unlike the intellectual politicians, he knew the German people, his knowledge stopped forty years before. The only men of the people with whom he exchanged a word were the labourers on his estates, where an antiquated social order was kept artificially alive. When he spoke of industrial conditions, his illustrations were drawn from the Silesian textile industry—the centre of eighteenth-century industrialism—not from the Ruhr. He never saw a coalmine in his life, was never in the Ruhr, and did not visit the Rhineland between 1871 and 1892. Even his attitude to Marxism was old-fashioned. Marx died in 1883, his best work done twenty years before; and Bismarck knew nothing of tradeunion development or of the practical points in the Socialist programme. For him the Social Democrats were always 'the red revolutionaries' of 1848, just as he still saw the Roman Catholics with the eyes of Luther.

Bismarck complained that the Reichstag was a chaos of factions, but this chaos was largely of his own making. He had forced a split in both the Conservative and the National Liberal parties; and, still worse, by launching universal suffrage, he had cleared the way for parties which were not 'upholders of the state' at all in his sense. To defeat the middle-class politicians by universal suffrage turned out to be itself a middle-class idea. Bismarck reacted by denouncing others, not by confessing his mistake. In the first years after 1867 he had almost ignored the Prussian diet. Later he praised it as a truer expression of the national will, and in 1885 actually sought a vote of confidence from it when he had been defeated in the Reichstag over his Polish policy. Again, he had found no words strong enough with which to criticize the German princes—their lack of any national feeling, to say nothing of the trouble that they caused him. In the eighteen-eighties he turned round and exalted their patriotism above that of the politicians. He even included in his *Reminiscences* a passage, contemptuous

of German nationalism, where he asserted that the dynas-
ties were the only effective bond of union. This was to fly
wilfully in the face of the facts; and Bismarck knew it.
He did not value the princes or respect them; he merely
wanted to repay in kind the exasperation which the
politicians had caused him. He claimed to serve 'the State',
almost to worship it. Yet he criticized the Prussian
bureaucracy, complaining that it was as 'intellectual' as the
politicians—'there is no difference between the man at the
green desk and the man at the orator's tribune'. The
State was, in fact, a name for that 'heroic will' which
Keyserling had seen long ago as Bismarck's dominating
characteristic. When Bismarck said that the state should be
served, he meant that he ought always to get his own way.

Bismarck owed his difficulties with the Reichstag to his
own success. He had constantly preached that interest-
groups should be substituted for parties based on national
principle; the voters and even the party-leaders took his
advice. The Old Conservatives of the eighteen-seventies
became spokesmen of the Junker estates in the eighteen-
eighties; the National Liberals became spokesmen of heavy
industry. But now Bismarck told the electors and the
deputies that they should consider only the national good.
Was not this a principle like any other? In practice he had
usually to promote the national good by concessions to the
interest-groups, a horse-trading that grew ever more
elaborate. A small section of Conservatives, called the
Empire party, and a small section of the National Liberals
tried to turn support of Bismarck into a principle, accepting
his identification of himself with the nation; but this
adherence to principle ruined them, as Bismarck had foretold. The two parties outside the national fold, the Centre
and the Social Democrats, were abhorrent to him both
because of their principles and because he disliked their
practical interests. Yet he often had to play for their support so as not to be taken prisoner by one of the respectable
parties. He jeered at the Reichstag for being unable to
provide a stable government-majority and asked: what

sort of a government would it be, where Windthorst of the Centre, Bebel the Socialist, and Richter the Progressive, sat side by side? As a matter of fact, this was exactly the coalition which sustained the Weimar republic; and it would have given Germany a secure parliamentary system if it had not been for the 'national' parties which Bismarck had patronized.

Bismarck's jugglery with the Reichstag in the eighteen-eighties rested on a simple calculation. The Conservatives supported him firmly once they were won over by agrarian protection; but he needed further votes to secure a majority. The National Liberals supported the *Kulturkampf*, but opposed protective tariffs and authoritarian government; the Centre opposed the *Kulturkampf*, but supported protective tariffs and perhaps would not mind authoritarian government if it were not applied against themselves. In 1879 Bismarck thought that he had out-manœuvred the Centre by promoting tariffs, without relaxing the *Kulturkampf*. The manœuvre did not work: the Centre went back to opposition as soon as the tariffs were passed. In 1880 he had a further, graver disappointment. Leo XIII was anxious to compromise. He disliked the head-on conflict with the modern state and in any case regarded the German Reich as the least of his enemies; if he could settle with Germany, he could play her against France or against his most dangerous opponent, national Italy. In February 1880 Leo XIII, not Bismarck, went to Canossa. He accepted Bismarck's principle that the age-long conflict could not be fought out: church and state should find a workable compromise. As a first gesture he agreed that Roman priests should henceforth register with the state-authorities; in return the May-laws would be more laxly applied. Bismarck and Leo XIII had reckoned without the Centre leaders. They refused to settle for anything less than repeal of the May-laws. Windthorst exclaimed: 'Shot in the field! shot in the back!' He thought at first of retiring from politics; then decided, despite Leo XIII's prompting, to oppose all Bismarck's measures.

7*

Bismarck swung back. He renewed his friendly relations with the National Liberal leaders almost for the last time; and in the summer of 1880 a liberal-conservative coalition carried the first renewal of the septennial army-law. Fortunately for Bismarck his diplomacy had promoted a peaceful Europe; and he asked only for renewal, not for increase, of the military establishment. He now embarked on a bolder manœuvre still. Since he could not shake the Centre, he would win over the Social Democrats—not certainly by appealing to their leaders, whom he was persecuting and sending to prison, but by a constructive social programme, which he hoped would detach the working-class voters from the Social Democratic party. It would be unfair to say that Bismarck took up social welfare solely to weaken the Social Democrats; he had had it in mind for a long time, and believed in it deeply. But as usual he acted on his beliefs at the exact moment when they served a practical need. Challenge drove him forward. He first avowed his social programme when Bebel taunted him with his old friendship with Lassalle. He answered by calling himself a Socialist, indeed a more practical Socialist than the Social Democrats; and he provocatively rejoiced in echoing Frederick the Great's wish to be *le roi des gueux*, king of the poor. Richter, the Progressive leader, called Bismarck's proposals 'not Socialistic, but Communistic'. The proposal was merely that part of the cost of Social Insurance should be borne by the state; and nowadays Bismarck seems the progressive, Richter the unenlightened reactionary.

The system of Social Insurance which Bismarck inaugurated in 1881 and completed in 1889 just before his fall would be enough to establish his reputation as a constructive statesman even if he had done nothing else. He recognized this and wanted to put into William I's mouth the words that 'it would be the finest work of our government which has been so clearly blessed by God'. William objected that unification ranked higher and struck the words out. Yet unification had been achieved by other countries. German social insurance was the first in the world, and has served as a model for every other civilized country. The great conservative became the greatest of innovators. Earlier it had been Bismarck's weakness that he did not share the basic principles of liberalism even when he worked with the National Liberals; now it was his strength. His very lack of principles gave him a clearer vision into the future. Of course, Bismarck did not promote social reform out of love for the German workers. Sympathy and affection had never been his strong points. His object was to make the workers less discontented or, to use a harsher phrase, more subservient. He said in 1881: 'Whoever has a pension for his old age is far more content and far easier to handle than one who has no such prospect. Look at the difference between a private servant and a servant in the chancellery or at court; the latter will put up with much more, because he has a pension to look forward to.' Social security has certainly made the masses less independent everywhere; yet even the most fanatic apostle of independence would hesitate to dismantle the system which Bismarck invented and which all other democratic countries have copied.

Bismarck's policy revealed the contradictions of his social outlook. He had always fought for his independence—from parties, from princes, from foreign countries. He believed that life was a ceaseless battle: 'Struggle is everywhere, without struggle no life, and if we want to go on living, we must be ready for further struggles.' Yet he wanted to combine this fighting independence with security, always seeking a verdict from the referee before he would enter the ring. His foreign policy was packed with insurances and reinsurances; and he kept away from war simply because victory could never be guaranteed. In his private life he was always beating down others, yet demanded security for himself. He hoarded money and estates, worrying endlessly about the old age that he did not expect to survive into. He would not tolerate any interference in his own concerns as landowner or industrialist and even

stormed at having to pay rates on the chancellery buildings. Yet his sensitive imagination was racked by the
thought of the worker who had no protection against
accident or old age. He preached rigour at one moment,
security at the next. He would not tolerate factory
inspection or any legal limitation of hours; the factory
owner must be 'master in his own house'. But he proposed
to insure every German worker against accident, sickness,
and old age. At the end he talked of 'the right to work'
and thought of insurance against unemployment—the
final step to the welfare state of the twentieth century.

These ideas were too novel for Bismarck's contemporaries. Most resisted them on the basis of liberal economics.
Even the Social Democrats were more interested in the
conquest of political power than in social reform. Even
when social insurance was carried, the Reichstag defeated
Bismarck on one essential point. It struck out the contribution from the state, and left insurance as a direct levy on
worker and employer. The politicians acted wisely from
their point of view. Bismarck wanted to make the workers
feel more dependent on the state, and therefore on him.
Ultimately he wanted to put the politicians out of business.
He talked of ending the representation of individual voters
and of substituting for it 'corporative associations', based
on the insurance system. The idea carried further his
emphasis on interest-groups instead of high principle. The
phrase and the device were to be picked up again by the
twentieth-century exponents of Fascism. But Bismarck
was not being a prophet. He was merely repeating the
medieval fantasies with which Frederick William IV had
long ago surrounded the first steps towards parliamentarianism in Prussia. Here was another illustration—
curious, rather than important—of the way in which Bismarck reverted to the outlook which he had despised in
his early years. He followed Metternich in foreign policy;
echoed Frederick William IV at home. The 'mad Junker'
of the rebellious eighteen-forties would have hard and
contemptuous words for such nostalgic regression.

Though social insurance helped to swell Bismarck's reputation in history, it was not a success as a move in practical politics; and this was what Bismarck cared about above all else. He put his proposals before the Reichstag in February 1881; the date was no accident—Bismarck was acutely conscious that the term of the Reichstag was running out, and he needed a new fighting cry for the approaching election. There was no chance that the emperor would be shot at again. There was no crisis in foreign affairs. Bismarck therefore must be made to appear as the sole champion of social welfare. The manœuvre was a failure. Certainly the Reichstag played into his hands. It reduced the employer's contribution and struck out the contribution of the state altogether—the liberals from individualism, the Centre in defence of federalism. Bismarck responded by getting the Imperial Council to reject the amended law. Then he dissolved the Reichstag. The electorate failed to respond, or rather it responded in an unwelcome and surprising way. Voters, even of the working-class, turned to the anti-Bismarckian liberals, who now over-topped the Centre as the largest single party. Add together these progressives, the Centre, the Social Democrats, and the various protesting fragments (Poles, Alsatians, Danes from north Sleswig, Guelfs from Hanover); and the German Reichstag had for the first time a majority consciously opposed to Bismarck, though agreed on nothing else.

Bismarck owed his defeat to his contempt for mankind. He always slipped readily into the mistake of underrating the power of ideas, particularly the great revolutionary ideas of freedom and equality; hence the admiration which disillusioned idealists profess for him nowadays. He was quick to assert his own claim to equality, and tolerated no encroachment on his own freedom. He never understood that others might feel the same. He was impatient enough with educated people who worried about principles and the rule of law; but he shrugged this off as an ineradicable effect of their education. What took him by surprise was that the uneducated cared just as deeply, or perhaps even more so. The Social Democratic party had been little more than a sect until the passing of the anti-Socialist law; then every working man regarded himself as persecuted and was not to be bought off by insurance against accidents. In 1881 the Social Democratic party was sufficiently hampered by illegality to lose some of its votes; but these votes, and many more, went to the parties which would oppose Bismarck on whatever ground. Many observers drew the conclusion at the time, and it was valid enough: the prospect of security cannot induce men to sacrifice their freedom. Yet Bismarck had perhaps anticipated the future, though he was wrong in the present. The men of the nineteenth century, even the most uneducated men of the lowest class, had the ideas of the French revolution in their bones. Freedom seemed essential to them. Three-quarters of a century later even educated men put security before freedom. Bismarck's dream has been accomplished. Men can be transformed into contented animals so long as they are secure and well-fed. Few care for great abstract principles at home or abroad; they ask only for a quiet life. This is exactly what Bismarck projected. But there is a difference between Bismarck and our present-day statesmen. He would at least have fulfilled his promise and provided the quiet life; our rulers find even this too difficult for them.

It was no consolation to Bismarck that his ideas would triumph fifty years after his death. He had to face the opposition which dominated the Reichstag between 1881 and 1887. Fortunately no septennial military-law fell in this period; and there was little damage for the opposition to do. As usual, Bismarck retreated when a gesture of violence had failed to achieve its end. He echoed, though with a wryer face, his threat to Andrássy in 1879: 'Accept my policy, if not . . . I must accept yours.' Before the election Bismarck had insisted that social insurance was worthless unless carried through according to his dictate. After the election he swallowed the Reichstag's amendments: 'You have rejected the contribution from the state, and I have bowed to this necessity in order to achieve something.' The state paid nothing; the levy on the worker was increased. With these changes health insurance was established in 1883; accident insurance in 1884. Bismarck lost interest in them once they ceased to be useful as weapons of political struggle. He did not devote a single sentence to social welfare in his *Reminiscences*. Admittedly the *Reminiscences* were designed for political effect, not as a contribution to history; still, it is strange that Bismarck forgot so completely what is now regarded as his most individual claim to fame. In the Reichstag of 1881–84 Bismarck attacked the opposing forces from a different side. Since he could not shake the Progressives and social welfare had miscarried, only concessions to the Centre remained. In 1882 Bismarck renewed German diplomatic representation at the Vatican after a lapse of ten years; and he weakened the obligation of priests to register with the state. But Leo XIII would not again risk the snub from the Centre which he had received in 1880. Rome remained silent; and the Centre, though less virulent, was not won over. Its votes were cast in favour of a renewal of the anti-Socialist law in 1884, but against Bismarck's old favourite, the tobacco-monopoly. Bismarck fell back on his final resort—a *coup d'état*. He talked of making the chancellor a pure figurehead, who should preside over the Imperial Council and no more. Then the Reichstag would find no responsible minister whom it could attack and would be reduced to impotence. The representatives of the states insisted that it was impossible thus to dismantle German unity; and he put the idea unwillingly aside. Yet he was determined to remain in power and to enforce his will. As he said in the Prussian diet a little later: 'I regard the minister as a wretched coward who does not risk his honour and his head to save his country even against the will of majorities.' These were brave words. All they meant in practice was that Bismarck intended to be the only permanent feature in the German political scene. He had always to be right even though this made everyone else wrong.

An English analogy again comes to mind. The years between 1881 and 1887 in Germany, when the groups in the Reichstag were strong enough to oppose the chancellor but were divided against each other, had much in common with the years of political confusion and instability in England which followed the Seven Years' war. There was restlessness and faction, but no uniting principle. In England a young king with weak ministers made the confusion worse. But suppose the old king, George II, had lived another ten years and suppose the political genius, William Pitt, had remained in full health, we might have seen a Bismarckian decade, with Pitt defying the House of Commons and refusing to bow to its temporary majorities. Even the younger Pitt, a lesser man, adopted much this attitude twenty years later. Maybe such analogies do not take us very far. But if we are to make them at all, they are better made for Germany at this time with an England that was still strongly monarchical and where the House of Commons had only the function of opposition than with the contemporary England which had two generations of full parliamentarianism behind her.

Bismarck's claim to be the indispensable man seems more justified when foreign affairs are brought into the picture. Here his uncanny sensitivity and his inexhaustible expedients had always made him a worker of miracles; and in the eighteen-eighties he developed a diplomatic mastery without parallel. He was the Napoleon of alliances; and, unlike Napoleon, he never met his Moscow or his Waterloo. He often used his domestic policy to strengthen his position in foreign affairs; and, with less excuse, he sometimes played tricks in diplomacy in order to influence affairs at home. The principal object of the alliance which he made with Austria-Hungary in 1879 was undoubtedly to make Austrian policy less anxious and aggressive; but he also paraded it in Germany as a national, even a nationalist, gesture—the diplomatic counterpart to protective tariffs and social welfare. This emotional coating which he had laid on the alliance, caused him difficulties later when he wanted to treat Vienna more coolly. The Austrians could always turn on him and claim that their alliance, unlike any other, was an affair of the heart as well as of the head. Bismarck disliked this: he had made the alliance in order to prevent a Balkan conflict, not to support the German cause on the Danube. His interpretation prevailed in the first years after the alliance was made. The Austrians wanted to oppose Russia in Bulgaria and at Constantinople. Bismarck insisted that they had no quarrel with Russia now that they had the security of the German alliance; and the Austrians were dragged reluctantly in his wake, particularly when the victory of the English liberals under Gladstone deprived them in 1880 of any hope of an alliance with England.

A surprising result followed—surprising, that is, to all except Bismarck. The Austro-German alliance of 1879 had been made against Russia. Less than two years later it produced a reconciliation with Russia, the so-called League of the Three Emperors. This was not, despite its name, a sentimental association of conservative monarchs; it was a hard-headed practical agreement, welcome to Russia, forced on Austria-Hungary by Bismarck. The three partners promised to remain neutral if one of their number were engaged in war with a fourth power. Since the only war Austria-Hungary would fight would be against Russia, this meant in practice a Russian promise of neutrality in case of a German war against France and an Austro-German promise of neutrality in case of a Russian war against England—this latter promise given most reluctantly by Austria-Hungary. Only a war against Turkey was excluded—for that Russia must first get the permission of her two partners. This was no real concession: it sprang from the nature of things and had always been true, in the Crimean war as in 1877. Germany got security; Russia got a firm promise that Austria-Hungary and Germany would give her diplomatic support against England in any dispute over Bulgaria or at the Straits; Austria-Hungary got nothing except the German alliance which she had already.

The League of the Three Emperors, signed in June 1881, represented the triumph of Bismarck's deepest wishes. It gave him what he wanted—escape from having to choose between Russia and Austria-Hungary. Russia's friendship was recovered at the expense of Austro-Hungarian and British interests in the Near East. Bismarck cared nothing for the first and was quite pleased to injure the second. The security of Germany's rambling eastern frontier was worth a high price, particularly when paid by others. Bismarck always held that it was more important for Germany to stand well with Russia than with any other Power. He took ˌhis line from beginning to end of his career. He said in 1863 when first in power: 'The secret of politics? Make a good treaty with Russia.' Almost his last public utterance in 1896 was to present himself, in contrast with his successors, as the man of the Russian alliance. Germans of a later age who advocated good relations with Russia could rightly claim to be 'Bismarckian'. Yet Russo-German friendship had a grave, indeed a fatal flaw for Bismarck, as for his heirs: it was intensely disliked by the overwhelming majority of Germans. The nation, divided in all else, was united in hostility to Russia. This was shown both at the outbreak of the first World war and in June 1941. It was equally clear in Bismarck's time. Only the old emperor, with his fading memories, agreed with Bismarck. All other Germans looked on Russia as their enemy, though the Russians asked nothing except to be left alone.

The liberals regarded Russia as reactionary and backward; the Centre disliked her oppression of the Roman Catholic Poles; the Social Democrats inherited hatred of Russia from the radicals of 1848; the conservatives had an agrarian jealousy of Russian grain; the generals, including even Moltke, eagerly planned war against Russia, the only power that they had not fought; the younger generation wanted to assert the German cause everywhere—on the Danube and in the Near East more than anywhere else.

Bismarck would have had a united nation behind him if he had gone against Russia; and he could have it in no other way. Instead he made friendship with Russia the keystone of his foreign policy. Social conservatism perhaps counted for something with him, fear of a revived Poland for more. Most deeply he feared that war against Russia would be a war to the death. Wars with other Powers could be fought, as he had fought them, for limited objects. War with Russia must end in the destruction of one or other combatant, as Napoleon had found and as Hitler was to find later on. Now Bismarck wanted a quiet life, however revolutionary he had been earlier. His greatest, and most admirable, quality was to be content with limited success; and this was the one thing which war against Russia could never give.

He was alone in his view. William I and a few elderly courtiers also wanted friendship with Russia, but on grounds of monarchical conservatism. Bismarck exploited their prejudices. The League of the Three Emperors was a conspiracy between Bismarck and William I against the German people. William I and Bismarck were also partners against the Reichstag between 1881 and 1887. But at least there were in the Reichstag some deputies who agreed with Bismarck over home affairs. No German politician would have applauded his foreign policy if it had been made known. Hence it remained a rigid secret. Bismarck boasted of the Austro-German alliance from the day that it was made; later, when Italy was added, he boasted of the Triple Alliance; later still, he boasted of his association with England. He never mentioned the League of the Three Emperors; and it remained an obscure mystery until thirty years after his death. In the same way, later German statesmen—whether Stresemann, Hitler or those of the present—have had to treat friendship with Russia as a guilty secret. German emotion has always been against it. Even when the second World war had made clear the full penalty of conflict with Russia, a German liberal writer could condemn Bismarck for seeking the friendship of

Russia instead of making an alliance with England, though this must inevitably have led to European war.

In 1881 Bismarck could ignore the German people; he could not ignore his Austrian allies, and they complained ceaselessly against the League of the Three Emperors. Bismarck did something to quieten them. He would not underwrite Austro-Hungarian interests in the Balkans. Instead, in May 1882, he brought Italy into the Austro-German partnership. The essential clause of this Triple Alliance was Italy's promise to remain neutral in a war between Russia and Austria-Hungary. The promise, Bismarck claimed, 'was worth four army corps'—the troops which otherwise Austria-Hungary would have to keep on her Italian frontier. The price for this bargain was paid by Germany: she, but not Austria-Hungary, undertook to support Italy in a war against France. This was a strange outcome. Bismarck despised Italy, who had, he said, 'a large appetite and very poor teeth'; and he did not rank her among the Great Powers—for him they remained five, not six. When Italy demanded territorial gains at the congress of Berlin, he asked: 'What, has she lost another battle?' Devotion to monarchy, even if it weighed with him, could hardly extend to the Italian royal house—at best, the Triple Alliance gave a convenient excuse for evading a revival of the temporal power of the papacy. His claim that the Holy Roman Empire had been restored and that 'the great powerful area of all central Europe had finally come together again after being torn apart by strokes of destiny and fierce struggles' was mere window-dressing to please German opinion. The Triple Alliance showed Bismarck's determination, almost his obsession, to keep the Pomeranian grenadier out of the Balkans. He would do anything rather than support Austria-Hungary there; he would even risk a war for Italy's sake against France.

The risk was not great. Bismarck used his alliance with Italy to prevent a war against France, just as he used his alliance with Austria-Hungary to prevent a war against Russia. As soon as he got allies, he took them under his control. He insisted that they must do what he wanted; and what he wanted was peace. The alliances had a further value: they fixed the limits of his concessions to France and Russia. After 1879 he was willing to do anything the Russians wanted short of sacrificing Austria-Hungary; after 1882 he would do anything to please the French short of sacrificing Italy. The parallel was not exact. He felt less committed to Italy despite the terms of the Triple Alliance. In 1879 he really came to believe, for whatever reason, that the integrity of Austria-Hungary was essential to the security of Germany, at any rate to the security of his Germany. Italy did not mean so much to him. Perhaps he feared obscurely that the Habsburgs might renew their claims in Germany if they recovered their predominance in Italy—and men in Vienna still talked of reconquering Venetia and Lombardy. But he jettisoned Italy's Mediterranean interests for the sake of French friendship; and he might even have let the Italian monarchy disintegrate if he could have won both France and the pope completely to his side. As it was, both, like Russia, remained too independent. They would not accept his control. Austria-Hungary and Italy had for Bismarck the attraction that they were the weaker and therefore the more subservient Powers. In foreign affairs, as in private life, men do not like equals; they like dependents—Bismarck more than most men.

Nevertheless he went on from the Italian alliance to an attempted reconciliation with France, just as he went on from the Austro-Hungarian alliance to a reconciliation with Russia. The reconciliation with Russia succeeded, at any rate for some years; that with France did not and has therefore attracted less notice. Yet it was the core of his policy from 1882 until 1885 and the most grandiose task that he ever attempted. For Germany would really be secure if France were reconciled. The Eastern question would lose its terrors; and Berlin would be the centre of a new European order. Alsace and Lorraine stood in the way, as Bismarck knew; and he attempted to win over the French by insisting rather clumsily that the two provinces would never have been annexed if it had depended on him. This was tawdry stuff. His more serious effort was to support France 'everywhere in the world except at that little corner on the Rhine'. He said to the French ambassador: 'I have had *one* aim in regard to France for the last fourteen years, since the making of peace: to get her to forget the war . . . I want you to forgive Sedan as you have forgiven Waterloo.'

The aim seemed more plausible in 1884 than it does now after half a century dominated by Franco-German antagonism. All the Great Powers had fought each other at some time, but resentment had died away. France had made it up with England after Waterloo; Russia had made it up with France after the Crimean war; Austria-Hungary, defeated in 1866, was now the ally of Germany. There seemed no reason why the Franco-German war should be any different in the long run. Bismarck was not alone in hoping for better relations. Gambetta, the great apóstle of resistance in 1870 after Sedan, shared this hope and was actually planning to meet Bismarck at the time of his early death. Though Gambetta certainly did not forget the lost provinces, he believed that they would be recovered by friendship with Germany, not by a new war against her. He pinned his faith to 'immanent justice'. Jules Ferry, prime minister of France from 1882 to 1885, had the same outlook. Though he, too, had an honourable record in 1870, he put Alsace and Lorraine in the background and sought to build a colonial empire for France, preferably with German backing. Tunis, Indo-China, Egypt, and central Africa were prizes which made patience over the lost provinces worth-while. Though the initiative came from Bismarck, the French were eager to accept his proffered hand.

Bismarck's diplomacy led inevitably to the isolation of England. Austria-Hungary and Italy were the two Powers on whom England counted—the one to resist Russia at the Straits, the other to resist France in the Mediterranean.

Alliance with Germany snatched them away from England's side, though it could not turn them into her enemies.[1] The League of the Three Emperors was implicitly an anti-British combination. By reconciling Russia and Austria-Hungary, still more by giving Russia security at the Straits, it cleared the way for a Russian advance in central Asia, which implicitly threatened the British empire in India. In exactly the same way, good relations between France and Germany left France free to press her colonial ambitions in rivalry with the British. Nor was she alone. In 1884 Bismarck, too, entered the colonial field. His reasons for this are obscure. Hitherto he had kept his gaze riveted to Europe and had insisted that Germany had enough to do in protecting her security and in developing her resources. He had rejoiced to be free from the rivalries which caused conflicts among others. He said repeatedly: 'I am no man for colonies.' Now he created a great colonial empire, each unit of it seemingly designed to exasperate British feeling. The first, which grew into German South-West Africa, was at the backdoor of Cape Colony. The Cameroons broke into an area where the British had monopolized trade for many years. German East Africa threatened the British control of Zanzibar. And finally, German New Guinea encroached on the British colonies in Australia.

There were, of course, domestic motives for Bismarck's colonial policy. Hamburg was on the point of entering the German customs-union at last; and colonial markets were perhaps held out to the Hamburg merchants as some compensation for the loss of their Free Trade privileges. There were wider grounds, too. Men everywhere—not only in France and England, but in Italy and even in little Belgium—were talking about 'the age of imperialism', and the Germans were anxious not to be left out. Colonies provided a new 'national' cause, which drove a further wedge between the Progressives, who opposed them, and the

---

[1] Italy insisted on adding to the Triple Alliance a declaration that it could never be directed against England.

remaining National Liberals, who still supported Bismarck. Moreover, Bismarck welcomed conflict with England for its own sake. He was always angered by British aloofness and independence, particularly when 'professor' Gladstone was prime minister. Still more important, the colonial disputes were a blow at 'the Gladstone ministry' in Germany which Bismarck always professed to fear. The crown prince would be crippled when he came to the throne if Germany and England were on bad terms. Herbert Bismarck later gave this as the essential motive: 'When we started colonies, we had to face a long reign by the crown prince . . . and therefore had to launch a colonial policy in order to be able to provoke conflicts with England at any moment.' It was not the first time that Bismarck had sought to discredit his supposed opponents by accusing them of favouring Germany's enemies. Once he had accused the conservatives of friendship with Austria; then he had condemned the south German states for their friendship with France; now the crown prince was to be smeared with English liberalism.

As usual, one hand washed the other. Probably Bismarck would not have developed colonial ambitions in order to win French friendship, if this had not suited his plans at home; but equally he would not have exploited German enthusiasm for colonies, if he had not seen the opening for a Franco-German *entente*. Whenever Bismarck advocated something, every argument went in the same direction—foreign policy, the balance in the Reichstag, dynastic calculations, all gave the same answer to the sum. It seemed inconceivable that there could be any other course. Yet he could change his mind overnight, and then every argument pointed just as decisively in the reverse direction. Only one thing remained constant: Bismarck was always right. Right when he was against colonies; right when he acquired them. Right when he went to war; right when he kept the peace. Loyal when he agreed with William I; loyal also when he disagreed with him. In other countries a change of policy needed a change of government. Bismarck made his own changes, ruthlessly attacking his own arguments of yesterday. Like a great man of our own day, he was a coalition in himself.

Bismarck's foreign policy brought him in the summer of 1884 unrivalled success. Serene in temper, recovered in health, he became, for a brief moment, the pivot of Europe. In September the three emperors—Francis Joseph, Alexander III, and William I—met at Skierniewice in Poland. It was the most open display of their League and seemed to be more—a revival of the Holy Alliance. Bismarck dominated the meeting, and the emperors hung on his words. Each of them could have said, as Nicholas I of Russia once said to Metternich: 'I come to sit at your feet, as the pupil at the feet of his master.' Scarce back from Skierniewice, Bismarck told the French ambassador that they should build up a maritime league, an Armed Neutrality, to resist British control of the seas. Bismarck's old friend Keyserling commented: 'Curious that Bismarck is being led in this way to a Continental System *à la Napoléon I* and that he has practically all Europe together for it.' Bismarck surpassed his prototype. The great Napoleon had had to fight many wars in order to impose his Continental System. Bismarck had done it by magic. There lay the weakness. The differences between the Great Powers had not been settled. They were conjured away, and they reappeared as soon as Bismarck's back was turned. Content himself, he had nothing to give the peoples and rulers of Europe except lassitude. They should forget their hopes, their ambitions, their enthusiasms, and should accept what life, or rather Bismarck, had to offer them. Bismarck wanted peace; therefore everyone else must want it too. He offered nothing positive, nothing creative, nothing which could make men square their shoulders and look hopefully forward. He should have lived in the despairing twentieth century, not in an age when men still believed in a progress without limits.

The colonial disputes gave a Bismarck a cry for the general election in the autumn of 1884—effective, but not effective enough. The Progressives lost a third of their

seats; the Conservatives gained. But the Centre was un-
affected despite its opposition to colonies; its roots were in
south Germany, remote from the sea. More dangerous still,
the Social Democrats doubled their representation. 'Imperialism' was never a cause which appealed to the masses,
despite all the arguments proving that it should do so.
It was a creation of middle-class radicals trying to be
popular, not of the masses themselves; and politicians
everywhere—not only Bismarck, but Jules Ferry in France
and later Joseph Chamberlain in England—were disappointed when they tried to capture the votes of the
masses with the Imperialist cry. In 1884 the German
Social Democrats became a serious force in the Reichstag
for the first time. The European economy was experiencing
its first depression since the great industrial expansion;
and social discontent was everywhere increasing. The
Social Democrats would make a formidable opposition if
they combined with the Centre. Bismarck sought to prevent this coalition by relaxing the *Kulturkampf*. Some
of the May-laws were repealed; and later in 1885 Bismarck
even invoked Leo XIII as arbitrator in a colonial dispute
with Spain over the Carolinian Islands. Leo XIII responded
by hailing Bismarck as 'the great chancellor'; Windthorst
was not won over so easily.

Bismarck did not discard his colonial claims and his disputes with England, even though they had failed of their
domestic purpose—proof perhaps that this had been a
secondary consideration all along. Reconciliation with
France was reward enough in itself; and this seemed to
grow stronger during the winter of 1884–85. An international conference met at Berlin to settle the future of the
Congo basin; and France and Germany made common
cause against the British. In the spring of 1885 Bismarck
launched a new colonial dispute over New Guinea. In
April the continental league made its most open demonstration. Russian forces were threatening Afghanistan. Great
Britain and Russia seemed on the brink of war; and the
British planned to attack Russia by passing the Straits

and entering the Black Sea. Not only the powers of the Triple Alliance, but France, too, warned the Sultan to keep the Straits closed against the British. Bismarck piously asserted that he had done nothing to promote the Anglo-Russian conflict 'on general Christian principles'. Herbert Bismarck was not so high-minded. He remarked to a friend: 'If England and Russia quarrel, I can only say, bad luck for every blow that misses.' Christian principles apart, a war between England and Russia would give Germany the effortless mastery of Europe; and Bismarck was not the man to overlook it.

The happy situation was too good to last. Bismarck's continental system tumbled down almost overnight. Russia and England failed to go to war; instead they settled the Afghan affair by negotiation. On 30 March Jules Ferry was overthrown in France. A trivial defeat of French forces at Langson in Indo-China brought him down. If his friendship with Germany had been known, he would have fallen all the sooner. Freycinet, Ferry's successor, took a more cautious line. At the end of May, Bismarck was complaining that the French would not play 'the great game'— the game of a continental league against England; and he warned them that he would win in a competition for English friendship. As usual, he did not confess that he had been wrong in his policy. He professed to believe that the old emperor was dying; then the crown prince would come to the throne with a pro-British policy. 'We are in for an era of Coburgs'; and tears ran down his cheeks for the benefit of the French ambassador. The tears were genuine enough—Bismarck had been sobbing for years whenever it crossed his mind that William I was mortal. But he did not intend either to change his policy or to lose his position merely because Frederick III was on the throne instead of William I. In any case, it was all a false alarm—William lived woodenly on for another three years.

The continental league was not really destroyed either by ministerial changes in France or by the failing health of William I. The Eastern question was always its most

vulnerable point, as in every continental league from that
between Alexander I and Napoleon in 1807 to that between
Hitler and Stalin in 1939. Russia would never allow
Austria-Hungary to dominate the Balkans; Austria-
Hungary would never trust Russia nor renounce co-
operation with Great Britain. The two could be held
together only so long as the Balkans remained quiet; and
Bismarck's miracle really depended on 'the sheep-stealers'
whom he so much despised. In September 1885 the Balkan
settlement of the congress of Berlin broke up and threatened to break up the European order along with it. Eastern
Roumelia, which had been made merely autonomous in
1878, revolted and joined Bulgaria. The Russians had
once sought a great Bulgaria; they opposed it now that
Bulgaria had broken loose from their influence. As a last
gesture of loyalty to the League of the Three Emperors, the
Austrians joined with Russia in demanding a new partition
of Bulgaria. The scheme was wrecked by the western
Powers, France and England, and by the Bulgarians themselves. In the summer of 1886 the Russians scored a last
success: they dethroned the Prince of Bulgaria, Alexander
of Battenberg—much to Bismarck's pleasure. However
unlikely it seems, he had detected in Alexander a possible
head of the 'Gladstone ministry' in Germany. The success
did Russia no good. The Bulgarians continued to take an
independent line; and a new crisis seemed to be approaching in the Near East, with Russia seeking to reconquer
control of Bulgaria, and England and Austria-Hungary
defending Bulgarian independence.

Bismarck was determined not to be drawn in. He cared
nothing for Bulgaria, though much for the integrity of
Austria-Hungary. 'We are completely indifferent who rules
in Bulgaria and what becomes of it. . . . We shall let no one
put a noose round our necks because of this question in
order to drag us into conflict with Russia.' The new crisis
in the Near East, together with the fall of Ferry in France,
had one important effect on Bismarck's policy: it led him
to drop his colonial ambitions, so as to make it easier for

Austria-Hungary and Great Britain to draw together. As early as September 1885 he was explaining to a British visitor that he had only developed colonial interests in order to please France and that he was now disillusioned. A little later he said to a German explorer of Africa: 'Here is Russia and here is France, with Germany in the middle. That is my map of Africa.' Bismarck made no further colonial claims after the summer of 1885. He had an occasional tiff with the British over Zanzibar just to keep his hand in, but usually he spoke of colonies with his old contempt. Germany had acquired a vast African empire which Bismarck did nothing to develop. Indeed, in 1889, he tried to give German South-West Africa away to the British. It was, he said, a burden and an expense, and he would like to saddle someone else with it. Not till the twentieth century did Germany draw profit from her colonies, and then only from the Cameroons.

Bismarck's estrangement from France had more important results. It provided him with a strong excuse for refusing aid to Austria-Hungary. Germany, he claimed, was in immediate danger of attack from France and could spare no troops for a war against Russia. The excuse had some reality. A French nationalist revival had certainly followed the fall of Ferry. The tinsel hero, General Boulanger, achieved an easy popularity by talk of 'revenge'. Bismarck deliberately exaggerated the danger. As he confessed afterwards: 'I could not invent Boulanger, but he happened very conveniently for me.' He ignored the opinion of the German general staff that a French attack was out of the question. He suppressed reports from Münster in Paris that French feeling was overwhelmingly peaceful. He whipped himself, and all Germany, into a state of anxiety and panic.

The Boulangist alarm did not merely serve the needs of Bismarck's foreign policy. It was even more effective in giving him his greatest victory in home affairs. The Reichstag elected in 1884 proved the most difficult that Bismarck had to encounter. The Centre was always threatening to bolt into an alliance with the Social Democrats and the Progressives. It would only agree, for example, to renew the anti-socialist law for two years—clear indication that it was keeping the door open for a change of course. Later in 1885 the coalition of *Reichsfeinde*, as Bismarck called his opponents, actually came into being. Bismarck had launched a campaign against the Poles—partly to offset the concessions he had made to them as Roman Catholics, more as a gesture of friendship to Russia. Poles without German nationality were expelled from the eastern provinces—30,000 of them, an unexampled number for those days. Bismarck followed this up by a compulsory expropriation of Polish landowners. He always regarded Polish nationalism as an upper-class affair and said contemptuously: 'It can't matter to us whether the labourers speak Polish or German.' Bismarck declared that this was a domestic question which only concerned the Prussian diet. The Reichstag insisted on discussing and condemning it. Bismarck was the more enraged because in his view this interfered with his foreign policy of good relations with Russia. As a matter of fact, his calculation was all at sea. The Russian government, looking forward to war against Austria-Hungary, were anxious to conciliate the Poles and were irritated by Bismarck's revival of the old anti-Polish front.

Now, in the autumn of 1886, Bismarck believed that he had found the winning card. Tariffs, the social peril, colonies, had all failed of their 'national' appeal. The cry of 'the *Reich* in danger' would do the trick; and what was more, Germany could evade foreign commitments while she was torn by political controversy. In November 1886 Bismarck presented a new army-law to the Reichstag, though the old one had two years to run. The Centre and the Progressives saw their danger. They tried to avert it by offering to vote 'every penny and every man' if Bismarck would compromise on three or even five years instead of seven. This would have been reasonable if the immediate danger of war had been the real motive for increasing the army. But it was not. Bismarck wanted a political victory, not greater armaments; and he wanted to drag out the conflict so as to turn his back on his allies. When the pope offered to influence the Centre in favour of the law, Bismarck brushed him off: 'Rejection would give the government a different and perhaps much more favourable basis for operations.' The military experts, half-convinced of the danger, made concessions to the Reichstag; Bismarck repudiated them as he had done in 1863.

Determined to provoke a decisive conflict, he remained quietly at Friedrichsruh until the majority against the army-law had consolidated itself. Then on 11 January, 1887, he appeared in the Reichstag and delivered his most powerful speech since the days of 'blood and iron'. It was a conjuring trick of the highest class. On the one hand Bismarck had to justify the increase of the army and therefore to display a Germany in imminent danger of attack; at the same time he had to claim that Germany was on good terms with all the Powers thanks to his unique diplomatic gifts. It is impossible for the reader, and must have been still more impossible for the listeners, to discover Bismarck's firm opinion, the summing-up of probabilities on which he acted. Was he really afraid of attack from France and not afraid of war with Russia? Did he inflate the French danger in order to glide over his greater anxieties in the Eastern question? Or were the dangers on both frontiers exaggerated for the purposes of home policy? At any rate, he was carried away, as often happened with him, by the excitement of his peroration, and let slip his real object: he wanted an army-law that would last for ever, not merely for seven years. 'The German army is an institution which cannot be dependent on changing majorities in the Reichstag. It is an absolute impossibility that the fixing of military strength should depend on the casual constellation and opinion of the Reichstag. Do not strive for such fantastical ideas, gentlemen!'

It was the old issue of a parliamentary or royal army, the

issue which had first brought Bismarck to power in 1862. Now it worked better for him. The limited Prussian electorate of 1862 had stuck to its principles; in 1887 the masses responded to the national appeal. On 14 January the Reichstag limited the army-law to three years by 186 votes to 154. Centre and Progressives had combined to defeat Bismarck. The Social Democrats abstained— ostensibly because they were unwilling to vote for the army at all, secretly because they were unwilling to vote against an army that might one day be used against Russia. The Reichstag was at once dissolved. Bismarck's opponents were massacred at the polls. The Social Democrats lost 12 seats (half their number), the Progressives 50. The Centre held its own as always (it lost one seat); but its moral strength, too, was broken when Bismarck published a letter from the pope, condemning its vote against the army-law. The National Liberals became the largest single party in the Reichstag—for the last time; and they joined the Conservatives in a 'cartel', sole basis of which was unconditional support for Bismarck. He had at last manufactured a subservient majority for himself after twenty-five years of failure or half-success.

The army-law passed the new Reichstag for its full seven-year term by an overwhelming majority—223 to 40. Bismarck enjoyed his triumph in silence and did not go near the tribune. Seven members of the Centre obeyed the pope's instructions and voted for the law; the other eighty-three, including Windthorst, abstained. Leo XIII got his reward. Most of the May-laws were repealed in March 1887, Bismarck personally inspecting the vote in the Prussian diet to ensure that it went the right way. The religious orders were allowed to return, the Roman church recovered control of its seminaries. Bismarck said airily: 'What do I care whether the appointment of a Catholic priest is notified to the state or not—Germany must be at one!' Once he had used the argument of national unity to justify the *Kulturkampf*; now he used the same argument to justify its end. Whatever his faults, he certainly did not lack resource. He showed the same opportunism over the cry of 'the *Reich* in danger' which had just won him the general election. For, as soon as the election was over, it turned out that the *Reich* was in no danger at all. A dispute over a French frontier official, Schnaebele, wrongfully arrested by the Germans, was amicably settled. Münster in Paris, poor old gentleman, was rebuked for sending reports on Boulanger, where earlier he had been rebuked for not sending them; and in May a resolute French government pricked the Boulanger bubble. It had all been a false alarm, very convenient for Bismarck, whether he was ever taken in by it or not.

The alarm in the Near East was less false. Bismarck did not invent the crisis over Bulgaria nor even exploit it. He kept control of Europe by the most elaborate diplomatic devices—dancing among eggs, one observer called it, juggling with five balls at once, said William I. Yet the basic principle of his diplomacy was clear and simple: maintenance of Austria-Hungary as a Great Power, but no support for her ambitions in the Balkans. It was a sort of 'Locarno' between Russia and Austria-Hungary; keeping the friendship of both and offering an additional premium to whichever followed the more peaceful course. Bismarck had followed this policy steadily since 1879; only its execution became more elaborate and difficult. His most immediate problem was the Triple Alliance. It had been made in 1882 for five years and was due for renewal in May 1887. Originally it had served to bring Austria-Hungary and Italy under German control. Now a flamboyant renewal would seem to capture Germany for an Austro-Hungarian drive against Russia and an Italian drive against France. Bismarck hesitated; and his hesitation pushed England forward. Great Britain had refused to back either Austria-Hungary or Italy so long as Gladstone was in power— hence in part the original Triple Alliance. Now, with Salisbury at the foreign office, British policy returned, more or less, to the line of 1878.

In February 1887 Salisbury made a secret agreement

8

with Italy to support the *status quo* in the Mediterranean, an agreement which Austria-Hungary soon joined. This first 'Mediterranean agreement', as it came to be called, was a mere declaration of policy, not a binding alliance. But it was firm enough to lessen the dangers of the Triple Alliance for Bismarck. Henceforth, if Austria-Hungary or Italy appealed for his assistance, he could reply that they should invoke British aid first. He made no further difficulties in renewing the Triple Alliance. Indeed, by a separate treaty, he gave Italy more binding promises against France than before. Since he was now confident that French policy was peaceful, these promises involved little risk. As always, Bismarck made them so as not to have to carry them out.

Russia was a more difficult affair. The Russians had never liked the League of the Three Emperors and the friendship with Austria-Hungary that this implied. They wanted a straight promise of German neutrality, which would leave them free to attack Austria-Hungary or at any rate to threaten such an attack if she interfered with them in the Balkans. Bismarck had refused to give this promise in 1876 and during the crisis before the congress of Berlin. It was still more out of the question now that he was bound by the Austro-German alliance. Always frank when it suited him, he showed the text of this alliance to the Russian ambassador. But he offered mutual neutrality of a limited kind. Germany would remain neutral unless Russia attacked Austria-Hungary; Russia, to make things equal, would remain neutral unless Germany attacked France. This was the basis of the Reinsurance treaty, which Bismarck concluded with Russia on 18 June 1887. In theory Germany was still exposed to the risk of war on two fronts; and Bismarck was wrong when he claimed later to have warded off this risk. Indeed the Franco-Russian alliance, as made in 1894, was strictly compatible with the Reinsurance treaty; for by it the Russians did no more than promise to aid France against a German attack. But war on two fronts was not the pressing danger in 1887. The

danger which Bismarck feared was of a Balkan war between Russia and Austria-Hungary; and the Reinsurance
treaty did something to lessen it. A secret protocol
promised Germany's diplomatic aid to Russia in Bulgaria
and at the Straits. Bismarck could not prevent Russia's
going to war; but the temptation for her to do so was less
if the tsar believed that he could get his way by diplomacy.

The Reinsurance treaty was Bismarck's last great stroke.
It has often been described as dishonest and immoral.
Dishonest against whom? Whom did it deceive? Bismarck
had told the Austrians from the beginning that he would not
support them in the Balkans; he had always told the
British that, in his view, the *status quo* implied the closing
of the Straits even against their fleet; and he had always
told the Russians that he would not allow Austria-Hungary
to be destroyed. The Reinsurance treaty did no more than
repeat these statements. When two Powers or groups of
Powers are contending, it always seems immoral to them
that another Power should try to remain friendly with both
sides. Prussia had come in for the same accusations of
'shiftiness' and unreliability during the Crimean war; Bismarck had been condemned both by the Russians and by
the Austrians and the British for acting as honest broker
in 1878. It all depends on the point of view. Germany was
in the middle of Europe. She had to keep in with both
sides, unless indeed she took the lead one way or the
other and became after a great war (if she won it) the
dominating Power in Europe. This had perhaps appealed
to Bismarck in his young revolutionary days at Frankfurt.
Now he was elderly, resigned, without ambitions for the
future—except to keep things as they were. His only object
was to maintain the peace of Europe. Those who admire this
call it operating the Balance of Power; those who do not,
condemn it as dishonest jugglery.

This is not to say that Bismarck's diplomacy alone pre-
served peace. Like all successful diplomacy it contained a
double bluff. He made the Austrians believe that he would
not support them; he made the Russians fear that he would.

But suppose either side called his bluff, what could he do then? It was no good saying that he would go against whichever was the aggressor. This was a moral conception of the sort that Bismarck always insisted had no relevance in international affairs: 'I have never judged international disputes by the standards which prevail at a student's duel.' Bismarck would have had to go to the rescue of Austria-Hungary, however aggressively she had behaved, if her existence was endangered. He managed to put over the bluff by the force of his personality; those who came after him were less successful. Bismarck did not make any exaggerated claims for the Reinsurance treaty at the time, whatever he said in bitter resentment later. All he claimed was that it made Alexander III feel more secure and there-fore made it easier for him to resist his bellicose advisers. This is the most that diplomacy can ever do. It cannot prevent war; it can merely make peace more attractive.

So events worked out now. Most Russians were weary of the Near East and were only anxious to leave it alone if it would leave them alone. In the summer of 1887 the Bulgarians elected a new prince in defiance of Russia; and she did nothing. It was the sign that there would be no war in the Balkans. But men took some time to read it. The Russians were angry at their humiliation in Bulgaria, even though they would do nothing to remedy it; and on the other side the Austrians wanted to launch a preventive war against Russia in Galicia. Bismarck repeated his diplomacy of the spring in more elaborate form. He con-jured up for the Austrians a tighter, more extensive 'Mediterranean agreement' with Great Britain and Italy; and he explained frankly to Salisbury the principles of his policy. 'We shall avoid a Russian war so long as that is compatible with our interest and security . . . but German policy will always be obliged to enter the struggle if the independence of Austria-Hungary is menaced by a Russian aggression.' On the other hand, he brushed the Austrians off with a sharp rebuke when they tried to lure the German generals into staff-talks preparatory to a Russian war; and he did his best to keep on good terms with the Russians, even coming out of his retirement at Friedrichsruh to meet Alexander III at Berlin in November. The interview was not very successful. Alexander III was sulky and resentful, using friendly phrases only to the French ambassador; and Bismarck talked to his intimates of a war against Russia for the resurrection of Poland—only to add that Russo-German friendship would be restored by a new partition of Poland afterwards.

This was a desperate remedy, and not much more than thinking aloud. His actual remedies were desperate enough. On 3 February 1888 he published the text of the Austro-German treaty without waiting for permission from Vienna. This is often described as a gesture against Russia. On the contrary it was a stroke against Austria-Hungary. The Russians had already learnt the terms of the alliance from Bismarck the previous year. Publishing them stressed the defensive nature of the treaty; it was a warning that German strength would not be used, as Bismarck put it, 'for Hungarian or Catholic ambitions in the Balkans'. He made one concession. He suppressed the final clause which limited the alliance to five years (though with automatic renewal), and thus unwillingly admitted its permanence. Three days later, on 6 February, he introduced a new army-law in the Reichstag, raising the age-limit of the reserve from 32 to 39 years, and spoke on foreign policy for the last time. Germany, he insisted, would defend her interests; she would not follow a policy of power or of prestige. Though she did not fear Russia, she would not be dragged by Austria-Hungary into a policy of Balkan adventure. Implicitly he repudiated the value of all alliances, and declared that Germany must rely on her own strength. 'The pike in the European carp-pond prevent us from becoming carp.' His last sentence rounded off a career that had begun with 'blood and iron': 'We Germans fear God and nothing else in the world.' It was a strange peroration for a lifetime of apprehensions, where God had often seemed to be the only thing that Bismarck did not fear.

Less than a month later, on 3 March, he appeared at the tribune to announce the death of William I. Tears choked his voice. He wept not only for a beloved master whom he had always claimed to serve though rarely obeyed. He wept still more for the end of his own mastery in Germany.

IX

THE FALL FROM POWER

BISMARCK made one of his rare public appearances at the
funeral of William I. Afterwards in the evening he sat with
his family, lost in thought, speaking softly and almost to
himself of the ruler whom he had served for so long. An
occasional tear ran down his cheek. Suddenly he pulled
himself up, straightened his back and exclaimed in a rough,
harsh voice: 'And now forward!' Forward to what? To
further struggle which became more and more personal.
Contemptuous of the new emperor, careless of public
opinion, Bismarck meant to remain in power till he died.
He believed that only he could rule Germany, indeed that
he alone was Germany. Everyone else was factious, particularist, or a *Reichsfeind*. For more than twenty years he had
played off Reichstag and emperor against each other.
A parliamentary majority could not overthrow him as long
as he possessed the emperor's confidence; indeed, every
parliamentary attack strengthened William I's conviction
that Bismarck was the only barrier against democracy.
On the other hand he could always get his way with the
emperor by threatening to resign and so open the gates to
the democratic flood. Now Frederick III was on the
throne—an emperor long critical of Bismarck's opposition
to liberalism and long friendly to the National Liberal
politicians.

Bismarck had been taking precautions against this
catastrophe for many years. He had surrounded Frederick
and his wife with his own creatures; he had broken the
National Liberal party; and now he had a majority in the
Reichstag pledged to his support. As a matter of fact, the
precautions were largely unnecessary. Frederick was a
National Liberal, not a democrat. Despite his occasional

disagreements, he belonged to the generation which had been enthusiastic for Bismarck's great achievements. The outstanding men of the National Liberal party supported the cartel of 1887. Bennigsen resumed his political life solely to advocate it; Miquel, once an associate of Karl Marx, was for the moment Bismarck's follower. The new emperor, too, would stand with the cartel and with Bismarck's policy. A few years earlier Bismarck told Frederick that he would be prepared to remain in office on two conditions: no parliamentary government and no foreign influences on policy. Frederick agreed to these conditions. By March 1888 he was ready to agree to anything. He was a dying man, cancer of the throat far advanced. He had already lost his voice and had only three months to live.

Bismarck remained master of the situation. There was no change of policy. But he wanted a public demonstration of his power. He had been ready enough to invoke Russian influence on William I when this suited him. Now he was determined to show that English influence counted for nothing, even though the new empress was a daughter of Queen Victoria. He soon found an excuse for conflict. Frederick's daughter had been in love for some time with Alexander of Battenberg, formerly Prince of Bulgaria. Bismarck had opposed the marriage as an offence to the tsar, with whom Alexander was on bad terms; and the old emperor had supported his objection. Now Alexander had abdicated the Bulgarian throne and was living a retired life in Germany. The political difficulties seemed to have disappeared, and Frederick wanted to do something for his daughter in the remaining few weeks of his life. He gave his consent to the marriage. Bismarck was up in arms. He made out that the marriage remained offensive to the tsar and would therefore ruin his foreign policy. Perhaps he himself still had some genuine resentment against one whom he had detected years ago as head of a 'Gladstone ministry'. Most of the fuss was pretence or imagination. The tsar cared nothing about the marriage one way or the other; Alexander of Battenberg had neither talent nor ambition for politics. Bismarck merely wished to show that his will was law. He threatened to resign (the first such threat since 1879) and he appealed to public opinion by giving the news to the press. Queen Victoria came to Berlin in order to sustain her dying son-in-law. Bismarck was a match even for this. He bewitched Victoria as he had once bewitched Napoleon III. She found him 'very charming, very reasonable' and joined his urgings against 'Sandro'. The wretched emperor gave way. Alexander was repudiated, the marriage forbidden.

Bismarck was radiant with success. He became more jovial and irresponsible as the shadow emperor sank into the grave. His last act in Frederick's reign was little more than a schoolboy prank. The cartel majority had just prolonged the life of future Reichstags from three to five years. This did not need Imperial assent.[1] The Prussian diet followed suit with a similar law. Frederick assented unwillingly. At the last minute Bismarck went to him and said: 'Show for once that you are king and care neither for ministry nor for chamber. If you'd rather, forbid the publication of the law.' Was he mocking the dying man? Teasing his Prussian colleagues? Or merely rejoicing in his power? At any rate, Frederick did not respond to the prompting. A fortnight later, on 15 June, he was dead. His last act was to press his wife's hand into Bismarck's as a gesture of farewell and reconciliation. Bismarck was not affected by such gestures. He carried his battles beyond the grave. Three months after Frederick's death a German periodical published excerpts from the diary which he had kept during the war against France. The passages, though harmless enough, revealed something of Bismarck's manœuvres with the German princes and his rejection of the crown prince's advice to appeal to the German people. Bismarck was enraged. First he denounced the diary as a forgery; then he tried in vain to prosecute the editor for treason. Only Bismarck, it seemed, was allowed to reveal

---

[1] Prussian assent to Imperial laws was given by the delegates to the *Bundesrat*. The emperor, as president of the confederation, did not assent to laws.

secrets of state. An observer commented: 'Bismarck regards the glory of creating the German empire as an
enormous cheese which is his sole property; anyone who
cuts off a slice is a thief.'

With the death of Frederick III, Bismarck seemed to
have come into undisputed possession of this property.
He had had to allow William I some grudging share of
historical glory, if only as his assistant (*Handlanger*); and
despite his intellectual superiority he had always been a
little afraid of the old emperor. Though he got his way in
the end, he had to fight for it; and William I expected
everything to be explained to him. Perhaps there would
have been harder fights if Frederick III had reigned longer
and been in good health. But Bismarck did not foresee any
trouble with Frederick's son, William II. The new emperor
was not yet thirty—impulsive, vain, untrained. Bismarck
supposed that he would be happy playing at emperor—
dressing up in fine uniforms, inspecting troops, making a
speech on some formal occasion. It did not occur to him
that a mere boy—born when Bismarck was already ambassador at St. Petersburg—might have ideas on policy,
still less want his own way. When Bismarck first became
prime minister, he never left William I's side until he had
established his personal ascendancy. He went to the palace
every afternoon or wrote long letters every day when
William I was absent from Berlin. He took no such trouble
with William II. He spoke to him casually at Frederick
III's funeral; then left Berlin and did not return for eight
months. He conducted foreign policy without reference to
the emperor, never explaining what he was doing. If
William II made a suggestion, Bismarck would write back
a few contemptuous lines, pointing out how dangerous and
silly his suggestions were. Then he would go back to serious
business.

Bismarck did not neglect William II altogether. He assumed that Herbert Bismarck, who was running foreign
affairs as secretary of state, would keep an eye on him.
Bismarck adored Herbert; and it did not cross his mind

that others might not share this emotion. William II certainly feared the elder Bismarck when he came to the throne; and he was perhaps impressed by Herbert's arrogance and knowledge. But there was never a tie of affection between them; and William II soon found other confidential advisers. Herbert was ill-suited to the part for which his father had cast him. He was forceful, assertive, even rude; and he had the technical training to run an office. But he lacked the charm which his father could use; and he had no understanding of men. Bismarck would have seen danger blowing up if he had been constantly in Berlin; Herbert noticed nothing until the last moment, and then it was too late. The starting-point was not any difference over policy. It was William II's desire, which many a young ruler has had, to be his own master. In William II's case, it was reinforced by impressions of an unhappy childhood and by resentment against physical disability. His parents had disliked him; and he had a stunted left arm. His behaviour in power could have been foreseen by any psychologist—ought to have been foreseen by Bismarck. William II said a few weeks after ascending the throne: 'I shall let the old man snuffle on for six months, then I shall rule myself.'

William II was mistaken over his timing. Bismarck's last bout of power lasted not six months, but a year and a half. It was the happiest period of his life. He was without a care in the world and looked serenely into the future. He was in splendid health—'I feel better than for many years past', as he insisted at the moment of his fall. The emperor was a figurehead; the cartel provided a subservient majority in the Reichstag; Herbert's succession was secure when he himself began to fail. He had at last managed to combine his contradictory wishes—supreme power and life in the country. He left Berlin in July 1888 and returned only the following January. He left again in May and only reappeared for an occasional day until the crisis of January 1890. English people complained of Queen Victoria's long absences at Osborne or Balmoral. What would they have said if it had been the prime minister, not the queen, who lived like this? Bismarck was not merely Imperial chancellor—the only 'responsible' minister whom the Reichstag could criticize or question. He was also foreign minister—needing to see foreign ambassadors, one might suppose, to say nothing of German representatives abroad. He was prime minister of Prussia, expected to preside at the Prussian council of ministers and to co-ordinate its policy. And he was Prussian minister of trade, conducting all economic policy. He had to wind up the remnants of the *Kulturkampf*; to introduce further measures of social welfare if there were to be any; and to hold together the parties of the cartel.

He could do none of these things when he was absent from Berlin. But he would allow them to be done by no one else. The Reichstag was ignored; and the cartel was always threatening to fall to pieces—the Conservatives moving towards a coalition with the Centre, the National Liberals looking wistfully towards the Progressives. A favoured ambassador was occasionally invited to Friedrichsruh; the others were sent brusquely packing by Herbert. The Prussian ministers met under their vice-president, but never to any purpose; they were not allowed to initiate legislation or to strike out on a new line. The minister of Finances collected the taxes; the minister of the interior directed the police. In everything else there was silence, stagnation. Meanwhile Bismarck, in the American phrase, was living the life of Reilly at Varzin or Friedrichsruh. He would get up late, swallow two raw eggs, and then ride or walk out into the fields and woods. In his long black coat and black cowboy hat, he looked like an elderly clergyman. And, in fact, he spent most of his solitary excursions in meditation. He would watch the birds and wild animals; examine the growing crops or admire the timber. Then he would dream for hours at a time; embroider in imagination his past triumphs, recall dead friends—Motley or Kathi Orlov; look with resigned melancholy towards death, with less resignation to Germany's future dangers.

He would come in wet, tired, but exuberant in the late afternoon; and eat, under Schweninger's watchful eye, a meal less enormous than formerly but still enough for two normal men. He would talk in his soft melodious voice—always recollections of the past, never a reference to the present; and these recollections improved at each telling. His first quarrels at the Frankfurt diet; his appointment as prime minister of Prussia; the disputes with William I over the peace terms with Austria; the manipulation of the Ems telegram; these were set-pieces of which he and his family never wearied. In these magical evenings he was more Henry Irving or Walter Scott than a practical statesman. At last, as night fell, he would work—scribbling pencilled comments in the margin of documents, throwing aside what did not interest him, and occasionally composing a literary masterpiece of diplomacy. And so on to another idyllic day, imagining that Germany, the emperor, the world would lie always under his spell. He wanted everything to remain unchanged, the balance of foreign powers and of German parties to produce a perfect equilibrium. His sons and his younger associates thought that he was losing his force with old age. But in truth he had always disliked steady routine work. He was only great in a crisis, driving himself then to exhaustion. He let things slide easily when he was not faced with some immediate challenge; and now none presented itself. He no longer wanted to create; he wanted to preserve, and this soon turns into negation. A negative foreign policy means international peace; and, therefore, Bismarck seemed to keep his grasp of diplomacy to the last. In home affairs negation is barren; and Bismarck seemed here to have nothing to offer. In reality his attitude was all of a piece at home and abroad. He had once condemned those who put the clock forward. Now he tried to make it stop.

His mastery of foreign affairs was most complete just before it fell to pieces. Though the great alarm of 1887 had blown over harmlessly, there was still great tension in the Near East. The Austrians could not believe that

Russia would remain quiet, and they pressed harder than
ever for joint military action against her. William II and
the young men round him were anxious to respond. Support for Austria-Hungary would have been overwhelmingly
popular. It was the 'German' cause; and it would have
shown that Germany no longer feared anyone in the
world. Besides, on a more practical level, the new generation of Germans were no longer Pomeranian grenadiers.
They were financiers and railway-promoters with a deep
stake in Turkey. If they fought Russia at Constantinople,
it would be for German interests, not for those of Austria-
Hungary or Great Britain. Bismarck would have none of
this. He disliked the Austro-Hungarian alliance more than
ever and talked wistfully of ending it. He remained firmly
indifferent to the affairs of the Ottoman empire, even
though he had to tolerate a visit by William II to Constantinople in October 1889—safely, as he supposed, under
Herbert's control. When the Austrians asked for German
backing, he referred them to London: they should make an
alliance with Great Britain if they wanted to fight a
Balkan war.

Bismarck did something to help the Austrians. Relations
between Germany and England were never closer than in
his last two years of power. He repudiated all interest in
colonies and even proposed to hand over the existing
German colonies to the British. In January 1889 he proposed to Salisbury a formal defensive alliance between the
two countries, and in March sent Herbert to London to
promote it. Salisbury saw through Bismarck's game. The
alliance was to operate only against France. If a crisis
arose in the Balkans, Germany would remain neutral,
and Bismarck would argue that, with French intervention
ruled out, England could safely take the lead against
Russia. Salisbury did not need an alliance against France;
rather he hoped to win her back to the side of 'the Crimean
coalition'. And he certainly did not mean to be manœuvred
into carrying alone the burden of Austria-Hungary. Bismarck's proposal was politely declined with the safe excuse

of parliamentary difficulties. Salisbury and Bismarck remained on good terms, each admiring the other's skill; but England was not caught for the Bismarckian system.

The 'natural alliance' with England was popular in Germany except among colonial enthusiasts. Bismarck talked of it openly and did not resent Salisbury's doing the same. But he never intended to commit himself wholly to the British side even against France and still less against Russia. If the written alliance had come off, he would have insisted on its defensive nature and treated Anglo-French quarrels much as he treated the disputes between Russia and Austria-Hungary—remote luxuries which were not Germany's affair. His essential object was to keep all these quarrels under control so that Germany should not be involved in a general war, from which in his belief she could gain nothing. He kept on good terms with France and what was more important, with Russia. This was the most difficult part of his policy—not from technical reasons of diplomacy, but from the current of German opinion. The Germans had no strong feelings against France; they were ready to be friendly so long as this did not involve any concession over Alsace and Lorraine. But German estrangement from Russia mounted apace; and William II reflected it. Bismarck alone adhered to the line of the Reinsurance treaty; and he had to do it in deep secrecy.

Tsar Alexander III was no fool. He knew that only Bismarck stood in the way of an anti-Russian policy; and it was this belief, not the failure in itself to renew the Reinsurance treaty, which made Bismarck's fall the prelude to the Franco-Russian alliance. Bismarck usually achieved what he set out to do; and his last great success in diplomacy was to retain the confidence of the sulky, suspicious tsar. When Alexander III visited Berlin in October 1889, Bismarck actually left his country retirement to meet him. The tsar asked him to sit down, while remaining standing himself; and Bismarck accompanied him to the opera, a tremendous gesture. It was his only appearance there since he became chancellor. He saw *Rheingold*, but made no

comment; it cannot have been much to his taste, which
stopped with Chopin. The meeting raised one cloud. Though
Alexander III expressed full confidence in Bismarck, he
asked: 'Are you sure that you will remain chancellor?'
Bismarck was taken aback. He muttered that he hoped to
enjoy many years of good health and that he would remain chancellor as long as he lived. It had not yet occurred
to him that William II might have different ideas. The
tsar's instinct was sounder.

Bismarck was not worrying about William II. His
thoughts in the autumn of 1889 were on the next general
election for the Reichstag which must come in February
1890.[1] He had made poor use of the cartel which he had
successfully manufactured three years before. He had
carried the army-law in 1887 and the increase of the
reserve in 1888. Otherwise there had been nothing.
Previously he had complained that the opposition parties
in the Reichstag prevented his legislative activity; now
he did no better in a Reichstag almost of his own choosing.
The session of 1888 was made entirely barren by the deaths
of the two emperors, William I and Frederick III. Bismarck did a little better in 1889. He took up the policy of
social welfare, which he had neglected since 1884, and
rounded it off with a scheme for contributory old-age
pensions. On 18 May 1889 he made his last speech in the
Reichstag, arguing that welfare was the true conservatism.
He spoke from genuine conviction. Yet there were tactical
motives also behind his policy. He had sensed something
of William II's craving for popularity and wished to ensure
that chancellor, not emperor, should get the credit for
social welfare. More than that, he was already planning to
use the social peril once more as the slogan for the elections
of 1890. Old-age pensions and a renewal of the anti-socialist
law (due to lapse just before the election) were the two
complementary parts of this policy.

His tactics always followed the same simple pattern. He

[1] The extension of the Reichstag's life to five years applied only to future
Reichstags, not to that elected in 1887.

translated the world of Grimm's fairy tales into political terms. Ogres and witches were waiting to chop Germany into bits, and Bismarck alone could defeat their spells. He acted from fear himself and expected it to work with others. He was always on the look-out for danger— liberalism, Roman Catholicism, red revolution. Even his constructive policy warded off perils—*defensive* alliances, economic *protection*, social *insurance*. First he raised the ghost; then he laid it. Security was what he wanted from life, and he supposed that everyone else wanted it too. He was often right, particularly with the Germans—an apprehensive, spook-ridden people. The danger of liberalism made William I Bismarck's prisoner from 1862 until the day of his death. Similarly, with the electorate, Bismarck always played on the alternative perils of revolution at home and enemies abroad. Foreign danger had the more effective appeal. It gave Bismarck the leadership of Germany in 1870 and again, more artificially, in 1887. But it was a clumsy weapon, causing too much stir in the world and reflecting adversely on Bismarck's diplomatic skill. It could certainly not be used two elections running.

Revolution was the other, though less decisive, card. The Roman Catholics had once provided an effective alarm in 1874. Now the *Kulturkampf* was over, and Bismarck was planning to recruit the Centre for his coalition. Only the Socialist peril remained. The danger from them had worked in 1878, though it miscarried in 1881 and 1884. Bismarck still took it seriously. For him the Social Democrats remained the barricade-fighters of 1848. He believed their threat of a general strike against war and said: 'If the *Socis* strike, then the war is lost before it starts.' He was alone in this belief. Most Germans knew that the Social Democrats had become respectable conservative trade-unionists. Bismarck had cut down his own flag. He had made the Germans feel secure; and they swung round from apprehension to an opposite extreme of confident arrogance. It was clear before the election of 1890 that the Socialist danger would not give Bismarck a majority in the Reichstag. This did not perturb him. He had talked often enough of tearing up the constitution and abolishing universal suffrage. William I had been reluctant to face new turmoil. Now, with a young emperor on the throne, Bismarck might do it. This would not only be a stroke against democracy and revolution; it would also be a stroke against the emperor. William II would become his prisoner as William I had been; Bismarck would be again the indispensable man, 'the chancellor of conflict'. Just at this time he hummed to the French ambassador the old song:

'Et l'on revient toujours
À ses premiers amours',

and added: 'Perhaps that will happen with me.' The great days of 1862 would come again. Maybe he would revenge the humiliations of 1848. Alternatively, he might switch the blame for repressive measures on the emperor and become again 'the republican and democrat' that he had been at the beginning. William II would be accused of seeking to destroy universal suffrage, and Bismarck would save it. At any rate, he would provoke a crisis of some sort. Then St. George would again slay a dragon.

Bismarck was in a gay mood when he left Friedrichsruh for Berlin on 24 January 1890. He had skilfully arranged to wreck the renewal of the anti-socialist law, much as he wrecked the renewal of the army-law in 1886. The National Liberals would support the law only if the clause were left out which allowed the police to expel Social Democrats from their home-towns; the Conservatives would accept this weakening only if Bismarck told them to. He remained silent. The National Liberals insisted on their amendment; and the bill was then defeated, only the National Liberals voting in its favour. Bismarck rubbed his hands: 'The waves will mount ever higher.' He looked forward confidently to industrial disturbances, strikes, civil war. Then 'blood and iron' would rule again. But when the Prussian council of ministers met, he discovered that his calculations had gone wrong. He had assumed that William II would be content to echo the policy of William I in 1862. The emperor would be the advocate of repression, Bismarck of conciliation. William II refused to play the part for which Bismarck had cast him. He refused to start his reign by shooting on Germans. Stealing Bismarck's own phrase, he said that he wanted to be *roi des gueux*, protector of the poor. Instead of fighting the Socialists, he would win them over by factory inspection, limitation of hours, guaranteed wages—all things which Bismarck had been resisting for twenty years. Worse still, the Prussian ministers backed William II, not Bismarck. He glowered at them silently, and they avoided his gaze. William II drafted his own programme of social reforms, and it appeared on 4 February without Bismarck's signature—the first imperial act since the founding of the Empire not to be countersigned by the chancellor.

On the other side, the Social Democrats, too, refused to play Bismarck's game. They had nothing to gain from violence. They were going to win the election. As Engels pointed out from his exile in London, the Socialists now had the law on their side; it was the reactionaries who appealed to force. Bismarck's family expected him to strike back at once. When he remained passive, his son Bill complained: 'My father can no longer wield the sledge-hammer.' But this had never been Bismarck's way. He was far more a diplomat than a fighter, despite his fierce appearance. He cajoled men, played on them, and gave a sharp bark only when he had got them safely into the pen. Now he appeared to retreat. He said of William II's social programme: 'I think we must go along with it'; he resigned the Prussian ministry of commerce; and he even talked of giving up everything except control of foreign affairs. He was really waiting for the results of the election on 20 February. These, he calculated, would be so disastrous that William II and every respectable German would be driven back into his arms.

The election certainly came up to his expectations. The

National Liberals and the Bismarckian conservatives each lost more than half their seats. The Social Democrats polled more than any other single party.[1] The three anti-Bismarckian parties taken together—Social Democrats, Centre, Progressives—held nearly two-thirds of the seats in the Reichstag. Now surely the time had come for a *coup d'état*. Bismarck assured William II that there could be no renewal of the anti-Socialist law and no new army-law with the existing Reichstag, or indeed with any other returned by universal suffrage. The princes who had made the German *Reich* in 1871 should now come together and dissolve it. This was a piece of constitutional nonsense, on a level with the famous 'hole' in the Prussian constitution which Bismarck had discovered in 1862. The *Reich* had been made by agreement between the German states, not by the arbitrary act of absolute princes; and Bismarck, who drew up the treaties of union, knew this perfectly well. But the theory served his turn. It would give him a fighting cause. William II was swept away for a moment. He grasped Bismarck's hand and exclaimed: 'No surrender'.

The emperor's mood soon changed. He was not by nature a man of violence, despite the theatrical utterances which subsequently made him a byword in Europe. As Bismarck said, he was more Coburg than Hohenzollern—conciliatory, anxious for popularity, and above all, high-minded. Unlike his grandfather, he had read the imperial constitution and understood it. He would not start his reign with illegality and bloodshed. Rather he would abandon the anti-socialist law, postpone even the increase of the armed forces, and seek to conciliate the working-classes by labour legislation. On 4 March Bismarck learnt that the emperor had again changed his mind and was opposing a repressive policy. According to the imperial constitution, the chancellor should resign if he lost the emperor's confidence. But

[1] The Social Democrats did not receive representation according to these numbers owing to the system of a second ballot where no candidate received an absolute majority at the first poll. At these second ballots all parties combined against the Social Democrats. They had therefore only 35 deputies, the Centre—with fewer votes—108. But the moral effect was the same.

Bismarck had threatened to resign only when he knew
that his resignation would not be accepted. Even now, he
was misled by the memories of his old successes against
William I. He did not understand that there was an
essential difference. William I always retained confidence
in Bismarck, even when he opposed his policy. William II
had no confidence in Bismarck and wished to be rid of him.

Bismarck would not believe that a mere boy could overthrow him. He tried to mobilize the forces which he had
resisted and despised for nearly thirty years—public
opinion, Prussian ministers, the parties. The news soon
leaked out that Bismarck was threatening to resign. It
made no stir. National feeling had been behind Bismarck
in the *Kulturkampf*; it had responded to the cry of foreign
dangers; it had even agreed with him over such a family
affair as the Battenberg marriage in 1888. The social peril
failed to work in March 1890, just as it had failed to work
in the elections three weeks earlier. How could Bismarck
claim to have public opinion behind him when the majority
of the electorate had voted for the parties hostile to him?
Even the propertied classes—the Conservatives and the
National Liberals—did not really believe in the Socialist
danger. They had acquiesced in the anti-socialist law
because Bismarck insisted on it; they did not regard it as
necessary. They certainly did not want the imperial
constitution destroyed merely to keep Bismarck in power.
Bismarck failed to grasp that, though he was still admired,
this was as a historic figure, not as a leader of the present.
The generation of Germans that had grown to maturity
in the *Reich* were impatient with Bismarck's caution and
restraint. They wanted great new achievements, not a
quiet life. William II, not Bismarck, represented German
feeling.

It was the same with the Prussian ministers. They had
long groaned under Bismarck's control; but they had put
up with it so long as he was 'the indispensable man'. Now
he seemed to be provoking civil war simply to keep in
power. The ministers sat silent when Bismarck developed

his plans for civil conflict; and Boetticher, the Prussian vice-president, ostentatiously accepted from William II the Order of the Black Eagle. Deserted by the ministers, Bismarck tried to silence them. He dug out of obscurity a royal order of 1852 that ministers could advise the Crown only with the knowledge and consent of the prime minister. Ironically enough, Frederick William IV had issued the order to strengthen the then prime minister, Manteuffel, against ambitious underlings of whom Bismarck was one. It had never been operated in the long years when Bismarck was far away at Varzin and Friedrichsruh. William II exposed its absurdity by asking: 'How can I rule without discussing things with the ministers, if you spend a large part of the year at Friedrichsruh?' Bismarck refused to annul the order. The breaking-point had come.

Bismarck's expedients were not exhausted. In despair he turned to the parties in the Reichstag. If he could only build up a majority, then he could impose himself on the emperor as a constitutional chancellor—the very thing that he had resisted since the founding of the *Reich*. He planned this new majority as a coalition between the Centre and the Conservatives, and even imagined that the Centre would bring over also his bitterest enemies, the 'separatists'—Poles, Danes and Alsatians. It was a wonder that he did not appeal to the Socialists; perhaps he would have done if they had had more deputies. On 12 March, Bleichroeder, Bismarck's man of business, brought Windthorst to the chancellery. It was the first friendly meeting between Windthorst and Bismarck since the attempted reconciliation of 1879. The interview was not a success. Windthorst demanded complete surrender: the Roman church should be restored to the privileged position that it had enjoyed in Prussia before 1872. He said as he left: 'I come from the political deathbed of a great man.' In any case, the Conservatives would not join in the game. Their leader refused to see Bismarck and told William II that his party would go into opposition if the government made a deal with the Centre. In resisting Bismarck, William

II was not only defending his personal power; he was reflecting opinion in the Reichstag and making it possible for the government to work with it.

Early on the morning of 15 March, William II came to the foreign ministry to have things out with his chancellor. His note, making the appointment, had miscarried. Bismarck was still abed. By the time he had dressed and come across to the foreign ministry, both men were in a bad temper. William told Bismarck that he ought not to have seen Windthorst. Bismarck replied that he must be free to meet the party leaders. 'Even if your sovereign forbids it?'— 'The power of my sovereign ceases at the door of my wife's drawing-room.' Bismarck's self-control seemed to desert him. He flung his dispatch case furiously on the ground. For a moment William II thought that an inkpot would come flying at his head. But Bismarck had a better trick. He fumbled at his case as he picked it up, appearing to conceal papers that he had in fact brought for the purpose. William demanded to see them. Bismarck pretended to refuse. William snatched the papers from Bismarck's hands and read that Alexander III had said of him: 'C'est un garçon mal élevé et de mauvaise foi'. Bismarck certainly remained true to his maxim: 'à corsaire corsaire et demi.' Though defeated, he had humiliated the man who defeated him. There was no more to be said. William stalked down to his carriage; and Bismarck accompanied him with every gesture of loyal subservience.

Bismarck's long reign was over. It was only left for him to resign. When Gladstone left power and political life under somewhat similar circumstances four years later, his only thought was to conceal the difficulties that he had had with Queen Victoria and to make things easy for the colleagues who had thwarted him. The truth became known only long afterwards. Bismarck had no scruples of this kind. He must have realized, in his calmer moments, that return to office was impossible for him after his quarrel with William II; and he ought to have hushed things up for the sake of the *Reich* which he had created. Bismarck did

not want a stable or quiet Germany, but revenge. He
intended to discredit William II and hoped that Germany
would become unmanageable. He laboured for three days
over his letter of resignation, coolly assuming that William
II would allow him to publish it. The letter was a manifesto,
not a statement of real differences, still less a testament of
political advice. It would not do to mention the anti-
Socialist law or his plans for overthrowing the constitution.
Though these had been the practical occasion for conflict,
they found no place in Bismarck's letter. They were quietly
rubbed out of existence, and rediscovered to everyone's
surprise only when the Bismarckian *Reich* had perished.
Bismarck now laid all his emphasis on the royal order of
1852, which had come late into the dispute, and presented
himself as the defender of orderly constitutional government against the arbitrary whims of the emperor.

Even this was rather thin as an excuse for resignation.
If Bismarck and William II were really in agreement, then
everything could be settled by Bismarck's spending more of
his time in Berlin. On 16 March, while still composing his
letter, he had a stroke of luck. Reports came in from the
German consul at Kiev, describing some Russian troop-
movements. William II, overwrought and highly-strung,
saw an imaginary danger of war. He insisted that measures
of precaution be taken and that the Austrians be in-
formed. At the very same moment, the Russian ambassador
called on Bismarck to propose the renewal of the Reinsurance treaty which was due to expire in June. Bismarck
redrafted his letter of resignation and added a new climax,
in which he appeared as the peacemaker of Europe,
William II as the firebrand who would lead Germany into a
disastrous war. In reality foreign affairs had played no
part in the immediate conflict between Bismarck and the
emperor. Domestic questions, and in particular policy
towards the Reichstag, had been the only issue. Even now,
though Bismarck's fall proved a turning-point in relations
between Germany and Russia, this was accidental. The
Russians would have been prepared to renew the Re-

insurance treaty with his successors, despite his allegations to the contrary; and William II at first intended to renew it. The new office-holders seized on the Reinsurance treaty as an excuse for marking their breach with Bismarck's 'system'. Its rejection gave them some better ground for a quarrel than if they had stood on merely personal jealousy. But this was unpremeditated and certainly far from being the motive behind Bismarck's overthrow.

Bismarck's letter of resignation gave a false picture of what happened in March 1890. But it represented, in however perverted a form, the underlying issues at stake. Bismarck wanted to stand still; William II and the men round him wanted to go forward. The appeal to the royal order of 1852 was not merely a bid by Bismarck for personal authority; it implied essentially that the emperor should be kept under control. If Bismarck had wanted to act, he would still have had to get the emperor's approval. It was because he wanted not to do things, and to prevent others from doing them, that he brought out the royal order. Nor was the dispute settled by Bismarck's fall. Later chancellors went on trying to control William II; and in 1908 Bülow succeeded. During the *Daily Telegraph* affair William II promised 'to respect constitutional responsibilities'—whatever that might mean; and Bülow imagined for a few months that he had won the battle where Bismarck had been defeated. He was soon disappointed; and his fall again showed what Bismarck had realized in his last fumbling negotiations with Windthorst—that the chancellor could control the emperor only if he had a majority in the Reichstag behind him. The order of 1852 was a poor substitute for genuine constitutional government.

In the same way, the course of German foreign policy was not settled once and for all by Bismarck's overthrow. Bismarck's and William II's foreign policy, or to speak more truly, a cautious and a forward policy, went on contending until the outbreak of war in 1914. Good relations with Russia implied abstention in the Near East and a

pacific policy at any rate in Europe; and though the
Reinsurance treaty was never renewed, there were long
periods when it existed in all but name. Wholehearted
support for Austria-Hungary was practised for two or
three years after 1890; and the enthusiasts for German
nationalism were preaching *Mitteleuropa* for a generation
before the word was invented. But they had little influence
over official policy. The statesmen at Vienna got firm
German backing only at the time of the Bosnian crisis in
1909; and this was an aberration. The decision to break
with Bismarck's policy of restraint was effectively taken
only on 6 July 1914, when William II and the then
chancellor, Bethmann Hollweg, committed themselves and
Germany to Austria-Hungary's attack on Serbia. Even
then Bismarckianism was not dead. Between the world
wars cautious German diplomatists still clung to the line
of the Reinsurance treaty—a line not altogether discarded
even at the present day. Bismarck in short dramatized in
personal terms a conflict of wider meaning; and even in
his letter of resignation asserted that he was the only
conservative, the one 'indispensable man'.

His letter was ready on 18 March. He refused to deliver
it personally, alleging that he was too unwell to leave the
house. No sooner was it gone than he called for his horse
and rode leisurely through the streets and the neighbouring
park. It was a last futile attempt to provoke a demonstration in his favour. The passers-by hardly acknowledged
him. After his rare visits to Berlin, he seemed like a ghost
from a great epoch of history that was already past.
William II tried to keep up appearances once he had won
the struggle. Not surprisingly, he refused to allow Bismarck's letter of resignation to be published, and gave out
that Bismarck was resigning for reasons of health. Bismarck
was implacable: 'I am better than I have been for years
past.' William II created him Duke of Lauenburg and
offered him a grant of money. Bismarck refused the money,
comparing it to a Christmas box given to the postman.
Though he could not escape the title, he announced: 'I

hope everyone will continue to address me as Bismarck; I shall use the title only when travelling incognito.' His last official dealing with the state which he had served so long was to receive a demand for the repayment of his salary for the period between 20 March and 31 March, when he was already drawing his pension. He commented contemptuously: 'By such means the Prussian state has become great.'

Bismarck spent his last days in Berlin strengthening his legend for the future. He was reconciled to his old enemy the Empress Victoria, widow of Frederick III, and said to her: 'All I want is a little sympathy.' The sentiment was not altogether sham. William II could have saved himself much trouble if he had occasionally sobbed during his arguments with Bismarck; though even this would hardly have prevented the final break. On 27 March Bismarck went ostentatiously out to Charlottenburg and laid three roses on the grave of William I, saying: 'I have been to bid farewell to my old master.' The flowers came to him on the cheap: he had chosen them hastily and at random from the tributes sent to him by admirers. On his return from Charlottenburg, he took Holy Communion in his drawing-room. The pastor announced a sermon on the text 'love your enemies'. Johanna bade him be silent and turned him out of the room. Bismarck, lying on the sofa, reviewed his life: 'I am seventy-five, my wife is still with me, I have not lost any of my children. I always believed I should die in service. I have been at my post for twenty-eight years, in sickness and in health, and have discharged my duties. I really do not know what I shall do now, for I feel in better health than for years past.' A very characteristic utterance. No human beings existed for him except his wife and children; there was no thought of his great achievements, no hint of policy for the future; the German *Reich*, it seems, had been brought into existence solely to save Bismarck from boredom—and now it could fall to pieces.

Bismarck did his best to create confusion for the future.

He refused to advise his successors, saying: 'Only Herbert knows my secrets.' William II made some attempt to persuade Herbert to stay on. Bismarck claimed not to influence him: 'My son is of age.' But he warned Herbert not to remain with a ship that was running on to the rocks; and Herbert resigned with a resentment even more bitter than his father's. No father and son were ever bound together by a deeper mutual affection. Yet the father had first ruined his son's private happiness and now destroyed his public career. Meanwhile Bismarck was packing his papers and planning future revelations. Knowing how he would have behaved to another under similar circumstances, he feared that his papers would be seized—they were after all official state-documents. He went through the files at random with Busch, his former press jackal; and the two old men grabbed at the most telling documents, Busch smuggling them out of the house at night and concealing them. These precautions were unnecessary. Neither William II nor Caprivi, the new chancellor, made any inquiry. The remaining papers were crammed into some three hundred packing-cases. Along with them went thirteen thousand bottles of wine and all the accumulated bric-à-brac of twenty-eight years, hideous little mementoes from every statesman and crowned head in Europe. Bismarck made it a great grievance that he was turned out of his house at a day's notice and even alleged, untruly, that he had heard the axe already being laid to his favourite trees. In fact he was given nine days' grace; and the chancellery was after all an official residence. It was not the fault of the *Reich* that Bismarck had no house in Berlin of his own.

Bismarck gave a dinner to the Prussian ministers, all of whom (save one) were remaining in office. It was an uneasy occasion. Bismarck would not offer his hand to Boetticher, and burst out towards the end of dinner: 'I see only smiling faces among you; it is your fault that I am no longer chancellor.' The ministers invited him to a dinner in return, but he refused to go. He did not exchange a single word of affection or regret either with his colleagues or with officials. The only man to whom he gave a parting present (extracted from one of the packing-cases) was the old messenger who had carried dispatches for twenty years between chancellery and palace. On 29 March Bismarck left Berlin. Crowds lined the streets. A guard of honour, and all the great dignitaries of the Empire—but not the emperor—were at the station. As the train drew out, the military band struck up a slow march. Bismarck leant back in the carriage and said: 'A state-funeral with full honours.'

X

INTO THE GRAVE—AND BEYOND IT

WHEN Metternich returned home on 13 March 1848 after
being dismissed, he said to his wife: '*Oui, nous sommes tous
morts.*'[1] Bismarck would not give up so easily. He was free
to lead the life of an independent country gentleman. But
forty years in the service of the state, twenty-eight years
in supreme power, had spoilt him for retirement. He had
always been easily bored; now he was bored all the time.
'I was turned out at 75, but I feel young, far too young
to do nothing. I was used to politics; now I miss them.'
He dreamt at first of an early recall, and said before leaving
Berlin: '*Le roi me reverra.*' When the public and the
politicians ignored him, he came to feel that he was already
dead, and he aimed instead at a revenge from beyond the
grave. He would appeal from the present to the future.
'What the newspapers write about me is so much dust
which I brush off. I only care what history will say about
me later.' Herbert dashed off a bitter, spiteful account of
his father's dismissal, which Bismarck approved,[2] and
took as his example. He would write a grandiose survey of
his entire career in the same spirit, exalting his achievements and scoring off all his enemies past and present.
Schweninger encouraged the project in order to give
Bismarck something to do. Cotta, the publisher, agreed
to take six volumes and to pay the fabulous sum of £5,000
a volume. Here was work which would last Bismarck's
lifetime.

Bucher settled at Varzin to organize the material and to
write at Bismarck's dictation. The work made slow pro-

[1] 'Yes, we are dead all right.'
[2] It ultimately appeared as the 'suppressed' third volume of Bismarck's
Reminiscences.

gress. Bismarck had never been a systematic worker. Now
he was more erratic than ever. He would dictate the dramatic episodes of his career to Bucher again and again, adding
new and less likely details at every sitting; but he could not
put his thoughts into order, and he was impatient when
reminded of the facts. Bucher was shocked at his disregard
for the truth. For instance, he denied all initiative in the
affair of the candidature for the Spanish throne, though
Bucher had been to Spain on his instruction and now
showed him a letter to Prim, the Spanish dictator, in his
own handwriting. He lost interest once he had dictated his
favourite stories, and he would lie for hours on a sofa,
flicking over the newspapers that he claimed not to care
about, while Bucher sat silent and disapproving, waiting
in vain for the dictation to begin. Bucher got down a good
deal, which he arranged in some sort of chronological
system and padded out with documents from Bismarck's
vast store. After a few months he fell ill, and in 1892 he
died. There was no one else to keep the work going. Cotta
set up the fragments, and Bismarck made a few verbal
changes in the proof. He dictated no more; and the presses
were still standing when he died.

Bucher had done enough to fill two volumes instead of the
six originally projected. The great set-pieces showed Bismarck's literary genius in all its grandeur, though he had
often told the same stories better at the dinner-table. But
there was little sense of history or of philosophic detachment. Men and women long dead were pursued with the
same relentless hatred. Judgements were inserted not for
their historic truth, but for their effect on the present—
jibes against the parties, attacks on Austria-Hungary,
hits at William II. There was little explanation of Bismarck's motives. This was not surprising. He had never
understood the secret of his career, and had been driven
on by unconscious forces which mastered him before he
mastered others. He was not interested in winning over
posterity; but even if he had been, he would have found
it beyond him.

Bismarck soon neglected the idea of a posthumous victory. He resolved to rise from the grave and to achieve victory even now. Like John Gabriel Borkman, he still expected to be recalled to life, and talked of those whom he would dismiss when he returned to power. No one associated with court or government was admitted to Varzin. The emperor's health was drunk on his birthday in disapproving silence; and laudatory references were allowed only to William I. Bismarck carried his dislike so far that he always laid out the coins from his pocket with the imperial eagle uppermost, in order—as he told Herbert —'not to see that false face'. He would not have minded, or so he said, if William II had told him frankly that he was not wanted; but he resented intrigue—forgetting the similar intrigues by which he had got rid of ministers throughout his career. Sometimes he emphasized his own moderation in contrast to that of his wife and sons: 'I am the only monarchist in this house. All the rest are republicans.' Occasionally he spoke with less restraint. He said to Sir Charles Dilke: 'Were it all to come over again I would be republican and democrat; the rule of kings is the rule of women; the bad women are bad and the good are worse.' A strange saying. No woman had a hand in his fall. But Bismarck did not forget his feud with Augusta even in his stronger dislike of William II.

The war was not kept within the family circle or carried on only for the benefit of visitors. Bismarck talked with equal freedom to journalists, even supplying a separatist journal in southern Germany with an attack on the Hohenzollerns. Soon he established a regular connexion with a daily newspaper in Hamburg, for which he dictated leading articles, unsigned but recognizable in every line. Here, of course, he appeared to rise above personal feeling. His theme was always the blunders and inexperience of his successors. Though he wanted rest and retirement, he could not stand silently by and watch his work being destroyed. He wrote mainly on foreign policy, and especially on relations with Russia. He hinted very early that he had been the only one who knew how to get on with the Russians, though it was not until 1896 that he broke all the rules by telling the story of the Reinsurance treaty and of the failure to renew it in 1890. No doubt he would have railed just as fiercely if his fall had been followed by cooler relations with England. As a matter of fact, Caprivi, the new chancellor, did not change much in Bismarck's line after the first dramatic months. Though he talked more about Austro-German solidarity for the sake of public opinion, he kept on good terms with St. Petersburg and was soon repeating Bismarck's refusal to back Austria-Hungary in the Balkans. William II got over his anti-Russian fever in a year or two, and after 1894 was far more intimate with Tsar Nicholas II than his grandfather had been with Alexander II, let alone Alexander III. Germany did not seem to need the wand of the magician—at any rate until well on in the twentieth century.

It was the same in home affairs. Caprivi turned out a sensible, efficient administrator—no genius indeed, but capable of one feat that had been beyond Bismarck. He kept on good terms with a Reichstag where the Centre, the Progressives, and the Socialists (Bismarck's *Reichsfeinde*) had a majority, and in 1893 even carried an increased army grant, a stroke which Bismarck had declared impossible with any Reichstag elected by universal suffrage. One National Liberal, anxious to support the imperial government and yet still devoted to Bismarck, journeyed specially to Varzin in order to be instructed in Bismarck's objections. He returned unenlightened and told his friends: 'I couldn't help saying to myself that Bismarck did or would have done many of the things for which he blames the present government.' In the last resort Bismarck had a very simple message. He had founded the Empire with some assistance from William I, his *Handlanger*. William II would destroy it.

There were those who tempted Bismarck to come yet more into the open. In 1891 a Hanoverian constituency

elected him to the Reichstag at a by-election on the
National Liberal list—an odd combination after Bismarck's
attacks on Hanoverian separatism. A constituency in
Pomerania or East Prussia would have seemed more
appropriate; but none presented itself, and Bismarck was,
in fact, more popular with middle-class German liberals
in the west than with the Junkers whom he is supposed to
have saved. Despite his desire to protest and to assert his
greatness, he never took his seat in the Reichstag. He
explained that he had no house in Berlin and was too old
to go to an hotel. Again, it would be improper for him to
criticize his successor over details. He would wait for some
great crisis; and none came. In earlier years, he had never
found it difficult to create a crisis when it suited him. Now
he had lost the gift; or perhaps, after all, feared to exercise
it. Despite his railings against the seclusion of Varzin, he
shrank from the harsh world outside. The Reichstag had
not been a docile audience even when he spoke with the
prestige of a chancellor. Would it listen to him at all as a
detached individual? Or would he be humiliated by some
despised 'orator'—Bebel or Richter?

Though Bismarck enjoyed the reputation of a fighter
and looked like one, he never fought on equal terms. He
always insisted on being in a unique position—the only
Junker with brains, the only politician with noble blood,
the only imperial minister, in short 'the indispensable man'.
His greatest gift was in packing the cards, not in playing
the hand. He confessed this frankly to Dilke: 'Cavour,
Crispi, even Kruger, were greater than myself. I had the
State and the army behind me; these men had nothing.'
Open debate in the Reichstag had no attraction for him.
He dreamt of returning to power, not by winning over
public opinion, but as the result of an appeal from the
emperor. There would be a dramatic reconciliation; then
Bismarck and William II would once more defy the world.
Hence his exasperation when William II remained coldly
aloof. He was indignant with the emperor, yet would not
burn his boats by openly denouncing him. He had gained

power by court-intrigue, and never learnt a better trick.

Nevertheless he made some approach to public opinion if only from force of circumstances. Crowds collected when he went on his yearly visit to Kissingen. Universities presented him with addresses. Societies elected him to honorary membership. He had to make some formal reply and, once begun, he could rarely break off without an attack on the present rulers of Germany. He developed, too, an affecting passage where he would look to the past and break into sobs before he could pronounce the words, 'my old master, Emperor William I'. In 1892 he went to Vienna to attend Herbert's wedding. He had meant it as a purely private visit, for, after all, his family was always more important to him than any political affair. Caprivi foolishly instructed the German ambassador to ignore Bismarck; William II, even more foolishly, followed suit with a private letter to Francis Joseph. Excluded from official circles, Bismarck had to play the popular hero whether he would or no. He stopped on the return journey at a number of German towns, ending with a speech in the market-place of Jena. William II's coldness brought Bismarck out as a liberal. 'Perhaps my dutiful behaviour has been the cause of the deplorable lack of backbone in Germany.' He urged his hearers to be more critical of the government, more independent in their views. Absolutism was bad, bureaucracy worse. 'It is a dangerous experiment to strive for absolutism nowadays . . . I was never an absolutist and shall certainly not become one in my old age.' The Reichstag was not powerful enough. 'I want a stable majority in parliament . . . I am anxious for the future of our national institutions unless the Reichstag can effectively criticize, check, warn, under certain circumstances direct the government.'

This was not new doctrine for Bismarck. Though he had always opposed parliamentary sovereignty, he had often, in his more restrained moments, preached the virtues of a balanced constitution, just as he had always upheld the

Balance of Power in foreign affairs. He knew his own love of power too well to trust unchecked power to anyone else. He did not invent constitutional principles merely because he was out of office; but he had failed to apply his own principles when he was in. He confessed as much in his speech at Jena: 'Perhaps I myself contributed unconsciously to depressing the influence of parliament to its present level'—a sentence in which only the word 'unconsciously' stirs a query. There was a deeper flaw in Bismarck's argument. Even now the stable majority that he desired was to be composed only of the parties 'that upheld the state'—'the old cartel' of Conservatives and National Liberals. This cartel had perished. Even if it were restored, it could not win a majority under universal suffrage. A German statesman who wanted to make the constitution a reality would have to win the parties of the masses for constructive ends—the Centre and the Social Democrats. Bismarck had always treated them as *Reichsfeinde*; and he established a tradition which made it impossible for these two parties to become supporters of the government until after the fall of the Empire.

In private Bismarck often foretold the victory of his old enemies. 'Perhaps God will send Germany a second era of decay, followed by a new period of glory—that will certainly be upon a republican basis.' The class war, he insisted, must be fought to a finish: 'When the final victory comes, it will be the victory of labour.' He was not the sort of conservative who admires existing institutions for their own sake and defends them for their intrinsic value. He was a despairing conservative, staving off a dreaded, though inevitable, future, clinging to the present for fear of something worse. Real conservatism is rooted in pride of class. Bismarck had no feeling for the Junkers from whom he sprung. In taste and outlook he was nearest to the rich merchants of Hamburg. It was no accident that he wrote for a Hamburg newspaper and died virtually in a Hamburg suburb. Here was his spiritual home. Merchant-princes are civilized, restrained, balanced, but essentially uncreative and without hope for the future. Bismarck resembled them. A gifted young observer, Harry Kessler, visited Bismarck with a party of students in 1891. He was impressed with Bismarck as a historic character, 'his white cravat in the style of 1848', but he was disappointed that the creator of the *Reich* had no vision for the new generation. 'He offered us young Germans as object in life the political existence of a rentier, the defence and enjoyment of what had been won; our creative urge was ignored . . . He was no beginning, but an end, a grandiose final chord—a fulfiller, not a prophet.' We might be at home with the Buddenbrooks.

Bismarck could always command an audience, but it was one that counted for nothing in the world of affairs. No German politician visited him until Tirpitz came in 1897. Even when a foreigner appeared, it was Dilke—a man excluded from political life in his own country. The enthusiasts for Bismarck were either those for whom life had not begun or those for whom it had ended—students or fellow-visitors at a watering-place. The university students were always ready to put on their corps-uniform, while Bismarck, also absurdly decked in a corps-cap, harangued in their midst. But they forgot his words when they became state servants, just as English students forget the rhetoric which delighted them at their university Union. The old gentlemen at Kissingen would cheer Bismarck as he walked across for his daily glass of thermal water; but rheumatism, not the future of Germany, was their real concern. Despite his explosions of rage and impatience, Bismarck could not step out of his grave.

For most of the time, he did not even attempt it. He was alone at Varzin for months on end—alone and bored. Johanna could offer him no real companionship. She had never had any intellectual or political interests, and was now failing fast. Herbert made his home at Varzin and continued to do so after his marriage. But Bismarck could only train him for a revenge that would never come. Bismarck needed friends. Where were they to be found? He had none in his own class. Motley had died in 1877.

Keyserling had not met him since 1868. On Johanna's promptings, Keyserling left his Baltic home in 1891; and the two old men spent some happy weeks together. When Keyserling left, Johanna implored him to return; and he did so. But apart from friendship, Keyserling had little to offer Bismarck. He advised Bismarck to cultivate 'a harmonious personality'. Bismarck replied fiercely: 'What have I to be harmonious about?' The two talked about religion. Bismarck confessed that 'during the struggles of the last decades he had moved further from God.' Some have seen in this a doubt as to the morality of his political actions. Nothing could be more mistaken. Bismarck's religion was pietistic, not ethical. It was active life in itself, not particular acts, which had taken him further from God. He gave Keyserling a more curious explanation. He had moved away from God, he said, as his erotic passions declined. That has the true Bismarckian ring. He had called in God to keep him away from pretty girls and to make him a respectable married man. When his desires faded—perhaps when Kathi Orlov died—he needed God no longer and had dismissed Him. On another occasion he expressed doubt of an omnipotent God directly controlling the universe. It seemed to him more likely that there were subordinate principles of Good and Evil in endless conflict; a Balance of Power, in fact, in the unseen world as in the world of states. His old rebelliousness blazed out still more clearly at the end of his life. 'I repeat the prayer "Thy will be done". I try to understand it, but I don't always succeed.'

Keyserling did not come again after 1891, and there was no one to take his place. In Bismarck's diaries the monotonous entries increased: 'bored'; 'tired'; 'bored and tired'. Though he still went out in the woods, he could not walk for long. After 1892 he could not ride. By 1894 he was condemned to a carriage, and soon to a wheeled chair. In November 1894 there was a worse catastrophe. Johanna died. Just before her death Bismarck took Holy Communion at her bedside—for the last time in his life. He turned even his wife's death into an excuse for resentment. 'If I were still in office, I should now work hard. That would be the best help; but this comfort is denied me.' In December 1894 Bismarck moved from Varzin to Friedrichs-ruh. He never saw Varzin again. At Friedrichsruh he was nearer the bustle of Hamburg and could hope to see more people, despite his growing weakness.

William II had already made it up with him. The open estrangement was humiliating for the emperor; there was no danger in ending it when Bismarck had so obviously lost all real influence. In January 1894, after much diplo-macy, Bismarck was invited to visit William II in Berlin. He went still hoping to be consulted on great affairs; and some of the men in office expected to be turned out. Yet at the same time he felt that he was venturing into the enemy camp; and he did not go unattended. He leant on Herbert's arm as he mounted the steps of the imperial palace. Herbert and Bill, his younger son, sat near him at the formal dinner in the evening. But nothing dramatic happened one way or the other. William II kept the talk firmly to polite trivialities. No serious advice was sought or given; no insults were exchanged. Bismarck was treated as a visiting royalty, not as the great chancellor. He realized fully for the first time that he had indeed passed beyond the grave.

It was much the same with the celebrations which marked his eightieth birthday on 1 April 1895. Every German prince and city, all the great public corporations, sent greetings. The universities joined in a common demonstration, the rectors glorious in their robes and golden chains, the students in their corps-uniforms. But they were celebrating the past, not acting in the present. They honoured the maker of German unity, not the living statesman. William II said ruthlessly: 'We honour to-day the officer, not the statesman'; and Bismarck accepted the distinction. He appeared for the last time in military uni-form, complete with helmet, and played his old mas-querade: 'The best in me and my actions has always been the Prussian officer.' There was one discordant note. When a motion to congratulate Bismarck came before the Reichstag, Progressives, Centrists, Social Democrats and Separatists combined to defeat it—Bismarck's old *Reichsfeinde* paid him the compliment of acting as though he were still alive. He had always hated more than he had loved; and no doubt it pleased him that there were still some who returned his hate.

There was little stir at Friedrichsruh after April 1895. Bismarck still spoke contemptuously of Germany's present rulers, even though he was supposed to be on good terms with Hohenlohe, who had followed Caprivi as chancellor in 1894. True to his rural affectation, he urged the Farmers' League against 'the drones who govern us' in June 1895. But the deputations, and even the individual visitors, dwindled. Bismarck's energy dwindled on the other side. In December 1897 William II came to Friedrichsruh for the last time, 'to see how long the old man will last.' Bismarck was by now confined to a wheeled chair; yet he played the host with the formal graces of the society that had perished in 1848. He tried to lead the conversation to serious themes. William II kept to the tone of worldly frivolity which he had learnt from his uncle Edward VII. Bismarck got in a last stroke. He told how he had advised Napoleon III to stick to personal government so long as he could count on the imperial guard; otherwise ministerial responsibility was the safer course. Then, speaking directly to William II, he concluded: 'Your Majesty, so long as you have your present corps of officers, you can do what you like; but if not, things will be very different.' He accompanied William II to the door in his wheeled chair. Later he said: 'Jena came twenty years after the death of Frederick the Great; the crash will come twenty years after my departure if things go on like this'—a prophecy fulfilled almost to the month.

Bismarck's last political visitor was Tirpitz, drumming round for a great German navy. Bismarck was enthusiastic for naval power; applauded torpedo-boats and coastal defences; but he could not be caught for an aggressive battle-fleet. 'Germany should keep within her frontiers.' It was his last political judgement, and an appropriate one. He had been as ruthless and unscrupulous as any other politician. What had distinguished him had been his moderation. In Goethe's words, which everyone quotes: *In der Beschränkung zeigt sich erst der Meister*.[1] He had reined in his political passions, and those of others; given to no one the victory; preached moderation and often practised it. He wanted Germany to remain content with the frontiers that he had drawn for her. Perhaps then she would have kept them. As it is, only Germany's frontier with Austria remains as Bismarck made it; and few would give much for its permanence.

In 1898 Bismarck fell into his last decline. He still harboured resentment, but now against his own weakness: 'There will be only one happy day for me: that is the day when I wake no more.' His mind remained fresh and alert, following political events even on his deathbed. Towards the end he lay sometimes talking, sometimes singing softly to himself. The only book by his bedside was a volume of Schiller's poems. Once, opening his eyes, he asked his daughter why she was so sad. 'Because you are so ill, Papa.' Bismarck smiled and whistled quite clearly, '*La donna è mobile*'—touching, though inappropriate. Six hours before his death, he raised his hand sharply and called out: 'That is impossible on grounds of general public policy! [*raison d'état*].' The great artist knew his lines to the last. It was not, however, his final word. Just before he died, he was offered refreshment from a spoon. He pushed the spoon aside, exclaimed 'forward', grasped the glass, and drank its contents unaided. This was even better than his prepared speech. He died on 30 July 1898, shortly before eleven o'clock in the evening.

William II was cruising in the North Sea when the news of Bismarck's death reached him. He hurried back for the funeral. It was an uneasy occasion. Bismarck had refused

[1] Genius is knowing where to stop.

*9

a state-funeral. He was buried at Friedrichsruh, separated
from his house by a railway-line—a modern note such as
had often appeared incongruously in his career. William II
and his glittering courtiers stood on one side of the grave;
Herbert and the family, glowering with renewed hate, on
the other. There was no gesture of reconciliation. William
did not even enter the house. This was hardly surprising.
The first shots in Bismarck's posthumous campaign had
already been fired. On the day after Bismarck's death
Busch released to the press the letter of resignation which
had been drafted with such care in March 1890. Cotta was
eager to publish the fragmentary recollections which Bismarck had left. Herbert jibbed at the narrative of
Bismarck's fall which, in fact, he had drafted. The Bismarck family, he insisted unctuously, could do nothing to
weaken the emperor's prestige; and it must wait until
William II's death. Perhaps he feared prosecution, and
with some reason. Perhaps he feared that William II would
make a telling reply. Here, too, he was justified. Cotta
regarded himself as freed from the restriction by the fall
of the Empire in 1918 and published the so-called 'third'
volume despite the protests of Bismarck's heirs. William II
had the leisure in exile to tell his side of the story, and did
so effectively. No one now would take the version of
Bismarck and Herbert at its face value.

The *Reflections and Recollections*[1] which came out later
in 1898 were more powerful without the bitter conclusion.
Bismarck appeared detached, aloof, an Olympian statesman; and his praise of William I pointed the contrast with
the present emperor sharply enough. As a further gesture
his tomb, on his own instructions, bore the words: 'A true
German servant of Emperor William I.' Herbert tried to

[1] The publisher Cotta put the words of the title in this order. Bismarck had
intended them in the singular and the other way round, *Memory and Thought*.
This was a truer description of the book, where Bismarck was stirred by
memory into reflecting on the past. It was also typical of this great man of
action that he should find thought more important than events when he
came to describe his life. The original title was restored in the Friedrichsruh
edition of Bismarck's collected works.

carry on the fight against William II in more practical ways. He entered the Reichstag and spoke often on foreign policy, criticizing the estrangement from Russia and the emperor's supposed friendship with England. To wreck this friendship, Herbert became a virulent pro-Boer. His criticism carried little weight. Even those Germans who were hostile to England did not wish to return to Bismarck's moderation and balance; they proposed to challenge both Russia and England at once. No Bismarckian party grew up in the Reichstag. Herbert fell ill, withdrew from the Reichstag, and died in 1904. His death passed unnoticed. The younger members of the family became unassuming state servants, and the name of Bismarck ceased to count in German affairs.

Yet there were Bismarckians, though there was no Bismarckian party. Bismarck became the hero of all those for whom the unification of 1871 was a great, but also final, step. The Junkers cared nothing for Bismarck. They disliked German nationalism and were now concerned only to defend their agrarian interests. The new generation of diplomatists ignored Bismarck's tradition. They had to make a 'world-policy', and his caution seemed irrelevant to them. The German masses wanted social reform and a greater Germany which would bring in the Germans of Austria-Hungary. The only Bismarckians were the former National Liberals, few in numbers but strong in intellectual influence. They were judges, university professors, solid bankers, steady men of affairs, the real *bourgeoisie*. In France this class had followed Thiers, one of the few statesmen whom Bismarck admired; and the France of Louis Philippe was their true ideal, as it was Bismarck's. They wanted a national state, constitutional monarchy, and the rule of law; and they admired Bismarck because he had given them these things without revolution or without forcing them into an alliance with the radicals. One of their number, Meinecke, who survived until after the second World war, confessed their error in extreme old age. They believed that they could have the rule of law without democracy. In Germany no Gambetta need follow Thiers; Gladstone, the follower of Peel, need not become 'the People's William'. The monarchy, the army, established authority, could go unchallenged; yet all that was meant by liberal civilization would be secure.

This was the theme for all the work on Bismarck between his death and the outbreak of the first world war. The great historians who wrote about him—Erich Marcks, Max Lenz, Erich Brandenburg—all concentrated on the period of unification. They were contemptuous of the Prussian radicals with their absurd moral scruples and insisted that liberal ends could be achieved, had been achieved, by unscrupulous methods. The wise liberal did not stick to his principles; he accepted the results of *Realpolitik* and rejoiced at doing so. If Bismarck had failed or if he had merely defended absolutism, they and their class would have remained fighting liberals. But the German *Rechtstaat* was in being. What sensible liberal could ask for more? They passed by Bismarck's social policy with uneasy embarrass-ment; and they neglected his later foreign policy. There was as yet little material for its study. Besides, this would have raised awkward contrasts with the present conduct of foreign affairs; and they had learnt from Bismarck not to criticize 'authority'. They did not approve the threats to France, the great navy, or the Baghdad railway; but they did not foresee disaster. The Bismarckian Reich, they believed, would always remain essentialy conservative and pacific.

The first world war belied their belief. It sprang from Germany's 'world-policy', from her determination to chal-lenge both Russia and Great Britain as world powers. But it was presented to the German people as a war of defence, especially against Russian aggression. This case was accepted by the Social Democrats, and by the Bis-marckians also. The great industrialists might dream of annexing Belgium and north-eastern France; the generals might claim all western Russia; the imperialist projectors might foresee a *Mitteleuropa* stretching from Hamburg to Baghdad. The sober German citizen of the middle or working class thought only of defending the *Reich* of 1871; and Bismarck was their common symbol. The centenary of his birth in 1915 saw him more truly a national hero than he had ever been. It was ironical that these celebrations were held in support of a war that was being directed, ostensibly at any rate, by William II.

The defeat of Germany and the fall of the monarchy in 1918 threw the admirers of Bismarck into confusion. What had perished—the Hohenzollern dynasty or Bismarck's work? A few former Bismarckians answered firmly: only the dynasty. Thomas Mann, for instance, had been Bismarckian to the core. Sprung from a line of Hanseatic merchants, he had drawn a proud contrast during the war between German culture and the decadent democracies of England and France. Now he urged that the high German *bourgeoisie*, his own class, should work with the Social Democrats to consolidate the republic. He was met with jeers and hisses when he preached this doctrine at Berlin university in 1923. Soon he left Germany and became an alien not only in place but in spirit. The great majority of the Bismarckians, with the university professors at their head, remained faithful to the dead monarchy. They wore their reservist uniforms with pride, as Bismarck had done; and they used his name as a stick with which to beat the republic.

The German universities became schools of nationalism. The professors condemned the policy of fulfilment and appeasement. They denounced Locarno and the attempts at reconciliation with France. Germany, they taught, could rise again only when she was freed from 'the shackles of Versailles'. They applauded secret rearmament, had no word of blame for the political assassinations. They still prized the *Rechtstaat*, the rule of law; but they supposed that it would survive the overthrow of the republic. The great event in Bismarck's career at this time was the Friedrichsruh edition of his works: nineteen stately volumes, presented with an opulence of type and paper which recalled a vanished greatness. Bismarck's despatches,

speeches and letters were brought together; every scrap of
talk was recorded; the text of his *Recollections* was edited
with meticulous scholarship. Thimme, the principal editor,
surpassed his pre-war colleagues. They had argued that
Bismarck had done wicked things, but that all had turned
out for the best. Thimme sought to show that Bismarck
had not behaved wickedly at all. Far from planning the
wars against Denmark, Austria and France, he had acted
in a purely defensive spirit. They had been the aggressors;
Bismarck had merely happened to get his blow in first.
The Danes had aimed to eliminate the Germans of Sleswig
and Holstein; Austria planned to destroy Prussia; France
was intending to dismember Germany and to annex the
Rhineland. Bismarck had been forced into war much
against his will.

Thimme was also the leading spirit in publishing the
records of the German foreign office between 1871 and 1914.
Here, too, he built up the case for Bismarck's pacific policy
—a case which it was indeed easy to make. But there was
a more doubtful implication. Not only was Bismarck's
policy peaceful and defensive; his method was the only one
by which peace could be secured. Hence Bismarck's legacy
was *Realpolitik*. Away with the League of Nations; back to
practical diplomacy. This lesson was drawn not only by
German professors. The most profound and scholarly
survey of Bismarck's diplomacy after 1871 was written by
the American professor, W. L. Langer; and *Realpolitik*
was taught to a generation of students who were to determine American policy after the second world war—not
the least of Bismarck's victories. Many causes combined
to win sympathy for Germany in England and the United
States. Sentimental regrets at victory counted most; the
complaints of economists against reparations for something.
But the name of Bismarck counted too. Previously Anglo-
Saxons had regarded him as the type of German power.
Now they began to believe that *Realpolitik* was right after
all and that the doctrines of Gladstone—or their modern
version, the doctrines of Wilson—were wrong.

The Bismarckians got their way. The republic was overthrown by Hitler in 1933. The shackles of Versailles were broken off: reparations ended, a great German army restored. Then the Bismarckians discovered to their horror that, while they had got everything they wanted, they had also lost everything that they prized. The *Rechtstaat,* the rule of law, had vanished. The Nazi barbarians ruled. The Bismarckians were helpless. They had never known how to oppose. Now they could not even protest. They clung to their official positions, trying to limit the evil, acquiescing in much of it, falling one after another by the wayside. They lost the army, the foreign office, the administration, even the universities and the learned world. Meinecke, for instance, was turned out of the editorship of the *Historische Zeitschrift* in 1936 for refusing to include a section of anti-Semitic history. A few, such as Rauschning and Hans Rothfels, left Germany for a new spiritual home in America, much as the defeated radicals had done after 1848. Most of them lay low. Bismarck had set them the example of acquiescence—wearing a revolutionary rosette in 1848, conforming to the prejudices of William I, talking the language of liberalism to please the Reichstag. The only method they knew was intrigue, not opposition. They hoped vaguely to manœuvre Hitler on to a saner, more moderate course, as Bismarck had drawn William I along unwelcome paths.

But Hitler was not an elderly gentleman of simple mind and political innocence. He was the greatest of demagogues, confident of his powers, marching somnambulistically to world-conquest. Instead of the Bismarckians manœuvring Hitler, he manœuvred them. They were his instruments; and he launched Germany into the second world war, despite the Bismarckians pulling at his coat-tails. Once more, as in 1914, the respectable Germans of all classes tried to present the war as one of defence, and they clung desperately to the hope that the *Rechtstaat* would be restored when the war was over. They continued to serve Hitler though they disagreed with him, just as Bismarck

had continued to serve Frederick William IV and Manteuffel between 1851 and 1858; and this grumbling service
would have gone on to the end if Hitler had continued to
succeed. Allegiance to Bismarck was their gesture of self-
respect, a sign that they were serving another Germany
than Hitler's. A. O. Meyer, for instance, who completed his
life of Bismarck in 1943, described it as 'my contribution
to national service during the war.'

By a strange turn of the wheel, Bismarck had now
become the symbol of opposition—no longer against a
foreign treaty, but against a German government. He was
the rallying point for all those Germans who were too
respectable to resist Hitler, yet also too decent to acquiesce
in his system. Meinecke records how a Danish historian
said to him during the war: 'You know that I cannot love
Bismarck; but now I recognize that he belonged to our
world.' It was this world of Bismarckians who made up
the silent German opposition, inactive, helpless, yet disapproving. In 1944 Hitler's failure, not his policy, drove
them to resistance. This was tardy, incompetent, in-
effectual. Yet the heirs of Bismarck attempted something
against Hitler, however late in the day. The outside world
puzzled over the objects of this German 'resistance'. The
answer is simple: they wanted the Bismarckian Reich.
They had no contact with the German people, no faith in
democracy. They still wished to combine militarism and
the rule of law, to find somehow an 'authority' that would
be moderate from its own decency.

The terror which followed the abortive rising of 20 July
1944 fell principally on the Bismarckians. Few survived the
end of the war. The Bismarckian tradition was itself in
tatters—Friedrichsruh ruined, Varzin in Russian occupation, Berlin no longer the capital. In the German universities the name of Bismarck was challenged for the first time.
A few unrepentant Bismarckians still praised *Realpolitik*
and even contended that there would have been nothing
wrong with Hitler if he had left the Christian churches alone
and not persecuted the Jews. But most professors had

doubts. They hinted that the academic world had been seduced by Bismarck's success. Perhaps it should have admired ethical values more, and worldly power less. Perhaps Gilbert Murray, not Treitschke, was the true example for a university professor. Yet was this more than a reflection of Germany's passing weakness? Did it not judge Bismarck by his own standards and condemn him solely because in the long run his work had failed?

Bismarck seemed to have nothing to offer the Germany that followed the defeat of 1945. The Roman Catholics and the Social Democrats dominated western Germany; the Communists had an artificial monopoly of power in the east. All alike were Bismarck's *Reichsfeinde*. And how could the Bismarckian tradition be applied in foreign affairs? No doubt Bismarck would have striven to liberate and to reunite Germany. But in what way? By co-operating with one world-antagonist against the other? Or by seeking to stand aside from their quarrels, as he had advocated neutrality in the Crimean war? Winston Churchill called Dr. Adenauer 'the greatest chancellor since Bismarck'— so completely had Bismarck's name become a word of praise even for non-Germans. But there was little parallel. Adenauer was a Roman Catholic from the Rhineland, for whom the unity of western Europe came first. The few German conservatives who tried to reunite Germany by negotiating with the Russians were perhaps nearer Bismarck's line—certainly they thought so themselves. But the essential conditions for a Bismarckian policy were lacking. He had counted on a strong Prussian army as the starting-point from which he made Germany the centre of Europe. Now Germany could not be a 'third force' so long as she was disarmed. Perhaps the days of German greatness have vanished for good. Even an independent Germany may still be overshadowed by the two world Powers, Soviet Russia and the United States, and may find herself much on the level of any other European country. But perhaps not. A new Bismarck may yet arise to exploit the antagonism of Germany's neighbours and to make her again 'the tongue in the balance'. At all events, Bismarck would be content that his name is still a symbol of policy and he himself a subject of controversy.

BIBLIOGRAPHY

THERE is an immense literature on Bismarck. A full list will be found in the latest edition of Dahlmann-Waitz, *Quellenkunde der deutschen Geschichte*. G. P. Gooch discusses 'the Study of Bismarck' with a survey of the outstanding books in *Studies in German History* (1948).

I. BISMARCK'S WRITINGS

Die gesammelten Werke, 19 vols. (1924–35). *Politische Schriften*: Vol. 1: to 1854. Vol. 2: 1 Jan. 1855 to 1 March 1859. Vol. 3: March 1859 to September 1862. Vol. 4: September 1862 to 1864. Vol. 5: 1864 to June 1866. Vol. 6: June 1866 to July 1867. Vol. 6a: Aug. 1867 to 1869. Vol. 6b: 1869 to 1871. Vol. 6c: 1871 to 1890.

Gespräche: Vol. 7: to the founding of the German Reich. Vol. 8: to Bismarck's dismissal. Vol. 9: to Bismarck's death.

Speeches: Vol. 10: 1847–69. Vol. 11: 1869–78. Vol. 12: 1878–85. Vol. 13: 1885–97.

Letters: Vol. 14/I: 1822–61. Vol. 14/II: 1862–98.

Erinnerung und Gedanke: The original text of *Gedanken und Erinnerungen* (first published in 1898).

The title of the collected works is misleading. Though collected, Bismarck's works are not complete. His writings on foreign policy after 1871, for instance, have to be sought in *Die grosse Politik der europäischen Kabinette*, Vols. 1–6 (1922). His speeches can be found in full only in the 14 volumes, edited by Hans Kohl (1892–95). There are many collections of his letters. For example: to his wife (1900); to William I (1903); to his sister Malvine von Arnim (1915); to Kleist-Retzow (1919); to his son Bill (1922); to Ludwig von Gerlach (1896); to Schleinitz (1905).

2. RECOLLECTIONS OF BISMARCK

M. Busch: *Bismarck: Secret Passages from his Life*, 3 vols. (1898).
H. Hofmann: *Fürst Bismarck 1890–1898*. 3 vols. (1913).

R. von Keudell: *Fürst und Fürstin Bismarck* (1901).
Lucius von Ballhausen: *Bismarck-Erinnerungen* (1920).
H. von Poschinger: *Bismarck und die Parliamentarier*, 3 vols. (1894–96).
C. von Tiedemann: *Aus sieben Jahrzehnten.* Vol. 2: *Sechs Jahre Chef der Reichskanzlei unter dem Fürsten Bismarck* (1909).

3. ANTHOLOGIES

H. Ameling: *Bismarck-Worte* (1918).
R. Ingrim: *Bismarck selbst.* (1950).
Tim Klein: *Der Kanzler* (1943).
Hans Rothfels: *Bismarck und der Staat* (1954).
A. Stolberg-Wernigerode: *Bismarck-Lexikon* (1936).

4. LIVES

Erich Eyck: *Bismarck. Leben und Werk*, 3 vols. (1941–44).
    Bismarck and the German Empire (1948).
J. W. Headlam: *Bismarck* (1898).
Max Lenz: *Geschichte Bismarcks* (1913).
Erich Marcks: *Bismarck. Eine Biographie 1815–1851* (1940).
Paul Matter: *Bismarck et son Temps.* 3 vols. (1907–09).
A. O. Meyer: *Bismarck. Der Mensch und der Staatsmann* (1944).
C. Grant-Robertson: *Bismarck* (1919).

5. BOOKS ON SPECIAL TOPICS

G. Anschütz: *Bismarck und die Reichsverfassung* (1899).
Otto Baumgarten: *Bismarcks Religion* (1922).
C. W. Clark: *Franz Joseph and Bismarck* (1934).
W. H. Dawson: *Bismarck and State Socialism* (1891).
Georg von Eppstein: *Bismarcks Staatsrecht* (1923).
    Fürst Bismarcks Entlassung (1920).
Maria Fehling: *Bismarcks Geschichtskenntnis* (1922).
E. Franz: *Der Entscheidungskampf um die wirtschaft-politische Führung Deutschlands 1856–67* (1933).
H. Goldschmidt: *Das Reich und Preussen im Kampf um die Führung* (1931).
H. Kessler: *Gesichter und Zeiten I* (1935).
G. Mayer: *Bismarck und Lassalle* (1927).

A. O. Meyer: *Bismarcks Kampf mit Österreich am Bundestag zu Frankfurt* (1927).

Bismarcks Friedenspolitik (1930).

Bismarcks Glaube (1933).

W. Mommsen: *Bismarcks Sturz und die Parteien* (1924).

B. Nolde: *Die Petersburgen Mission Bismarcks 1859–62* (1936).

N. Orloff: *Bismarck und Katherina Orloff* (1936).

A. Richter: *Bismarck und die Arbeiterfrage* (1935).

Gerhard Ritter: *Die preussischen Konservativen und Bismarcks deutsche Politik 1858 bis 1876* (1913).

Hans Rothfels: *Bismarck und der Osten* (1934).

K. von Schlözer: *Petersburger Briefe* (1921).

Carl Schweitzer: *Bismarcks Stellung zum christlichen Staat* (1923).

E. Schweninger: *Dem Andenken Bismarcks* (1899).

Helene von Taube: *Alexander Keyserling* (1921).

A. J. P. Taylor: *Germany's First Bid for Colonies* (1938).

Walter Vogel: *Bismarcks Arbeiterversicherung* (1951).

W. Windelband: *Bismarck und die europäischen Grossmächte 1879–1885* (1940).

E. Zechlin: *Staatsstreichpläne Bismarcks und Wilhelms II* (1929)

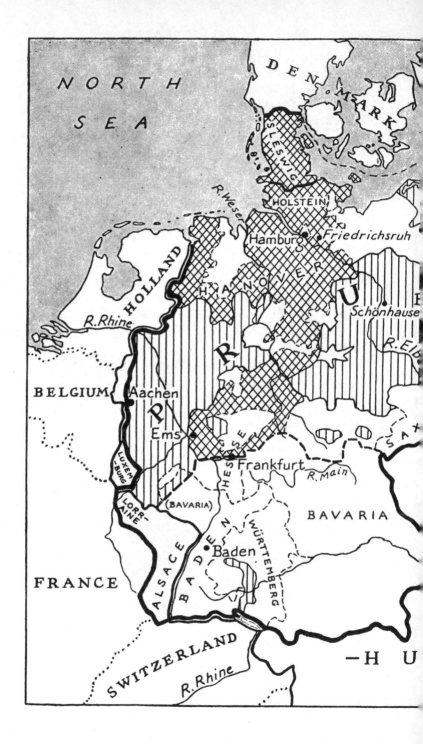

NORTH SEA

DENMARK

SLESWIG

HOLSTEIN

R.Weser

Hamburg   Friedrichsruh

HOLLAND

HANOVER

U

Schönhause

R.Rhine

R.Elbe

BELGIUM   Aachen

P

Ems

R

HESSE

SAX

LUXEM-BURG

Frankfurt

R.Main

LORR-AINE

(BAVARIA)

BAVARIA

FRANCE

ALSACE

BADEN   Baden

WÜRTTEMBERG

SWITZERLAND

R.Rhine

—H U

Miles

40 20 0 40 80

DEN

BALTIC SEA

Königsberg

PRUSSIA

RUSSIA

R. Vistula

R. Oder

adova
✗

AUSTRIA—

Danube
Vienna

GARY

Boundary of German
Empire, 1871

Boundary of German
Confederation, 1815-1866

Southern boundary of
North German Confedera
—tion, 1866-1871

Prussian Territory
before 1866

Prussian Acquisitions
in 1866

INDEX